SAMUEL JOHNSON

Gabriel's Ladder

PENGUIN BOOKS

PENGUIN BOOKS

Published by the Penguin Group
Penguin Books Ltd, 27 Wrights Lane, London W8 5TZ, England
Penguin Books USA Inc., 375 Hudson Street, New York, New York 10014, USA
Penguin Books Australia Ltd, Ringwood, Victoria, Australia
Penguin Books Canada Ltd, 10 Alcorn Avenue, Toronto, Ontario, Canada M4V 3B2
Penguin Books (NZ) Ltd, 182–190 Wairau Road, Auckland 10, New Zealand

Penguin Books Ltd, Registered Offices: Harmondsworth, Middlesex, England

First published in Penguin Books 1997
10 9 8 7 6 5 4 3 2 1

Typeset in Adobe Palatino and Adobe Optima
Typeset by Rowland Phototypesetting Ltd, Bury St Edmunds, Suffolk
Printed in England by Clays Ltd, St Ives plc

PENGUIN BOOKS

GABRIEL'S LADDER

Samuel Johnson was born in London in 1963. In 1965 he became a ward of court and stayed at Drake House, part of a community of children's homes known as Beech Home in Banstead, Surrey. As a young boy he moved to Balham in south London. He has worked as a social worker, essayist and scriptwriter. In 1991 he joined a close friend in South Africa. He married Marcia Nair in 1996 and has two young daughters, Nesley and Willow. Despite a series of heartbreaking disappointments, he has faithfully worshipped snooker champion Jimmy White for over seventeen years.

For my mother, Neslynne.
I thank you for the gift.

One

Gabriel sat on the lower level of a double-decker bus filling with laughter as the driver slowed to keep pace with two men. The first, naked except for an enormous nappy, held water-divining rods out before him. The second, clothed only in strips of tin foil, carried an enormous metal detector. Both wore the inscription 'Unemployed, but talented' upon their backs. They walked on to the common and began to collect donations from those who were amused enough to part with their money.

The green was dotted with umbrellas shielding families and lazing couples. Those without sun-glasses found the harsh glare upon their magazines and newspapers unbearable. Battery-powered fans were cursed as non-rechargeable power units began to expire. Fingers slick with baby oil struggled to open packets of sun block as skin peeled and burnt. Pot-bellied traders from the local market handed out multi-flavoured lollies and overpriced ice-creams. Saturday boys with acne-ridden backs pedalled their iceboxes between ghetto-blasters, yelling out the price of their cool drinks.

Most of the activity took place on the north side of the common, for its centre had recently been disfigured by several flash-fires. A number of signs warning travellers not to drop cigarettes or matches had been posted. The local pond, too small for model speedboats, bereft of fish for two years since an 'anarchist from beyond' had taken to dynamiting it, was packed with animals and playful children.

The south side of the common was mostly deserted. In general, people avoided the short cut through the old railway bridge. They didn't bother to use the children's playground with its rubber base and new swings. Cyclists had no time for the brand-new throughway, laid down by the newly elected 'caring council'.

Reaching out from the disused railway lines – some said it had begun when the gypsies set up camp the previous summer, others that it was entirely the fault of the striking transport union – was a mammoth structure of uncollected garbage. An overwhelming preponderance of black plastic bin-liners, many of them melting, provided the reflective outer hide of the heap. Lumpy mucilage seeped out of brightly coloured supermarket carrier bags stuffed full of tin cans and wine bottles. Bloated maggots crawled out of blackened fruit and rotting vegetables.

The spoiled produce lay upon the ground much like the bruised veins of an unrepentant junkie. Squads of green flies buzzed everywhere, torn between laying their eggs within the fruit or feeding upon the many animal droppings which, despite protests from family groups and GPs, showed no signs of abating.

Several stray dogs roamed freely. Occasionally they stopped for a brief squabble before chasing after the scent of a discarded rib or chicken bone. Up and over the heap they went, darting over dented bicycle frames, dislodging limbless dolls and empty packets of washing powder.

These ejected packets were in turn crunched under the feet of youngsters with baseball caps and designer pumps as they efficiently filtered out the salvageable from the hopeless. The elderly worked alongside them, as did veterans of the street, contemptuously tossing aside chipped radio sets for chairs that could be broken up into firewood and soda bottles that might be exchanged for cash or a cigarette.

The bus came to a halt by a shelter that leaned over like an arthritic giraffe. Its shaky structure presented an advertisement for Lamb's whisky and a poster of an elongated dole queue with the words 'Labour isn't working'. An elderly woman came on to the bus complaining, 'What an awful smell. I thought I was going to die out there.'

The conductor pulled the overhead cord. 'They say that a body has been found underneath all that.'

The older woman's exquisitely pencilled eyebrows formed a smooth arch over spotted, diligently oiled skin. 'Really, is that what they say? It's disgusting. I can't believe people could do this to their own.'

'Everyone's got a right to decent money, including the likes of me.'

Grateful to leave them behind, Gabriel hopped off the bus and made his way towards a sprawling cemetery. Row upon row of headstones filled his eye. Some rested comfortably on flat surfaces. Others leaned precariously out of tiny humps, their cereal-box shapes ground away by past rainfalls. On he went, along a poorly maintained pathway, noting the varying quality of the headstones, contrasting the humility and unrestrained extravagance of the engravings. All the time slowly but surely nearing the chapel.

Within the walls of the chapel, Martin paused as he turned the grey, fingerprinted page of the five-generation King James Bible, his weary sigh causing the flame from the once elegant candle stump to lean away.

Again the sound of someone knocking.

Martin moved slowly through the familiar dust of the curtain-drawn dark and found a young man standing before the chapel door. His eyes contained a bright, fox-fleeing-from-hound intensity. A long, tightly woven plait of hair fell to the small of his back. 'Hello,' he whispered. 'My name is Gabriel DuBois. I've come to visit my mother.'

'You'd best come in . . .'

Gabriel followed Martin into the darkness. The caretaker's voice was still, after decades in London, Yorkshire-deep. 'Haven't I seen you before?'

'This is the first time I've been here.'

'I've a memory for faces. Do you live near here?'

'No.'

Martin grunted an acknowledgement before returning to his office. Under his desk, two single-bar electric fires glowed. The desk was bare except for a mug, filled with pens and pencils. A red bouncing ball and a Rubik's cube rested upon a completed crossword torn out from *The Times*. Pride of place went to an enormous book, in appearance much like an accounts ledger, that Martin gave the lightest of caresses.

'If you could tell me your mother's name and the year she died –'

'Her name was Jocelynne Wills. She died in 1963.'

Martin, struggling with the boy's low modulation, began to thumb through the book.

On certain pages black numerals denoted the passing of twelve months and the arrival of another cycle. Carefully printed names formed an endless tabulation of individual misery and pain, rendered almost inconsequential by the collective toll of anguish. Signatures upright as grey tower blocks were followed by shamelessly inchoate markings of identification that were little more than indecipherable conundrums. Each passed before Gabriel's eyes as, one by one, the years fell away and 1963 approached.

Martin smoothed out the pages, running his index finger over a series of columns. Then on to the next page, then another and the next, where the column ran out and 1965 appeared. As he carried on to 1966, he asked, 'Are you sure she died in 1963?'

'Yes, I'm sure.'

'Sorry?'

The boy spoke up. 'Yes, I'm sure.'

'Jocelynne Wills, you say? I'm sorry, I can't find anyone by that name. Are you sure you've come to the right place of rest?'

'Yes.'

'Hm.'

'Can we check the Ws?'

Martin examined the pages again, then stopped at SOPHIE WARRING. Next to Sophie's name, her age – thirty-two.

'No,' said Gabriel. 'My mother was twenty-three when she died.'

Martin went on until he reached a JOSIE DUBOON who died in 1963. 'That's her,' said Gabriel, 'Josie Duboon.'

Duboon's age at the time of her death was given as twenty-three.

'I can't see how that could be – I don't see how I could have . . . ?'

'My father buried her under another name.'

'Why did he do that?'

'Can we go?'

'Yes, well, maybe.' Martin closed the book. 'I'll take you to the lot, then.'

They walked through the cemetery, passing dry cobble-stones stained with the crush of cherries, until Martin came to a short row of headstones spotted with fallen peaches. 'This must be it. Yes, this is it.'

His stoop increased as Gabriel's shadow came to share the unmarked grass with him.

'This is it?'

'Yes, this is where your mother is buried.'

Gabriel examined the grass for a time and the surrounding markers of respect and love. 'How much does it cost to maintain a grave?'

'About ten pounds a year. The council wants to put up prices, but we've got to try and keep them down so that we remain competitive.' Martin sneaked a look at Gabriel.

'I remember your mother, she was a very beautiful woman. I used to see her walking about the market doing her shopping. She was very popular, very sweet. It was very sudden. Yes, I remember everybody being surprised. She was very popular. I remember when I was preparing the grave for her –' His feet performed a little shuffle. 'Yes, I buried her. I thought I'd seen you somewhere before.'

The boy's face told him it was time to leave.

Alone, Gabriel struggled to hold back his tears, the unexpected words from the caretaker proving too much. 'Don't,' he whispered, 'don't.' His arms slid behind his back as his consciousness embarked upon a journey to somewhere peaceful and quiet.

An hour passed without movement before his posture relaxed and awareness returned, without any knowledge of how he came to be within his present environment.

He reached into his back pocket, he wasn't sure why, and removed a miniature writing pad. On the first page:

YOUR NAME IS GABRIEL DUBOIS. YOU SOMETIMES HAVE PROBLEMS WITH YOUR MEMORY. DON'T WORRY, IT WILL COME BACK SOON.

These words were followed by an address, and:

YOU HAVE COME TO SEE YOUR MOTHER'S GRAVE AND PAY YOUR RESPECTS. THIS IS YOUR FIRST VISIT.

He looked over the grass beneath which she lay, sure of her presence, unaware of how he came by this knowledge, before moving off.

He found himself at a locked exit-gate. Which way was out?

Eventually, he set off back up the path again. In the distance, a small chapel. Gabriel was fond of old buildings and took an instant liking to it. An old man emerged and gave him a slight wave. He returned the gesture, but quickened his pace to prevent any conversation.

There, about twenty metres ahead, an unlocked gate. Beyond it, hopefully, a road leading to something he could make sense of. Once he was through the gate, the sounds of mechanical things and stuff that rattled within hulls converged upon him.

A few minutes into his journey he came across a parked TR7 hemmed in between two police cars. The driver, a tall, elegantly dressed black man, was being body-searched. At the instruction of one of the constables, he removed a ring from his finger. His angry eyes settled on Gabriel. Sensing he was drawing attention to the younger man, he turned away.

On he went, allowing himself a glance over his shoulder as he turned the corner. The police were handing the man his driving-licence back. Gabriel continued down the hill until he found a telephone booth. A tampax lay on the telephone directories. A puddle of urine surrounding a syringe covered the floor. Someone had painted 'Street Life' across the phone.

At the bottom of the hill was a row of streets. Perspiring shoppers carried heavy bags and pushed supermarket trolleys past people who took refuge in shadowed doorways with tiny electric fans held up to their faces. A crowd had gathered outside a pool hall full of black teenagers. The balls were still, the speakers silent as a squad of police officers moved about the premises, saying things that no one outside the shop could hear. Many of those who watched were uneasy and expressed their agitation, telling the police to move on and go about their business. The police separated out the protestors and cracked the odd joke with the curious and the bored.

On he went, head down, suppressing a growing sense of vulnerability, determined not to attract attention. When he found a booth with a working phone he closed the door behind him, happy to muffle the sounds of the street and the city.

He dialled quickly and received a few rings, a click and then a voice. 'Gabriel, this is Gabriel. I left this for you, just in case something happened. Don't worry, do what you've written down and you'll be home in no time. Relax. Everything will be fine.'

Another search through his pockets produced a small leather wallet that contained a wad of money and a note – GO TO THE NEAREST CAB FIRM. So he did.

The office of the taxi outfit resembled an overrun skip. On the floor, next to some broken pencils and a book of crossword puzzles, he spotted an old copy of the *Clarion*, a local publication. Its headline read, 'MISSING BOY FOUND DEAD AFTER TEN YEARS!' On the front page the tale unfolded of a Brian Smith, found, murdered, on a rubbish heap after he had disappeared from a London street over ten years ago. The boy had been badly beaten and apparently poisoned. The newspaper blamed his death on the decline of a once-great nation that may have ruled the world and defeated Hitler, but had lost the long-term war against social revolutionaries, anti-family groups and 'a generation of lost souls with no respect for family, Christ, government or the flag, which would inevitably breed criminals who prey on the young, the old and the defenceless'. The *Clarion* trusted that 'Margaret Thatcher, the only politician of vision and conviction in this country, can lead us back to a time when we had good reason to take pride in ourselves and our communities.'

A blank-eyed man with luxuriant, permed hair stared at a horse race upon the fuzzy screen of a portable television, a dwindling Rizla drooping from his bottom lip. After Gabriel asked for a cab, Rizla man pressed a button. A door was forced open. A colleague slipped out and, without greeting or introduction, headed for his parked Ford Capri.

Gabriel's seat was covered with a representation of the national flag of Nigeria. A pair of enormous fluffy dice, with mummified heads as spots, hung from the rear-view mirror. The car stalled several times before the driver managed to crawl away from the kerb.

Gabriel found himself outside a semi-detached house with the correct number on its black front door, as the cab sped away with Nigerian jazz funk beating from its speakers. The latchkey turned without any resistance and the door swung open.

The downstairs area was completely open-plan: everything was visible from where he stood. He went for it. A step inside and a slam of the door. No shouts. No sounds. It was safe to look around.

The kitchen was immaculate. Its cupboards were filled with an extensive range of cooking materials and a wide selection of spices and dried fruits. The refrigerator contained a host of goodies; his eyes came excitedly to rest upon a bowl filled with a creamy brown liquid smelling of beer and nutmeg. Enough.

Swigging liberally from a bottle of wine plucked from an expansive wine rack, he examined his surroundings. The shelves were packed with books, mostly hardback. An endless array of African and West Indian poetry and folk stories waited for his hand, though these were far outnumbered by books on astrology, psychic phenomena and the occult. Other interests included the board game *Go* and photography.

As he climbed the stairs he wondered how often he had visited this place.

Just looking at the bathroom, with its white walls and wooden floor, made him feel good. So he ran a deep bath, stripped and lay down in the hot water. In no time at all, tension eased from him and his penis rose with the steam. Soon he was stroking himself into a warm calm, the movements of his hand quickening until he directed his erection beneath the water and ejaculated. Later, when the heat of the water had faded and the sweet dreaminess broke, he developed a powerful fascination with the toilet, and to his utter surprise began to sob. So he buried his face in his hands until he was ready to face the memory that waited for him.

It is early morning. Gabriel is four months away from his sixth birthday. He gets out of bed, walks along the landing, enters the bathroom and sits down upon the toilet. The smell of the loosening is strong, but for some reason it causes him to laugh. Done, he stands and begins to clean himself. His legs weaken, and as he flops down again a thin liquid seeps from between his legs. Even the slightest push results in more liquid falling free.

Eventually, when his urgings fail to bring forth any more material, he stands and flushes the toilet. Water swills into the basin. The paper and stool move downward, but then slow and stop. The water level begins to rise. Mercifully it does not spill over. Just.

He considers what to do.

Eventually he goes to his father's bedroom.

It takes him quite some time to awaken his father, whose breath smells heavily of alcohol.

Matthew mumbles, 'What is it, Jocelynne?'

'It's me, Daddy.'

'What is it?'

'Something's happened with the toilet.'

'What?'

'I've broken it.'

Matthew pushes back the blanket to reveal white boxer shorts, over which his paunch has staunchly grown. The smell of his body is quite strong, but Gabriel finds it reassuring. The whites around his eyes are tinged with red roots, as delicate as fairy toes.

'You broke the toilet?'

'Not exactly.'

Matthew sits up and coughs into his hand. 'Don't look at me while I'm thinking. And don't think anything that you shouldn't be thinking.'

Gabriel looks at the floor and tries to erase every thought from his mind.

Matthew leads him back to the bathroom. They study the basin together.

'Why haven't you flushed the toilet?'

Gabriel notes the putty-like appearance of the expanded paper. 'I've tried, but it doesn't work.'

'Clear it away.'

'Clear it?'

'Now.'

Gabriel walks over to a bucket and pulls out a plunger.

Matthew barks, 'Use your hands.'

'My hands?'

'You heard me. I'm tired and I want to go back to sleep. Please, get on with it.'

With cupped hands, Gabriel collects a small amount of filth and pours it into the sink.

'Gabriel, why are you smiling?'

'I didn't spill any.'

'There's a lot more to go.'

'I won't spill any.'

'I've got a headache coming on. Hurry up.'

Gabriel scoops up some more paper and trots back to the sink. Several drops fall to the floor. Still, he continues on as if nothing had happened.

'What are you doing?'

'I'm going to get some water.'

Matthew points at the spillage. 'You can't be trusted with your hands. Use your mouth!'

Gabriel stares at his father.

'Do it.'

Gabriel kneels down by the basin and studies its contents. Holding his nose, closing his eyes, he leans forward, but it is too much and he turns away. 'I can't do it.'

'Get back!'

'No. I don't want to do it. Please.'

'Don't disobey me.'

'I'm not, I'm not.'

Matthew reaches for his belt, but it isn't there. Frustrated, he storms out of the room. The door is slammed shut. From the landing he shouts, 'Don't open that door, Gabriel! Don't you open that door!'

Gabriel panics and runs forward, punching and kicking at the door, his hair becoming flecked with paint and dirt, his finger nails filling with splinters until the strength fades from his limbs and he slides to the floor. Within the mirror he sees himself pick a little tail of mucus off his forearm, get up and drop it into the toilet.

Matthew enters the room with a leather belt. He sees the boy's eyes widen and something hard and strong rises in his belly. 'You forced this upon me.'

'Please, Daddy, don't hit me. Put it away.'

The belt unravels down to the floor.

'Do what I told you! Now!'

He beats the carpet, the door, the wall before grabbing Gabriel by the hair and licking his thigh with the buckle. 'Do you want more?! Do you want more?!'

Gabriel takes too long to answer and the belt lashes him again. 'Bastard!' shouts Matthew and yanks hair. The boy forgets himself and kicks out at his father. Matthew smacks him across the face, knocks him to the ground and sits on him. 'You want to fight?! You want to fight me, boy?!'

'No, no.'

Matthew swings the belt over Gabriel's body and orders him to stand. Gabriel hurries over to the toilet basin.

Matthew slumps down against the door, complaining righteously about his son's stupidity.

Gabriel opens the medicine cabinet and grabs a packet of aspirins. He offers them to his father, but Matthew's head has lolled over to one side and he is staring off into nowhere. So Gabriel kneels down and opens his father's mouth. He drops the pills on to his tongue, then closes the jaw. 'Daddy? Daddy, you've got to swallow them. If you don't swallow them you've going to feel bad.'

'Why? Why do you make me do these things? Why can't you behave yourself?'

'I'm sorry.'

'It's not good enough, is it?'

Gabriel begins to cry.

'You know what you've got to do.'

The boy jumps.

'Stop your crying, boy! Stop crying like a blasted baby. Get up, when you've finished your stupidity.'

The boy gets to his feet and returns to the toilet basin.

'Now, do as I ask.'

Gabriel, whispering to Jesus for help with his stomach, kneels down. Eyes closed, he leans into the toilet basin, lowers his lips to the water and begins to suck. A brown solid begins to move towards him in a turtle-like fashion. The stench spreads all over his face, but he tries to ignore it and when his cheeks are full spits once more into the wash-basin. He repeats this routine until all the relatively clean excess water has been disposed of. Then, with the resigned acceptance of a petal bobbing rhythmically upon the breeze, he kneels, fills his mouth with the nearest stool and carries the melting lump over to the sink.

Matthew can't resist. The opening's too good. He lashes out with his belt against Piglet's leg. The shock causes Gabriel to cry out and swallow the material. The tears start to come again as he runs to the sink and throws up the filth and yesterday's food. Behind him, Matthew lashes the belt against the wall.

Gabriel quickly fills his mouth with sizeable amounts of paper, his discomfort receding as he sees the water level begin to fall. A tug at even more paper and the water level drops.

Matthew, breathing hard, points at a trail of excreta caught on the side of the basin. To Gabriel his motion is as relaxed as spreading shadow and his face, though distorted by alcoholic abuse, has the unconscious dignity of an intelligent, rebellious pup, slapped for the first time. 'What is that? Take it!'

Gabriel wipes the remaining stain away with his palm and heads for the basin. But he doesn't make it. His legs fail and he crumples to the floor, clutching his throat, gagging his life away into ten plus a hundred can still make a thousand and everything can be wrong with the world.

Matthew leans over Gabriel and starts to pull the mottled paper from his mouth. Gabriel vomits over his fingers. His father flicks the emission into the toilet basin and pulls the chain. It flushes easily. With a tinge of satisfaction he calls out, 'Gabriel, make sure you clean all of this up. You hear me?'

Gabriel calls out weakly, 'Yes.'

'Good. Don't let me find anything in the morning when I come in here.' And with that, Matthew leaves the bathroom.

Gabriel sits up, waits for his head to clear, then begins to wash himself. Soon his skin is cocooned in a thick white froth. He rolls his tongue about his teeth removing brown specks and scrubs his gums. Done, he slips his pyjamas back on and leaves the bathroom. Off he goes to the cupboard at the bottom of the stairs for some cleaning agents.

A hiss.

Sobers, his cat, has his amputated-paw stump raised in greeting. Together they return to the bathroom. It takes Gabriel about fifteen minutes to clean the room, though his pleasure is muted by the knowledge that his father can find imperfection in whatever his eyes settle upon. Still, he returns to his bed, his muscles throbbing with accumulated fatigue as his eyes water.

Sleep continues to elude him, so he listens to his father through the bedroom wall, shouting in his sleep, weeping, cursing, calling out her name over and over again. Then there is silence. Gabriel prepares himself, then walks to his father's bedroom.

He finds Matthew spread-eagled across his bed, an empty whisky bottle lying between his legs. One hand still clutches the open pages of a pornographic magazine, the other holds his flaccid penis, from which drops of semen fall. Gabriel takes away the magazine and places it underneath the bed on top of a pile of rival publications, before lifting up the bottom sheet and wiping his father's groin with it. When he is finished he turns to leave the room. His father calls out to him. 'Gabriel?'

'Yes, Daddy?'

'What lesson did you learn tonight?'

Gabriel thinks hard on this. 'I'm not sure.'

'Amongst other things, you learned that the strong can do anything they want to those who are weaker . . . You learned that you can do your best and that it isn't enough . . . What else?'

'I don't know.'

'The lesson will come to you. When it does, you must pass it on to me.'

Gabriel waits for his father to fall asleep and watches him from the door. Morning light creeps into the room. The sound of growing traffic swells. His back begins to ache. When it proves too much, he leaves the room.

Gabriel blew hard through pursed lips and eased the bad times away, before towelling himself dry. Much to his disappointment an erection came on, bringing with it a spiky panic. So he squeezed the bottom of his penis, causing the veins to bulge. Then, at the right moment, he scraped a fingernail over his nipple and ejaculated across his chest and throat. Soothed by the warmth of the white he lay down on the floor and fell asleep.

Hours passed before he awoke into a deeply sensual afterglow that suffused his every limb. Happily, it didn't fade as he went to where the bedroom was sure to be.

The room was empty except for a king-size mattress and a reading lamp. As he lay down, a series of images – some fractured and warped, others gently blurred – came to tease his interest.

A street full of the smell of freshly laid tarmac. A cotton skirt containing bright peacock colours. A thumb bleeding on the metal of a newly opened tin with lacerated edges. A nail clipping dropped between some toes. Hot water flowing out of a kettle on to a cracked pavement where a group of ants congregated, the ants desperately scattering as the hot water falls upon them, their corpses curling up into tight balls.

Someone was at the door.

Standing underneath the bedroom window was a tall, reed-like figure.

Gabriel couldn't hide his irritation. 'What do you want?'

The stranger held up a photograph. The back of his hand was lined with scars. 'Dis is fe yu.'

Gabriel closed the window and headed for the front door.

The man held out the photograph for him. It showed him sitting in Gabriel's kitchen.

'Who are you?'

'Me is ya uncle, Rupert. Rupert Wills.'

Gabriel looked the man over before inviting him in.

His 'uncle' came inside and handed over his coat, averting his eyes from Gabriel's naked form. 'Wi doan' yu get dress or someting?'

'Are you cold?'

'Not at all.'

'Neither am I.'

Gabriel put the coat on a hook before heading over to the kitchen. He poured himself a beer.

'Uncle' hovered at the kitchen entrance. 'Eif de good Lord mean fe us to walk so, den Eve wud still be smilin wen she look ovah her husband.'

'Would you like something to drink?'

'Do yu remembah wat me 'ave?'

Gabriel finished off his own drink without any more conversation before refilling it. 'Who are you?'

'Rupert. Rupert Wills. Me is ya modah's brodah. Yu find out fram me, weh ya modah lay.'

Gabriel's eyes strayed to the scarred hand.

Rupert stroked the skin. 'Me do it inna press 'bout twenty t'ree yeah ago, wen we mind stray back to ya modah.' A broad grin skipped across Rupert's face. 'Yu truly doan' remembah me, do yu?'

'Remember what?'

'Dis conversation, we 'ave it befoh.'

'When?'

Rupert relaxed into his chair, his accent flitting fluently between his Jamaican and English pronunciations, with vowels and consonants effortlessly forming new phonetics. 'We talk plenty. Yu explain de way tings is wid ya head, so we tek precaution an' put ah likkle chat 'pon de video machine.'

Gabriel raised his glass high and swallowed the last drop. After removing another beer from the fridge he went over to his lounge, sat down on a bean bag and picked up his remote control. Rupert joined Gabriel as a recorded image of himself appeared, sucking upon the stem of a smokeless pipe. Only his head and lower torso were in shot.

'Yu suah about dis?' the recording asked.

The disembodied voice of Gabriel replied in stereo, 'Yes.'

'Dis ting yu got, it mus be dangerous, eh?'

'Not always. Just sometimes under stress or for whatever reason it chooses.'

'Lord,' said Rupert, his eyes rolling up to the ceiling, 'yu place a powahful cross on dis younsta, doan' let it crush ihm.'

'It takes a lot to pressurize me.'

'So yu seh. Anyway, back to de story. Me look a long time fe yu. All de family look wen ya fadah jus' up an go like dat.'

'It doesn't matter.'

Rupert twiddled the pipe stem between his front teeth. 'It mattah to me. Ongle God can change de pas'.' The camera moved into a tight shot. 'As soon as me lay me eye 'pon yu, me knoh yu. Yu an' ya modah like peas in a pod. Peopal always seh we look alike, but yu outdo me easy.'

Gabriel's voice eased out of the television speakers. 'What was she like?'

'Wat she like? She was a good woman. Full of life, like it gwine burst fram her. Wen she enta a room, it go an' light up like a Christmas tree. Do ongle time she evah lose dat light is wen me tell de family, me leavin fe Engalund to mek me fortune. But me 'ave to come, yu see, deh was nuttin' in Jamaica fe a man of my social calibre hu wan' to move on.

So to cut de long of it short, dat is how me an' ya fadah meet up. We live in de same house. One day, he see a piccha of ya modah an' tek a fancy to her. Wen he mek his offah to bring her ovah, well at firs' me tink he a foolin', but he was serious fella, ya fadah. Yu knoh dat as well as me. So me write to her about his offah. Me caan rightly seh hu get de biggist shock, ihm or me, wen she write back.

Deh exchange lettah, an' wen de family happy, we na wan tings to move too fas' yu understan, we give permission, an' he pay fe her to come ovah.'

Rupert took the remote control from Gabriel and pressed the pause button, before sitting down with his nephew. 'We concern 'bout it, naturally, but eif nuttin' else gowan', it mean me sistah in England at least. As it was –' He paused. 'Yes, me remembah de day she come to us like it was yestaday. Yu knoh, Gabriel, me ongle got to close me eye an' me see it all again.' He produced a handkerchief from his pocket and wiped his nose. 'It was a good day.'

Gabriel took a swig from his drink and whispered, 'It was a good day.'

'Yes,' chanted Rupert. 'It was a good day.'

Gabriel watched Rupert's fingers tap as he dwelt happily within the cosseting warmth of nostalgia, before inducing the stalled images upon the television screen to become fluid again.

17

'Evaryting was fine,' said the image. 'Evarywun be deh to greet Josie, an' soon she be holdin' court like she use to, back home. She got dat from her granmodah, de gift a speakin'.' He looked over to Gabriel. 'Trut' to say, me can see ya grandmodah in yu.' He brought out a photograph from his wallet.

It was a black and white print. An Asian woman, wearing traditional clothing, sat before her desk. About her neck a pair of heavily rimmed bifocals. In the background, on the wall behind her, a framed picture of a black man in white cricket flannels, leaning against a curved bat. 'Me modah an' fadah good lookin', eh?'

'What was her name?'

'Sharika. Her name was Sharika. She meet ya granfadah wen dem bot' study in London. She join ihm in Jamaica a yeah afta de course end. Her fadah nevah speak to her again. We ongle see her modah once. Wen we reach seven or so, she come an' see us. But dat was dat. By de way, Sharika is not her real name. Afta her parents kiss her off, she change it.'

'How did my mother take to my father?'

'Let us just seh dat she took to ihm.'

Rupert is in the kitchen cleaning the dishes. The last friends and relations left over ten minutes ago. Jocelynne, having kicked off her shoes, rests in a chair and wriggles her toes as she surveys a small plate with a large slice of carrot cake, and a white china cup, half-filled with tea lush with evaporated milk. He calls out along the hallway, 'Josie?'

'Yes, Rupert?'

'Yu all right?'

'Yes, Rupert!'

'Yu sure?'

Rupert enters the room and sits down upon the floor. 'Me caan' tell yu how good it is to see yu.'

'An' yu. Yu shud write moah.'

'Me knoh, me knoh, but me caan' always mek de time. Tings go at a diffrant pace ovah heah.'

'Me hope so.'

'Yu will see.'

'Weh is Matthew?'

Rupert shrugged nonchalantly. 'Matthew is very shy.'

'Shy?'

'Yes. Very, very shy. Yu can run ya mout' off til de heavens open, an' get nuttin' outta de man.'

'Dat is not very kind.'

'De trut' is de trut'.'

'Yu go off Matthew, oah someting?'

'Well, me like him, but as a friend. Me knoh de man well an' he is not fe yu.'

'Let me decide dat.'

'Friendship shall not come befoh blood. Mark me words an' tek care.'

The conversation stops as they listen to the sound of a key turning in the front door and wait in silence until Matthew enters the room, his hair gleaming with gel above an immaculate suit.

'Hello, Matthew,' says a surprised Rupert.

'Hello, Rupert.

'Come in an' meet me sistah, Jocelynne.'

Jocelynne holds out her hand. 'Hello, Matthew, it is a pleasure to meet yu at las'.'

Matthew gently shakes Jocelynne's hand. 'And you. I've looked forward to this moment.'

Rupert says, 'Well, Matthew, weh yu been? We expec' yu soonah.'

'I didn't want to intrude so I waited.'

'Intrude?'

'I knew your family wanted to see your sister and I was determined not to get in the way.'

'Well, yu wrong, mos' definitely wrong. We all appreciate all yu a do fe us. Nevah let anybody tell yu diffrant. Me likkle sistah get a big, big opportunity now, an' it all stem fram yu.'

'I felt it was for the best. Anyway, here I am. Nothing is ever certain, but I kept faith that you'd arrive.'

'Oh, is dat so?' said Rupert. 'Yu surprise me, considerin' yu doan believe.' His eyes flicked over to Jocelynne. 'As we do.'

'True, I am not one for going to services regularly. I leave that for others.'

'De ongle reason we might miss out on a Sunday is eif we too sickly to attend.'

'I hope that both of you always have reason to attend church, then.'

'Tek a good look aroun' de world an' see what it tell yu. Any fool can see dat dese peopal hu doan' atten' church, doan' really lead a full life. Dem caan' function or do anyting right.'

'Perhaps.'

'Perhaps?' Rupert turns to his sister. 'Jocelynne?'

'Yes, Rupert?'

'Well, wa' yu ah seh to dat?'

'Nuttin'.'

'Nuttin'? Nuttin'? Me find dat strange, to say de least.'

'Why, Rupert?'

'Why wat? Yu got nuttin' to seh to a man hu got no interest in de Almighty Saviour an' his miraculous works.'

Matthew's voice hardens a touch. 'I never said I was uninterested in God, Rupert.'

'Oh, really. Maybe me doan' heah right. Bein' a simple man, wid simple habits, me tought me heah yu seh someting once about man not havin' a spirit. Yu knoh, dat we is like de animal, even de lohest of dem. Accordin' to yu,' he patted his body, 'we nuttin' but dust an' food fe worms.'

'I meant that spirituality, my spirituality, holds no interest for me, since I do not believe in the metaphysical nature of man.' Rupert's eyebrows edge together. 'The notion of God, however, does interest me. Or rather, mankind's interpretation of God and godhead, his will, his law and emotion.'

'Emotion?'

'Yes, I like the Old Testament model. He's vengeful, capable of jealousy and anger, an extremely sensitive and egotistical deity as all the best ones are. But no, I do not for one moment believe that this supposedly superior being exists.'

'Yu speak dem words wid plenty a' contempt, Matthew.'

'Cynicism perhaps, but not contempt.'

Rupert's finger starts jabbing. 'Contempt!'

'If I do have contempt, it is for those whose belief in this God has kept us soft and easy.'

'Gowan, gowan, let me heah it!'

'I mean that no higher celestial being who I can possibly imagine could have allowed our race to have suffered the indignities that have been cast upon it by the white colonials.'

'Colonials,' stammers Rupert.

'No God, no God that I can possibly conceive of who could rightly claim the title could have allowed the exportation, exploitation and degradation of my people and indeed all the coloured peoples through-out the world.'

Rupert's bottom lip began to tremble. 'Yu nevah 'ave occasion to speak like dis befoh, Matthew.'

'The truth is that you have never really taken the time to speak to me about anything, Rupert.'

'How was I to knoh yu got dese kine a' tings meesin' up ya brain?'

'You only had to ask.'

'Well, me ask yu now. An' now me heah it, me no longah certahn me like it.'

'As Lenin said –'

'Lenin!' screams Rupert. 'An' wa' de hell dis got to do wid bloody Lenin! Wa' now? Yu tellin' me yu is a communist, Matthew? Is dat it?'

'All I said –'

'Is yu a communist, Matthew? Eif yu is a blasted communist yu can forget all a' dis right now! No way is mi sistah about to 'ave anyting to do wid a Marxist, communist, God-hatin' non-beleeva, hu sneak, yes, sneak undah me bes' will an friendship! Carryin' on like a slippery snake, writin' wurtless poetry an' God ongle knoh wat to my blessed likkle sister, befoh speakin' dis kine a' – dis kine a' heathen bullshit!'

Jocelynne tries to calm him down. 'Rupert, deh is no call fe language like dat.'

Rupert wags a finger before Jocelynne. 'Stap ya silly chat an' sit de hell down! Me is de rulin' powah heah, gal!'

Matthew, alarmed, gets to his feet.

Rupert, sensing movement behind him, spins around. 'Wat a piece of liberty! Wat a blasted cheek! Yu can get out a' me house right now! Me woan' heah any more a' ya blasphemin'!'

'I live here, Rupert.'

'What?!'

'I live here. Like you, I rent a room from the landlord. Neither you or the other tenants can throw me out.'

Rupert begins to splutter something, but Jocelynne rests a hand on his shoulder. 'Rupert, calm down will yu?' Turning to Matthew, she asks, 'Can yu leave us alone, please?'

The Wills watch him leave.

Jocelynne pinches her brother's arm hard.

He jumps away. 'Stap ya nonsense girl. Yu caan' hold back de trut' like Queen bloody Canute. Yu caan' expec' me to jus' stahn' by an' listen to dat kine a' filt'.'

'Since wen yu come on so like Moses, dishin' out gospel an' stone?'

'Jocelynne, yu caan' let dis pretty boy blind yu to de trut'. Open ya eyes an' listen. Yu act as like de man put some kinda spell on yu!'

'Wa' wrong wid yu, Rupert? Me nevah hear yu speak like dis befoh.'

'Yu is me sistah, it is me duty to protect yu.'

'No! Me warn yu —'

'Warn me?! Hu de Ras ya a warn?!'

'Yes, me warn yu good. Eif yu ruin dis for me, me nevah forgive yu! Nevah!'

She leaves the room.

Rupert flops down on to a chair.

Rupert avoided Gabriel's gaze. 'Yes, she certainly took to ya fadah. Took to ihm well.'

'But you weren't surprised.'

'No, not really. Ya fadah was a good-lookin' man. He was a truly fine speaker. I s'pose he remind ya modah of ya grandfadah. Every man she meet, she compare to ihm.' He sighed. 'Yu nevah did get to see de best of ya fadah.'

Gabriel turned the machines off.

Both men kept their own counsel for a time before the older man said, 'Anyway, I got to go.'

Many years ago his sister had stood outside a post office waiting for her exam results, her introspection and focus upon some inner point as strong and resistant to intrusion as her son's was now.

'Now, Gabriel, yu mus' come to me house an' meet me family, propahly.'

These were the last words between them before Rupert left and drove home.

Alone again, Gabriel sat in his lounge and thought through the encounter. He undid the plaits in his hair, stood by a mirror and tried to imagine himself as Rupert's sister. He began to perspire. With the small finger of his right hand he drew the letter G upon his moist belly, before wiping this out and inscribing the letter J. After his perspiration erased this, he etched out more lines and played a game of noughts and crosses. The game and the grids were repeated until his stomach was covered and he had to move down to his legs. The toughened skin about his ankles required more pressure.

Later on, he strolled about his garden in his favourite black cotton gown. At the garden's end a variety of flowers bloomed, their colours and scents pleasuring his senses as he stood before a tree-infant supported by a thick piece of wood. He rocked back and forth to an inner melody, a silent arrangement of sounds from the garden and music from other times, vaguely aware of the intermittent ringing of telephones from nearby houses. Done, he went back into the house, dressed, took two bottles of Champagne from the fridge, slipped into his blue Volvo 1800 and drove to the graveyard where his mother was buried.

Taking care with the Champagne, he climbed the graffitied high brick wall, his foot scraping over 'Keep this place free from Jews'. Safely over, he turned into a faint wind and headed for his mother's grave, his gaze constantly returning to an old tree, an ancient stooped soul whose memory had been chased away by the advance of senility. Saddened, he attempted to count the stars, but gave up at 237 before laying upon the ground which contained Jocelynne. The Champagne cork was loosened and the wine splashed over the ground.

Fingers were pushed deep into the earth as far as they would go. He imagined them stretching out and travelling through the ground, past stone, weed and worm towards his mother, as he sniffed the green before retracting his fingers and examining the insects that clung to them. Tired, he nibbled at some blades of grass until all the flavour had gone.

He lay there for a time, retaining a consciousness of the corpse a small distance beneath him, before entering a soft, liquid mood for the next hour or so, during which he unzipped his trousers and began to stroke himself. Unable to come, he directed his erect penis under his shirt, zipped up and went home.

Late in the morning of the next day, Gabriel once again found it impossible to achieve ejaculation and so decided to go for a long run. He watched parents at play with their children in a park and grew absorbed for a time with the stride of tiny arms, the pumping and kicking of short legs, the breaking of grins, the arrival of pain-induced tears and the constant rubbing of sore knees and bruised flesh, before returning home. Once there, he washed himself and dressed in a pair of old jeans before cleaning the house. When he was finished, he changed his clothes again and drove to the address his uncle had left with him.

A short ring and the door was opened almost immediately by a smiling Rupert.

'Good, yu come.' He stepped lightly back into the hallway. 'But listen, we in a prayer meetin', so eif yu doan' mind waitin' in de kitchen befoh we come?'

Rupert led him towards the kitchen, but paused as they passed a closed door. He held a finger up to his lips, leaned his head against the door and encouraged Gabriel to do the same.

Several voices reached them.

'Donald,' said a woman, 'try to fight de ailment. It is a phase, nuttin' moah. One day, wen dis all ovah an' yu sit widdin de Lord's embrace, it will all seem like a bad dream.'

Rupert tapped Gabriel's hand. 'Dat is me daughtah, Ruth. She counsellin' a boy wid her brodah.'

Another voice, strained, anxious, came to them. 'I hope so. I really do.'

'Prayah will cure evaryting. It can heal de sick, lif' mountains.'

'I know it can. I pray every day, every hour. Some days I pray so hard, I think my hands will bleed.'

'De Lord bleed fe yu, nun a' us need to bleed any moah. He love yu, Donald. Though yu turn ya back on ihm, he nevah lose sight a' yu.'

Rupert pressed his ear even closer to the door.

'Donald, yu is me friend. Dis ting, wat yu is, was, woan' stap anyting. We will nevah tell yu go, nevah.'

'The people, the group, they told things.'

A new voice entered the exchange. 'You don't need these people. They're no good.'

Rupert smiled proudly and whispered, 'Dat is me son, Jeffrey.'

'We won't accept them on to our forums. They're just a front for white perverts who want to live amongst the community. We know that group. Every one of them was abused by some white man.'

Rupert beamed his approval.

'All of them have white lovers. That kind of behaviour is not normal, especially not with us. You know that. You know who we are, what we're like. What did they do? Tell you that their numbers were growing?'

'Yes.'

'That you weren't the only one?'

'Yes.'

Rupert shook his head. 'Dem white peopal bad, eh? Tryin' to corrupt de yout' wid deh renk ways. Dem is bad, bad, bad.'

Jeffrey's reassuring voice was filled with utter conviction. 'It's all right, it's all right. There are perverts in every group. You mustn't mistake one incident.'

'Listen to Jeffrey, Donald. Let ihm help yu.'

'They said I was normal.'

Something, a chair leg perhaps, made a scraping noise. The girl's voice lowered, but was still audible. 'Yu can lead a normal life. Evaryting yu want can be. Listen to Jeffrey. Let ihm lead yu to de cleansin' light. Tek my hand. Deh. De homosexual peopal, dem can ongle do as deh physical aspect command dem to. Deh got no spirit. Tell ihm, brodah.'

'The word will cleanse you. The word will make you strong.'

Someone began to weep. It was a pitiful, broken sound.

Rupert led Gabriel away. 'Come, leave dem to deh work.' They walked along the corridor, passing various portraits of Jesus Christ performing miracles. On the facing wall hung photographs of Margaret Thatcher. Inside the spacious kitchen, a blown-up photograph of Rupert shaking hands with the Prime Minister took pride of place.

Rupert poured Gabriel some tea. 'Personally, me tek de view dat all a' dem batty boys shud get drap off an' drown in de ocean. Jeffrey has de patience of a saint. He can stomach dem. Me, well me jus' grateful me picney turn out right.'

Gabriel sipped his tea.

Rupert excused himself and left the room.

Gabriel waited at the long table as song and prayer filtered through the house. When the session ended with much exultation and clapping, Rupert, closely followed by his wife and children, came back and introduced Gabriel to the family. 'Dis is Jeffrey.'

'Wa 'appnin', star,' said Jeffrey, his eyes distant and cool, moving on before the greeting was completed. Ruth's lip curled disapprovingly as she asked, 'Have you got colour contacts on?'

Rupert chided her, 'Stap ya chirpin, me tell yu it run in de family.' He moved on. 'Dis is Peter, my first-born.'

Peter was taller than Gabriel, with greater muscle definition beneath his high-quality blue turtle-neck sweater. 'Hello, Gabriel, it's a pleasure to meet you,' he said, with near-perfect enunciation.

'And Mary.'

Mary smiled weakly before Rupert moved on.

'Now meet me wife, Marianne.'

Marianne squeezed Gabriel's hands. 'Welcome to ah home, welcome.'

Rupert took his place at the table. 'Please, forgive us. Wen we get de chance to free up some space, we like to spend it wid me family.'

'You never mentioned that you were involved with the Church.'

'Well, ya fadah an' me always argue about anyting religious. For all me knoh, yu might follah de same godless approach.'

Mary sipped some punch from her glass. 'Dad is the Pastor of the largest Pentecostal church in the whole of London. He's the best speaker, too. He whips up quite a storm when he gets going.'

Behind her head, a picture of the actor Robert Powell in the role of Jesus of Nazareth shared space with an anti-abortion picture of a foetus, apparently in pain, crying out for help. The words: 'We must never forget this holocaust!'

Rupert took a leaflet out of his pocket listing rehearsal times for all choir members. 'We got de bes' choir in de whole of Engalund, by a long, long way. Next week, we defend ah title at de Albert Hall. Yu mus' come.'

Marianne asked, 'Can you sing, Gabriel?'

'No.'

'Speak up, me caan' hear eif yu whisper.'

'No, I can't.'

Mary put on a posh accent. 'No, I can't.'

Her father scowled at her. 'Wat is so funny?'

The bark in his voice was like a whip that immediately cowed her. 'Nothing's funny, Dad.' Her voice fell away to a whisper and she struggled to finish, 'I was just mimicking Gabriel's voice.'

'Perhaps yu can tell me why a man shud not speak clearly? His fadah was an educated person, an' wud not raise his son to speak any diffrant.'

Mary changed the subject and said nervously, 'This is really bad timing, you know. I'm going to have to leave for this party soon.'

Ruth, spotting her father's growing anger, quickly asked, 'By de way, Gabriel, how is ya fadah?'

'I have no idea.'

'Why not?'

'We don't keep in regular contact.'

'It is none of my business, but −'

'You're right, it is none of your business.'

As Ruth's mouth dropped, Rupert said, 'Doan' look to me. Me warn yu yesterday, so de fault is wid yu' an no one else.'

'What did you warn them about?'

Rupert grinned a Duke Ellington grin. 'How yu was not a run-of-de-mill charactah, how yu 'ave a penchant fe doin' an' sayin' tings ya own way. Do yu disapprove?'

'I'm not overly concerned.'

Mary tapped Peter's knee. 'Not overly concerned. You should watch this guy, he can teach you a thing or two.'

Her brother checked his wristwatch. 'Speaking of teaching, I've got a new teacher lined up for the accountancy classes. I really should be there for when she starts.'

Mary offered Gabriel a slice of strawberry cake. 'We do a lot of charity and social work. As Dad's ministry has grown, so have his social responsibilities. We've set up various bodies within the institution to deal with the problems of the local people. The local council has given us grants and, what with money from various business institutions, we manage to intervene quite successfully. I'm afraid the work tends to take over our lives. That's one reason why we try to have a weekly prayer session just for the family.'

Peter called out to his brother. 'Which brings us to this meeting tonight, Jeffrey. Are you still planning to go?'

'Yes, as soon as Rachel comes to pick me up.'

Ruth sucked her teeth. 'She a bad influence an' nuttin' moah.'

'No she's not. I'm doing what is right.'

'No one is telling you not to do what you think is right,' said his older brother. 'But we caan' afford any bad publicity at de moment. Not at a time when we've major grants up for renewal.'

'I'm only doing what's right.'

'That's very brave of you, but –'

'Nuttin' brave or big about it.'

'Just so long as you go as an individual and don't pledge any support from the church or the community centre.'

'Do me a favoah an' doan' tell me wat to do. Me doan' need permission fram yu!'

'That's my point, you can do it for yourself, but not for any of our organizations. And you have to agree, Jeffrey, that they will ask you for our support as an organization. Otherwise they wouldn't want you to go.'

'Everybody needs help. If Dad hadn't got help to start up, the church wouldn't even be here. You carry on like he did everyting himself.'

'I was there, you weren't. You was just a boy when his friend lent him the money.'

'Don't talk shit, you were a baby when dat business happened.'

'I was told about it when I grew up. You don't know anything.'

The door bell rang, sending Jeffrey rushing out of the kitchen.

Mary told Gabriel, 'This will be Rachel. You'll like her.'

Jeffrey returned with a green sports jacket hanging off one arm. Behind him came a striking woman whose thick dreadlocks, bound by several multi-coloured bands, brushed the underside of the door. Her skin was the same tone as the milky tea Gabriel had just tasted. Her leather jacket bore a collection of paper clips, miniature cars, buses, airplanes and shuttlecocks. Ear and nose rings glittered with reflected light.

Mary chuckled, 'Rachel, it's great to see you.'

Underneath the jacket was a black vest with holes in. A pair of black jodhpurs with various representations of the African continent sown into them covered extremely long legs, which ended in sandalled feet with golden toe-nails. Just above her left ankle, the tattoo of a black snake, undulating upon her skin as she moved across the floor.

'And you, Mary.' Her voice resonated like that of a trained singer. 'You're looking very glamorous.'

Mary winked at her. 'Evaryting is relative, my dear, evaryting is relative.'

Peter kissed Rachel on the cheek. 'Look at you. What the hell have you been up to?'

'Working hard on the market stall, coming up with new goodies for the customers.'

'I'd have thought you'd have scared them off with all that stuff through your face. It looks sick.'

'And I'm glad to see that you're your old charming self.'

Ruth's whisper scolded, 'It too much, Rachel, too much. Ya modah mus be horrified.'

'Talking of my mother, she sends her best to you, Uncle Rupert. Auntie Marianne, she says it's been too long since you last saw each other.'

'Me call her tonight after six.'

Rachel's eyes came to rest upon Gabriel. 'And you, dark, silent and beautiful. What do you say?'

Ruth could hardly bring herself to speak politely to her cousin. 'Rachel, dis is ya second cousin, Gabriel.'

'Oh, you're Gabriel? Uncle Rupert's talked about you for years. You're quite a mystery man.'

Mary warned, 'Careful, Gabriel. Rachel can't stand someone else being the centre of attention.'

'Maybe you're right, but my attention is clearly focused on the prodigal son. Are you going to answer me? Are my clothes too much?'

'It's not for me to say.'

'I assume you have a mind, therefore you must have an opinion and all opinions are relevant, or do I presume too much?'

'Only in presuming that your manner of decoration should hold as much fascination for me as it so clearly does for you.'

'If I do, it is only because I'm used to being an object of complete and utter fascination for men.'

Howls of laughter peeled about the room.

'And on dat note,' said Rupert, 'let us put all dis distempah to one side an' move into de oddah room.'

Jeffrey whined, 'I'm sorry Dad, we've got to go.'

Rachel said, 'Don't panic, Jeffrey. We've still got time – we won't be late.'

Mary slapped Gabriel's thigh. 'You've done it now. She won't rest until she's given you the biggest tongue-lashing of your life.'

Rupert led everyone into the living room. Though it was quite formally stylized with heavy chairs and two large sofas, the room had a friendly, relaxed quality which was emphasized by its enormous, reproduction open fire. Over the mantelpiece hung a bronze cast of Christ, wearing a particularly nasty set of thorns.

Mary informed Gabriel, 'Peter made the thorns. His order book is full into next year.'

'I wasn't going for any beauty,' said Peter. 'I don't find anything attractive in what happened to the Lord. It seems to me that what happened was horrible and barbaric, and I wanted to capture his suffering. I think that is something people tend to forget.'

'How can you object so much to my rings,' snorted Rachel, 'and yet find beauty in the torture of another human being? I don't see what the difference is.'

'Don't be ridiculous. Why do you always have to go over the top?'

'I don't think I'm going over the top. Christians are the ones who worship the drinking of blood and the eating of flesh, not me.'

Ruth's features glowed with a heartfelt anger. 'Not all Christians, Rachel! Yu shud not speak so of dose wid true faith.'

'Each to her own.'

'Each of us is God's own.'

'That's why we're going to this meeting tonight. I don't claim to be some sort of super-Christian, like some people, but I know when my people need my help.'

'We intavene every day.'

'I'm not talking about singing on the streets and handing out leaflets, I'm talking about campaigning to release innocent men.'

Ruth's voice rang out. 'Christ's innocence is de salvation of us all.'

All of her family chanted, 'Amen.'

'Watevah yu do fe dese men, it is Christ who will eventually be deh salvation, Rachel. Doan' forget dat!'

'I'm sure that is a great help to them while they're rotting in jail.'

'Me sure it is, too. Doan' tell me dis Rastafarian nonsense gwine save dem eida!'

'Who mentioned Rastafarianism?'

'Wen yu las' look in de mirror?'

'What has −'

'One of dese killahs yu is so intent on defendin' is a Rasta, is he not?'

'Ruth,' wailed Jeffrey, 'that is not the point.'

'Now wa kine a' religion get peopal to carry on like dis? All dis ganja, it too bad. It do tings to de brain, yu knoh? All dis murderation an' killin' an' –'

'The prisons', snapped Rachel, 'are overflowing with so-called Christians.'

'Deh na real Christians, anyone can see dat!'

'Rastafari is not a cult.'

'It is a cult. De good Lord seh, "Thou shalt not worship any oddah God but me." '

'Dese innocent men believe Jah is God.'

'Yu seh yu no longah tink like dem, a long time ago. Yu can see de way, but yu let dese lost souls carry on dun de wrong path. Yu allow dem to believe in dis wickedness!'

'Really, Ruth, control yourself.'

'Yu knoh, yu knoh deh caan' find salvation, while deh carry'n on wi' dis foolishness, but yu doan' seh so, do yu?!' Ruth's voice filled the room with the casual ease of someone used to projecting their voice across a church hall. 'Ansa me question!'

'Not while you're in this hysterical mood.'

'Just ansa de question!'

'All me seh is dis, deh be a damn sight bettah off believin' in a black God den some blue-eyed bwoy hu doan' give a damn fe dem!'

Ruth tried to say something, but her mouth would not work. For a moment it seemed she was about to strike Rachel, but then, with her jaw firmly set, she marched out of the room and slammed the door behind her.

Peter took a deep breath. 'That was uncalled for.'

'She shouldn't have shouted at me.'

'Why do you always have to go over the top?'

'Eif yu caan' see it, yu caan' see it.'

'Are you asking us to believe that some jumped-up tin-pot dictator who spent all his people's money on big cars and women is really the Saviour?'

'I doan' believe in Rastafari any more.'

'You still have the hair – that's the same as us wearing crucifixes.'

'It's a political statement.'

'A political statement? And I suppose those rings through your flesh are a political statement as well?'

'In a way, yes.'

'Perhaps you could tell us what it is?'

'It's personal.'

'Just because you have no regard for our personal feelings doesn't mean that we have no regard for yours. How is it a political statement?'

'It's symbolic. It is for all those of my ancestors who were kept in chains.'

The door burst open and Ruth thrust the poster of Robert Powell into Rachel's face. 'Deh! See dis? See it! Heah is de perfect Jesus! De perfect Christ! Wen me see dis, it inspiah me! Wen me see dis man gwine play de Lord, me knoh de Almighty send ihm to light up me fait! An' yu, yu dare to gowan 'bout de colour of his eye! Why, yu shud get dun on ya knees an' tank ihm!' She slapped the poster. 'Yu shud tank ihm, tank ihm over an' over dat Ruth follah de Christian value an' doan' scratch ya damn eye out heah an' now!'

The poster was thrown on to Rachel's lap.

'Look at it! Look an' behold de awesome wondah a' de Christ an' be tankful dat he is forgivin' an' allow ya black soul into heaven!'

And with what she stormed out of the room.

'What did I say?'

'You know how much she believes,' said Peter. 'You shouldn't mock her.'

'I wasn't mocking her.'

'You were. It's too easy, Rachel, taking it out on her. She hasn't got the necessary humour to laugh what you say off, or the cynicism to see that you're winding her up.'

'I was not winding her up.'

'You should go and apologize to her.'

'Forget it! I've got beliefs as well. If it's not right for me to offend hers, then she should respect mine.'

Peter threw up his hands. 'Mom, Dad, I've got to go.' He kissed his parents goodbye. 'Gabriel, I'm sorry you had to see this. Things aren't always like this.'

'Go on,' said Rachel with a sneer, 'play the good guy till the end.'

Mary also prepared to leave. 'Look, everyone, I've got to go. I can't hang on any longer, I'm supposed to be helping out.' She blew kisses to her parents. 'Gabriel, it was nice meeting you, I'll see you again.' Then she, too, disappeared out of the room.

Jeffrey mumbled something under his breath and followed his sister.

Rupert wagged a finger at Rachel. 'Gabriel, me trust tonight woan' put yu off de family completely. Me bring all me picney up to express demselves freely, widdout fear or recrimination.'

Rachel's eyes rolled upwards as Rupert ushered Marianne upstairs after she had kissed Gabriel goodbye.

The two cousins sat together in silence until Rachel commented, 'It's unsettling, the way you look at people. Is that why you do it?' She didn't wait for an answer. 'What would you say if I told you that sweet Uncle Rupert had a chat with his family in which he described you as – what was the phrase? – "Disturbed". Yes, I think that was the word. How do you feel about that?'

'It's not a description I would volunteer of myself. But I accept that it may well be a valid interpretation for someone else.'

'You don't mean that?'

'Ruth worships a figure whose followers have decimated a host of ancient cultures and practised world-wide slaughter in the name of Christianity. If that is an act of sanity, I have no problem in declaring myself completely and irrecoverably insane.'

'I'll try to quote you next time that mad bitch comes at me again.' She sat down on the carpet before him, an action that clearly unsettled him. 'It's OK, I'm only looking at you. You shouldn't be worried about saying what you've got to say. I always say what I think.'

'Then why is there so much unsaid between you and Peter?'

'I hope things aren't as obvious as you make them out to be. In fact, I know they're not. Why is there so much unsaid? Who knows? Peter's intelligent and that's a rare quality in a man.

'Much to my undying shame, he was the president of the Conservative students at his college when we were seeing each other. All we did was argue about politics. He has this almost pathological hatred of the Labour Party. He thinks they've never done a thing for us and that Margaret Thatcher is the best thing to happen to black people since Frederick fucking Douglas. For all that, I liked him. It made me laugh to fuck a black man who actually stood up when the anthem was played on the telly. He was useless in bed, but that almost made up for it.

'You can see how vain he is, he couldn't handle just being a fuckmate and came down on me. OK, now I'm not so blasé about exchanging fluids without love, but there's no going back for us. He can't handle not being "the one". It doesn't matter if he's got three women on the go, he's got to be "the one" for each one of them. Me, right now, I'm not into adoration, I want to be worshipped. I want a man to pay homage with his love. I want a black man who's got the balls to make a gesture, who will woo me. I want an adventure, an opera. I want it, because I can give it. If I ever find it, that's it.

'I read this story once, about this architect and this missionary who'd been together for over sixteen years. In that time, because of her various missions, they only got to spend three weeks of the year together, but it was enough for them. Not because they weren't into sex or anything, they were incredibly passionate people, but they each knew the other was the love of their lives. Each was all the other wanted. I read it and I knew I could do it. I don't ever intend to, but if the right man came along, I could.

'I think my heart can handle, at the most, three, maybe four great loves in my life. I want to know that each one of those loves, whatever pain they might bring me, is worth it. I will not look back at any man I spent time with and think he wasn't worth it.'

She rubbed her eyes. 'All this talking is draining. So, black man, tell me something interesting about yourself. How's it going with your fuckmates?'

'I don't have any fuckmates. I've never had one.'

'What do mean?'

'I'm celibate.'

'Celibate? You mean you're a virgin? Are you saving yourself for the right woman?'

'Not at all.'

She burst out laughing. 'I'm sorry, I didn't mean to laugh.'

'You can do anything you like. Nothing you do or say will hurt me.'

She stared at him, then, frowning, edged forward. 'Why don't you like to be inside a woman? What are you afraid of?'

'I'm not afraid of anything.'

'Yes, yes you are.' The frown lifted. 'You think we're dirty, don't you?'

He crossed his arms.

'You think you have to remain pure?'

She reached out to touch him.

'Don't, please.'

'Gabriel?'

34

'I don't want this.'

She stroked his face before kissing him on the lips. As her tongue moved in deeper, he cried out into her mouth and fell to the floor in a faint, taking her with him.

'It's all right,' she whispered, removing his shirt from a body without any strength, 'I won't hurt you.' As she knelt over him, he tried to push her away, but she forced his arms underneath his body before clamping her hand over his mouth, whispering, 'Shush, shush.'

Someone entered the upstairs toilet.

As her fingers flattened out his bottom lip, the upstairs toilet flushed, causing the pipes of the house to resonate with the flow of water. 'What are you afraid of? Tell me.'

He awoke in her arms.

She watched him sit up and said, 'I want you to come home with me tonight. If you don't, I'll never forgive you.'

From the top of the stairs came her name.

'Yes, Uncle Rupert?'

'It's getting late.'

'All right, Uncle, we'll be off soon.'

'All right. Good night, Gabriel.'

Gabriel called out good night and tried to get to his feet. Rachel put an arm about him. 'I said I want you to come home with me.'

Unsteady, slightly dizzy, he left the house and tried to start his car as quickly as possible. She followed and asked for a lift home.

She took him the long route, through Clapham Common, back down to Streatham and up into Brixton before turning left at the town hall along Acre Lane, and a sharp right on to her road. She handed him a card as they parked outside her apartment block. 'Gabriel, I'm glad we met. My studio is on the card. You can meet me there for lunch if you like, when you're ready.' She went inside without a look back.

He drove home to the sound of Radio Luxembourg and a news programme, on which a member of the cabinet was defending a speech by his colleague Norman Tebbit, who had told people to get on their bikes and look for employment. The chairman spoke eloquently of his own father, who had walked for miles in search of work on the odd occasion when unemployment struck him.

By the time Gabriel entered his bedroom his heart had grown heavy and a mood of foreboding was upon him. He lay down upon his bed, only slightly comforted by the close proximity of the walls, his legs pressed together, his hands clasped to his side, and pleaded in the dark, 'Please be a good dream.'

Gabriel's dream carried him along hardened cobwebs wipped in pale silver and powered frankincense, until he came to a dark, cold place filled with cushions. On the top of the cushions sat the Dark Man of Gabriel's dreams and half-forgotten memories.

Each strand of his hair was bonded with dirt and scum, forming thousands of dry, endless, corrugated plaits, that fell to the ground and stretched out into the tunnel behind him. Attached to the hair at gravity-defying angles were hundreds of thousands of pots, each filled to the brim with a thick composition, from which puffs of steam swirled upwards.

His halva-coloured epidermis slid over his bones and joints like thick porridge in a tipped pan. At his elbow, the skin was lumpy and scaled, on his stomach, dry and cracked. He was naked except for a rotting, lilliputian cloth about his groin. Dirt-encrusted finger-nails wound to the ground like charred apple shavings.

A mighty sea came to a crashing halt several feet behind Gabriel and throbbed with incalculable power as it lapped back and forth.

The Dark Man dipped a nail into a pot and sucked the rotten dew with an unashamed infantile delight, before dropping the pot on to the ground and, with a voice like the last breath of a frail octogenarian wasted by disease and pain, spoke. 'Aren't you afraid, brother?'

Gabriel denied that he was.

The Dark Man brought a finger-nail up to his stomach and slit his stomach open. A foul-smelling substance seeped forth. A nail was dipped into the liquid and another pot skilfully moulded as the creature, wriggling his nose as if he were consuming snuff, drifted on the sweet pain of his magical catabolism.

The pot was offered to Gabriel.

Gabriel saw within it a sleeping child. The child's skin was whiter than anything he had ever seen before. Its hair shimmered like the brightest gold. Gabriel reached out for the child, but the Dark Man pulled the pot away and laid it on the ground, out of his guest's reach.

The Dark Man frowned the frown of a beautiful infant refused food for the first time. 'Come hither, sirrah,' he said. 'Dis entity is fresh of spirit and resolved to be constant in the humility I hold for me fellow men.'

Gabriel heard someone wail. It was a pathetic sound, full of loneliness and longing. As he tried to find its source, the Dark Man held out his hand. From behind him came a number of children. Their sex was unclear. They walked stiffly as if they were unused to walking. One by one, without making a sound, they began to climb into the pots.

Gabriel began to ask a question of the Dark Man, but was silenced with a wave of his hand. 'Sweet yout', me do wat me need to do an' seh wat me wan' to seh. But it also hold dat de full beauty of godhood doth oft lie in de denial of greatness an' de humble assumption of de mortal aspect.'

Gabriel walked over to a pot.

The Dark Man did not prevent him.

He found one of the children rocking back and forth in the container. He asked for the child's name.

The Dark Man ignored him, took out his penis and began to urinate into the pot. The child seemed to be comforted by the urine and began to sing himself to sleep.

Once again, Gabriel asked for the child's name.

The Dark Man let out a sigh that bubbled heatedly upon the air. 'Irritant yout', de fate of man is inborn and evah certahn. De certahnty of death do discolour the babe's first breath, an' inspire de infant to capture its own expiration and hold it widdin its straining cheeks for ever. The knowledge of de ending doth foul de babe's first smell, for de innocent cherub be cognizant that it doth inhale, no matter how well perfumed, de sugar-plum scent of curdling, decaying flesh.

'Chile, death is a righteous woman. For it be she who must encompass the suffering people of the world and give succour from breasts which hold no milk. It is her ear dat hear de las' sigh. She who mus' hold de trembling hand. She who mus' witness de giving up of de las' secret.

'She be a mighty woman, the mightiest of all! Mightier even than Gea, for it is she who mus' place a hand over de lip which mek de mos' passionate, fearful plea. It is she who mus' force her cloth down de throat of de mos' beautiful chile and cause suffocation! She who mus' break de neck of de falling parent beneath her sandalled feet. And who be de creator of the misery dat de chile and de parent do always suffer? He dat lives above!

'Yea, de Lord be a coward! The shittiest, shit-eating, turd-stroking coward of cowards! My mistress is de bravest of de brave, de boldest of de bold!'

He began to hop from one leg to the other, his long toe-nails leaving deep marks on the ground. 'Tall, she walk, like de brightest angel! She be de star dat do lead de sufferer away from de most painful pestilence! Her song doth lift de spirit, so dat de dying do leave their shells with disrespectful haste and join in de glory of her righteous ballad! And her ballad shall rise! Yea it shall rise ever upwards and shatter de paper walls of heaven and fill de puff palace of de shit-eater!!'

The Dark Man bustled forward, his hands reaching out to scar Gabriel's face. Though the youth appeared to move much slower than the Dark Man, he had time to pick up the pot before leaning away from danger. The Dark Man's clicking finger-nails, dangling like the feet of hunting crows, fell still as Gabriel lifted the pot to his lips.

'Chile, yu na wan' to taste me brew?'

'Why not?'

'Why not indeed? Why not, as yu say? Why not, anyway? Yu hold a most powerfullest concoction. No one but me and my own may drink from de pot. Since there is only me, it doth follah dat ongle I can drink de brew widdout suffering de most severe consequences.'

Gabriel took a sip from the pot, slapping his lips together to savour the taste properly, before drinking fully without any apparent ill-effects.

The Dark Man, mightily offended shouted, 'Give it back to me! Give it back to me, I say!'

Gabriel downed the last remnants from the pot.

'Give it back! Give it back! This caan' be so!'

Gabriel threw the pot to the Dark Man, who smashed it with a vicious sweep of his hand. 'Hu are yu? Declare your intent! Yu sip me potion brazenly, widdout sign of ill-effect or discomfort! No diseased dog, dat even de bes' vet caan' lead to betteration, can mek a fool outta' dis entity. Either express de purpose of ya intrusive visit, or withdraw!'

Gabriel stood his ground.

The children began to toss and turn, mewing like frightened kittens.

The Dark Man gobbed at Gabriel. 'I na shake in me britches jus' cos thy wretched blood promise misrule upon my head. Me na need a likkle boogooyagga like yu to cuss an' slag me! If yu tink me prowess be bettah suited to de boudoir dan de battlefield, I shall endeavour to raise ya callow estimation by de most bitter of means!'

Slime swam out of the pores of his skin and plopped on to the ground, where it grew readily into abhorrent miniature gargoyles, who snapped the air with gleaming razor teeth. 'Come, ignorant clodpoll, take up arms! Fear not the bite of me loving cockatrices.'

Gabriel tried to make peace. But his words stoked the anger of the daemon, causing him to stamp upon the rabid gargoyles. He plucked some shit from his anus and flung it at Gabriel.

'Be done, yu arrogant quashie, wid your kinky hair and rude lips. Effect wid care your malicious intention lest your folly match that of your exigent mother, Eve; fe truly the combustible filament which inspire her son Cain to his spiteful deed is as nuttin' to mine own elemental nature.'

The Dark Man's mouth filled with angry froth, the spittle flying forward with every heated word. 'I see dat your ancestors have known de mark of heated metal. I see deh forms pressed up against each other. Upon dem, vomit, blood and filt! Above dem, thru de dark and wood, de smell of salt widdin de foreign sea! Below dem, de smell of curdling sweat and thickening grime 'pon de dying.

'I see 'pon deh lip de beaten leather of de muzzle! Across deh back, de stripes of de flickering bull whip, which cracks wit de rise o' de sun an' doan' stap crackin' to de fall o' de moon. Their gait be unnatural, de riddim of deh muscle long broken by movement widdin the manacle.

'Hear me now! No steel has touched my skin. My lips have never known the taste of animal fodder. My stomach has never digested the weight of a master's sufferance. Who are yu to threaten me?!

' 'Tis true. Dis soul of mine has made a religion of insurrection and pain. Vile an' bloody are my thoughts, to which I have dedicated de infinite sureties of body and mind.

'The cruel noble who doth tax his tenants beyond their means weeps in pain as the leech buries its likkle head beneath his skin, because of my will. The Archbishop, fresh from straddling a smooth-faced youth, cries out in agony, like a small-hipped girl in labour, when he passes water, because of my doing. I have writ my name large upon the world! Show me weh yu have made the slightest imprint! Show me!'

The Dark Man rose to his full height. 'Hear me now! Dis spirit do stake a claim to your flesh, and no plea will stay my hand. Me gwine create a stick from your pussyclat head! Ya Nygwo skin shall be as dat of de finest cheese! Your hog blood shredded into de finest garlic! My powah shall reach out and consume all yu hold dearest, man-chile, and crucify thee!'

The Dark Man grabbed Gabriel's scalp, screaming, 'Harlot chile! Suffer de same fate as thy whore mother!' Finger-nails began to slice through bone towards –

Two

Gabriel ran into the bathroom, the morning light stunning his eyes as he retched into the basin. So that he might relax he washed and conditioned his scalp.

Later, he sauntered down the road to collect the morning papers, then settled down at the table to the music of Phylis Hyman.

The *Sun*'s headline screamed, 'Burned to Death!' The story below was peppered with words such as 'Horror', 'Nightmare', 'Tragedy', and in a florid, emotive style told of a fire at a house party.

The party, referred to as a 'blues' by locals, was being held in an apartment building in New Cross. It came to grief in the early hours of the morning when a fire broke out, killing at least sixteen people, mainly teenagers. The party had been held by a local community centre to raise funds for a sculpture of Nelson Mandela.

Gabriel scanned the other papers on the table, all of which featured the fire. Pictures of survivors from the party, standing around in a state of shock, were prominent. In all the papers, the face of a strikingly beautiful teenager weeping, her eyes up to the heavens, her skin stained with smoke, featured dramatically.

A Labour councillor was quoted as saying, 'This is an enormous blow to the black community. We have lost some wonderfully gifted youngsters, all of whom we were immensely proud of, and who had enormous contributions to make.'

An anonymous person offered, 'These parties are always being held without guidance or supervision. It's got so that people can't sleep at night. They're always having them. Something like this was bound to happen. I only hope that this bad thing leads to the government trying to control this sort of thing, for everybody's sake.'

The *Guardian* provided a small piece that commented upon the cultural significance of the 'blues':

For the black youth, social deprivation and limited job opportunities combine with a feeling of alienation and the increasingly draconian SUS laws. The 'blues', a colloquialism for an all-night party, offers an escape from the daily oppressions of a society which is often less than warm, and provides a place where identity and roots can be reaffirmed and revelled in. Last night's tragedy may give the organizers of such events cause to consider the safety implications, but is unlikely to lead to a lessening of the constant demand, indeed need, for such celebrations.

He telephoned Rachel at her home without success before opting for her business number. 'Hello, my name is Gabriel DuBois. I'd like to speak to Rachel Wheeler, please?'

'I'm sorry, she's not in today. A cousin of hers was in that fire that happened down in New Cross last night. Is there anything I can do for you?'

He put the phone down, checked the address of the fire in his A–Z and left the house. On the doorstep he found a crumpled newspaper wrapping. As he picked it up, he spotted a young boy staring at him from across the street. The boy watched him unwrap the package, then turned and walked away. Gabriel found an egg within the paper, with his name written on it. He slipped it into his jacket and set off.

Ten minutes before he reached the street, he encountered a stream of traffic moving so slowly that he decided to park his car and walk the rest of the way.

Barriers had been erected to prevent access and a number of police officers stood about, encouraging people, the vast majority of them black, to move on. All the attention was directed upon an old five-storey building. The four lower sections were untouched, but the top floor had been destroyed by fire. People who lived in adjoining buildings stood on their steps, marvelling at how close they had been to disaster. Television crews still moved about, interviewing people, preparing reports for broadcast.

From the crowd came a scream, 'How many of us have to die before you people do something?' It was immediately repeated by others. The police ignored the calls at first, but soon a senior officer strolled over to the barrier and began a conversation with an extremely agitated old-timer. People edged forward and tried to listen to the exchange of dialogue between the two men.

'Listen, Sir, screaming and shouting won't do any good.'

'Well, what good have you done? All these poor children killed and you haven't done one single thing about it!'

'That's not true. Now why don't you just calm down before you make any further trouble.'

'And what kind of trouble is that?'

The officer, seeing that some television cameras had turned upon him, signalled for the lenses to be turned away, inspiring some youngsters to run over and taunt him. Several constables moved in and squared off with them.

A megaphone appeared in the hands of the senior officer, who asked for the crowds to disperse immediately. An object struck him on the back of his neck, sending him to the ground. Some constables chased after a woman who sprinted away. Gabriel was pushed to one side as three men barged past him and screamed at the police. He walked away.

Jeffrey led Gabriel into a guest-room filled with a gathering of friends, family and supporters. Two tables had been placed in the centre of the room. Pots of tea and coffee, cake and fruit had been laid out. The curtains were open and Gabriel was able to see for the first time an expansive, exquisitely cultivated garden, through the windows.

Peter came to the door and called for everybody's attention. 'As you all know, Mom and Dad have returned from the morgue. They didn't find Mary's body among the dead.' He raised his hand. 'Mom's depressed, understandably. Dad will be here in a minute. There's nothing we can do now until we receive further news from the police. But we'd like to thank everyone for their support.'

He turned and left, but was followed by those determined to know more.

Rachel's reflection appeared in the glass of the garden window. It smiled at various people and made small greeting signals before approaching him. 'Hello, stranger. Heard anything I haven't?'

'No.'

'I hope she's all right. With a bit of luck, she won't even have been there.'

'Meaning?'

'Mary's been seeing a boy, he lived in Streatham. She wouldn't tell your parents about it, but I know she goes there. I've just come from there, but he hasn't seen her.'

Peter, clearly agitated, returned to the doorway and signalled for Rachel to join him. Scowling, she patted Gabriel on his thigh and went with her cousin into another room, their raised voices filtering along the hallway. A girl of about eighteen, wearing a blue suit, introduced herself to Gabriel. 'I'm sorry to be rude, but I don't know your name. I know everyone else here.'

'I'm Rupert's nephew.'

'Is that all your own hair?'

'Yes.'

'It's not fake, then?'

'No.'

'Do you attend church?'

'No.'

'I don't approve of men having long hair. It says in the Bible that it is wrong for men to have long hair.'

Gabriel walked past her and sped upstairs to the toilet. Heart beating, he locked the door and quickly unbuttoned his trousers. A few strokes and the anxiety began to subside as he told himself that this would all be over soon. Somehow he massaged himself to a full erection. He came into some toilet paper, flushed it away, washed his face and hands, then went back to face the crowd downstairs.

Rupert and Marianne were at the bottom of the stairs saying goodbye to the guests. Gabriel slid past them and into the kitchen. Rachel and Jeffrey were preparing to leave, much to Peter's displeasure. 'Can't you put your family first at a time like this?'

Jeffrey was having none of it. 'You know where I'll be. Being here won't change anything.' He laid his hand on Rachel's shoulder. 'You coming?'

'Sure,' she said. 'Gabriel, will you come with us?'

'Where to?'

'Have you heard of Delroy Richards?'

'Yes.'

'There's going to be a meeting for him in about twenty minutes at the youth centre. We're going to show our support.'

Peter sucked his teeth. 'I can't believe you two think it's more impor-
tant to go to meetings about Delroy Richards than wait for news about
Mary.'

Jeffrey turned red. Rachel grabbed him and pushed him out of the
room. Gabriel followed.

Rachel and Jeffrey led Gabriel into a rather dilapidated building covered
in dirt encrusted murals and sloganizing graffiti. The windows on the
ground floor were boarded over. A heavy security gate covered a
battered door. They went past damp walls up a flight of dusty stairs.
On the top floor they entered a long hall.

A number of tables had been laid out. Some displayed books on
African and Caribbean literature; others contained brochures and fliers
on the National Health, welfare benefits, law centres, libraries and civil
rights. The smell of spiced food, fruits and vegetables hung in the air.
Bins filled with empty cans and soiled napkins dotted the floor.

On the back wall were two banners. The first read: 'This youth centre
was built in 1976. Since that year over thirty black people have been
murdered in this country by racists.' Posters of a group of men hung
on the wall with several names and accompanying information: 'Gurdip
Singh Chaggar – aged eighteen, stabbed to death in Southall by a gang
of white youths; Altab Ali and Ishaque Ali, murdered in Brick Lane;
Michael Ferreira, murdered in Hackney; Akhtar Ali Baig, murdered
in Newham; Mohammed Arif and Malcom Chambers, murdered in
Swindon; Sewa Singh Sunder, murdered in Windsor.' The second
banner contained the words, 'Delroy Richards has joined this list of
hate and shame. Don't let your son or daughter be next!'

A group had seated itself in a circle. A tall Rastafarian standing in
the centre, his hair covered by an enormous woollen hat, welcomed
them. His accent was pure Hampshire. 'Thank you for coming, Jeffrey.
For those of you who don't know him, Jeffrey is a director of the
Battersea Bridging Centre, one of the many facilities set up by the
Swansea Road Pentecostal Church, which is arguably the most influen-
tial black church in the country. Jeffrey's centre was set up to try and
intervene directly within areas of stress for black people. It has taken
a very active part in publicizing the reasons which have brought us
here today.' He sifted through his papers. 'These reasons are laid out
on the information sheets which you have been given.'

The room filled with the sound of paper rustling.

'As you will see, we have many complaints to discuss. There is the old chestnut of the SUS laws.'

This set off a host of disapproving murmurs.

Rachel smiled reassuringly at Gabriel, who glanced over the sheets of an elderly man to his right.

'From all over London, black organizations are reporting the draconian style in which the police are harassing the black youth, forcing them into spontaneous acts of aggression, so that they can lock them up. One of the purposes of this meeting will be to organize a march through London protesting at the SUS laws. I'm sure that we're going to come under pressure from the police to react badly, so stewarding will be vitally important.'

The man next to Gabriel raised his hand. 'Edwin, I raised this very point last week at a union meeting. Several of the drivers said that they would be more than willing to sort out their shifts, so that they could help out with stewarding.'

A grey-haired woman with a slight stoop spoke up. 'Edwin, I believe dis may turn out to be one of de most important areas. De last ting we want is to be splashed across television screens makin' fools of ourselves.'

A number of people voiced their agreement.

Encouraged, she continued, 'De youngstahs have to remembah dat havin' a right to march brings with it responsibility.'

Someone said, 'Right to march. What's that supposed to mean?'

Edwin held up his hand. 'I think it'd be better if we stuck to the agenda –'

'We have a right to march. It's not something we have to beg for.'

'Otherwise, this meeting will seriously overrun. Contributions are welcome, but let's try to keep discussion down while we go over the necessary points.'

Edwin turned to another Rastafarian who wore a yellow jumper with a representation of the African continent woven on to the left side of his chest. 'Clive, you have something to present?'

Clive cleared his throat as he turned the pages of a small pamphlet which sat on his lap. 'We 'ave heah a likkle report wid big tings in it. De report consist a' testimony fram many of de yout' an' certainly back up all we have been sayin' about de pohlice.' He paused for a dramatic scratch of his nose. 'It certainly a bad report, very bad. Tings caan' be allowed to carry on so.'

Elizabeth shook her head furiously. 'Noh, noh, it woan' carry on so.'

Edwin came in again. 'Thank you, Clive. Copies of this report will of course be circulated to all interested parties. I'd like to personally thank Daniel for all the work he put into getting this report together. If he hadn't given up many hours of personal time, there's no way it would have been as comprehensive and thorough. As it is, the facts are indisputable and we can back them up all the way. Daniel?'

Daniel sat up, his papers in order. 'Thank you, Edwin,' his Trinidadian lilt thick and sing-song. 'The stopping and searching of our youth has been getting out of hand. Drive down any street and you'll see a policeman stopping some boy and hassling him. Everybody knows it's happening – the schools, the parents, everybody. So, I am more than happy to report that our counteraction has been going so smoothly over the last few months. All the youth clubs we've contacted have been more than positive. We've hit countless walls, job centres, halls, discos, churches – you name it, they've got our leaflets and posters there.'

Applause rang out.

'I'd like to thank the representatives of the Southall Women for Women Organization and the Brick Lane Defence Group for the amount of work they've done in their areas.'

A well-built Sikh, wearing a BLAIR PEACH WAS A FRIEND OF MINE T-shirt, flashed a bright smile and held up his hand to identify himself. His colleague, an Indian girl dressed from head to toe in black, with lipstick to match, looked away in embarrassment.

'Guptah and Rowena's work has been invaluable in addressing the problems in Southall and other Indian communities. The most valuable aspect of this report, I suspect, will be the way in which it has built up a conclusive picture of the number of stop-and-searches carried out by the police and of their target areas.'

Daniel turned over a page, his action mirrored by most of his listeners. 'You'll see a table on page one. It lists areas such as Brixton, Balham, Clapham, Battersea, Peckham, Norwood, Camden, Hounslow, Finsbury Park, and so on and so on, and records the amount of reported stop-and-searches over a period of six months. With eye-witness accounts by workers who spent weeks in sensitive areas and recorded what they saw. The pattern is not a pretty one. You won't be surprised to hear that the metropolitan police forces that we've sent this to have flatly rejected our findings. That rejection hasn't prevented our phone from being bugged.'

Edwin looked up from his copy of the report. 'So if anyone has a private phone call to make and you don't want it going into a computer —' About him, heads gently rocked in disbelief as dry, mocking laughter lifted up from the group.

Daniel continued, 'We have sent this information out to interested parties, i.e., sympathetic trade unions and certain left-wing publications, but I would not hold my breath to see it passed about where it could do most good. And if it reached those areas, I suspect it would either be distorted or made light of. The main thing is we have it. We know it to be true and we can start to do something about it.'

Daniel finished to a steady stream of applause which lasted for almost a minute until Edwin brought the attention of the group back to himself. 'And now, without further ado, I suggest we move on to the main source of interest for everyone here today.'

He turned and squeezed the hand of the woman seated on his left. 'This, as most of you will know, is Sonia Richards, sister of Delroy Richards. Delroy was murdered within the doors of a police station which is situated only 200 yards from here. We have marched past this station once before, and will be doing so again over the next three weeks. Sonia is here to help us drum up some more support for that march, to cast some light on Delroy's personality, which has been maligned by the police, and to help us understand his mood that day, the day of his murder.'

Sonia got to her feet and pulled down the hem of her skirt as a smattering of applause broke out from the attentive circle of listeners. She began slowly with her head down, avoiding direct eye contact.

'I don't really know how to describe his mood, the way he was feeling that day. My brother's the sort of person who can be sitting next to you at a table and you wouldn't notice him. Sometimes you're eating and you ask where he is and there he is, right next to you. I know it sounds a bit much, but there it is.

'He isn't the brightest of people. I don't think that he would take offence if I said that. Well, he can't now, anyway. But he wouldn't. He weren't like that. I ain't saying he was a saint, 'cause he wasn't, he did bad things like anyone else. He didn't do them out of spite or badness, 'cause he wasn't bad. He was – he was just – a bit slower than most people, that's all. But he wasn't bad, that's the point.

'They say that Delroy shot himself with a shotgun. Well, I can't believe that. I mean, who shoots themselves with a shotgun and who does it in a police station? But that's what they're asking us to believe, that my brother walked into a police station and shot himself.

'I mean, what kind of nonsense is that? Delroy wouldn't know how to work a gun, never mind find one! Yet all of a sudden he's supposed to walk up there and blow his head off!'

Angry exclamations of disbelief from her audience caused her confidence to spiral.

'No one has said where he got this gun.' She brought up her hands, 'Sorry, sawn-off shotgun. Not a gun, a revolver, a pistol – a sawn-off shotgun! No one says how it is that he walked that far without anyone seeing the thing.'

Her lips flared, baring clenched teeth. 'And no one's said why he should do it! They've said that he had a history of mental illness! They've said that he was having trouble at college! But no one – not me, not my mother, his father, not his brother Henry, his brother Steven, or any of his cousins – can say why he did it! And if we can't say it – if we can't say it was girl trouble, or learning trouble, or 'phrenia this, or 'phrenia that, then who can? Who?! How many people – how many have to die before something is done about it? How many? Just show me one policeman who's paid for all the killing. Where are they?'

Someone yelled, 'Getting in more practice.'

Sonia nodded righteously as the temperature in the hall rose, holding out her hands as if she could feel their heartbeats within her palm.

'They shoot that boy down in Brixton and nothing happens. A child – a child crawling under the bed, and nothing happens.'

The calls came quick.

'A baby!'

'Nuttin' but a baby!'

'How a chile gwine shoot a pohlice officah?'

'How his face fit dat of a killah!'

Clive's voice rose above the others, 'De bwoy dun nuttin'! Nuttin'!'

Sonia jabbed a finger at him. 'That's right! He was doing nothing! The same as my brother was doing! Nothing! Nothing at all!'

'But de bwoy dead now! He gone now!'

Sonia grabbed a roll of paper from underneath her chair and let it fall open. On the poster the face of an overweight boy of seventeen, hair army-regulation short, the eyebrows meeting over the bridge of a wide nose.

'Dat right. He dead now. Dead. Me fadah work fe British Rail fe ovah twenty yeah, an' in dat time he ongle tek two day off. Two day to mark his modah passin' on! Now, now he caan' get ihmself outta bed. He caan' do anyting – eat, watch de telly, nuttin'. Me modah de same. She inna heavy, heavy shell dat nobody can touch. Me family been torn apart by dese fools, carryin' on about mental illness dis an' mental illness dat! Wen we all knoh! We all knoh deh is nuttin' but murderin' filthy white scum, hu mus' pay, pay fe wa' deh done to my brodah!'

As Sonia's audience congregated about her, Jeffrey made his way over to Gabriel, who stood by himself. 'Quite a scene, eh? Rachel and Sonia are good friends. Over the last few months she's given her a lot of support. Sonia's come to rely on her a lot lately.' They were joined by Guptah and Rowena. Jeffrey greeted them as old friends before introducing them to Gabriel.

'I thought I knew all your family,' said Guptah.

'Whatever, whatever,' said Rowena. 'If you want us to get people on the march, we can do it easily.'

'Yeah, your organization has been doing a lot of work down there.'

'Jeffrey, you always assume that everybody is like you, a well-to-do, middle-class boy who turns up when there is trouble and returns to his thick carpets and packed fridge when the going gets tough,' said Guptah.

'That's not very fair.'

'No, I suppose it isn't. I take it back.'

'We always turn up to help you guys, you know that.'

'Any help is always welcome, but this is specifically an Asian problem.'

'Tell that to Sonia –'

Guptah rose to the bait. 'The only people who have been attacked in Hounslow are Asians. Not one black has been –'

'I thought we were all black as far as the racist attackers were concerned?'

'You know that's not what I meant.'

'It seems to me that's what you meant.'

Rowena asked Guptah, 'Maybe you could explain what you did mean?'

'Don't you two gang up on me.'

'Guptah, you should know by now that that sort of talk is only divisive and ultimately destructive.'

'Rowena –'

'Guptah, just because only Asians are being attacked on the streets of Hounslow, it doesn't mean it's an issue that is ours entirely, not when Afro-Caribbean kids are being treated the same way in Arsenal and Tottenham. Why bother to segregate us into our various cubby holes, when the point is that the people who are attacking us see us as one thing – black?'

'Don't put words in my mouth! I'm simply saying that it is a valid strategy for Asians to highlight the issue of racist attacks which are specifically directed at Asian kids. I'll give you the phone number of the Bangladesh Youth League in the East End, and you can talk to them about Pakistani kids being stabbed by black youths.'

'Didn't we stroll around Hyde Park together, about two years back, on an anti-racist march? You were carrying a 'Blacks against Racism' banner, if I remember correctly.'

'Yes, you do remember correctly.'

Guptah aimed some punches at Jeffrey's arms. Rowena was not impressed. 'Boys will always be boys, I suppose, but could we finish this discussion?'

'Rowena,' snapped Guptah, 'lighten up, will you?'

'What is there to be light about? I thought this was a serious discussion about serious events.'

'Jeffrey, talk to her, will you?'

'Oh, I see, Jeffrey must talk to me, shut me up. I'm out of line, am I?'

'I didn't say that.'

She turned towards Gabriel. 'He did say that, didn't he?'

'Hey, hey, leave my cousin out of this.'

Rowena told Gabriel, 'You should smile a bit more. I haven't seen you smile since you came in here.'

Guptah didn't let this comment slide by. 'Rowena, no one, but absolutely no one, is sterner on a day-to-day basis than you.'

'Is that so?'

'Yes, I think so.'

'Yesterday we admitted a woman whose back was covered in scars from regular whippings from her husband. Her family wouldn't talk to her and the so-called community had shunned her. Like the rest of our women, she's been denounced as a trouble-maker, a whore and worse. After dealing with her this morning and having to wash obscene graffiti, yet again, off the walls of the Refuge, it is little wonder that I am a tad, as you put it, stern.'

Gabriel saw Rachel signalling to him, and after excusing himself, joined her and Sonia.

'Not too bored?' she asked.

'Not at all.'

Sonia said goodbye to Rachel and left the room. Edwin, dropping papers, chased after her. 'Come on,' said Rachel, 'let's go.'

'Shouldn't we wait for Jeffrey?'

'No,' she said, leading him away, giving a perfunctory wave to her other cousin. 'He's on a mission.'

When Rachel and Gabriel left the building they found a group of skinheads demonstrating across the street. At their appearance, the group started to chant and wave boards with slogans such as 'Rights for Whites' and 'Support Your Police against Violent Immigrants!' One of them shouted, 'Come on, love, try some white meat! Get it while you can!'

Rachel said to Gabriel, 'Ignore them. They're just animals.'

As they climbed into the Volvo, someone shouted, 'Monkeys shouldn't drive white men's cars.'

Gabriel accelerated into the group. Mouths dropped, teeth were bared, cheeks prepared to hurl spit, before bravado burst and they scattered. Rachel, clapping her hands together and roaring with laughter, gave them the V sign and got many in return. As they sped on she kissed his cheek. 'Gabriel, they're just stupid, they don't know any better. I know them, they aren't hard-core.'

'Why bother to differentiate?'

'Sometimes, it's important to.'

'Why?'

'Because. That's all.'

*

They were both out of breath by the time they'd climbed to the top of her building and reached the apartment. Rachel swung open the door with, 'There's a roof garden up on top, you can see over everything. I'll take you up one day.' She sniffed her hallway. 'The smell is an incense – I got it from Rowena. I love coming back to it.'

A series of boxes were stacked along the hall, overflowing with books and magazines. Rachel and Gabriel went into a bedroom devoid of cupboards or drawers, piled with clothes in all manner of prints and colours. On the bed lay a plethora of toy animals. Golden teddy bears lay alongside green hippopotamuses, furry tigers, monkeys, plastic dogs, fluffy cats and leather mice.

It took her a few minutes to find a kettle and cups. 'Did I say tea?'

'Coffee will be fine.'

'If you look in the other room you'll find some bean-bags. Bring them in here and we'll sit and talk.'

While he was gone, she picked a pint-sized blue monkey off the bed and told it, 'Mommy's missed you, missed you badly today. Hope you haven't missed Mommy as bad as she's missed you? Mommy doesn't want you to feel bad.' When Gabriel returned with the bean-bags she offered the monkey to him. 'Go on, take him. His name is Marvin.' Gabriel held the monkey. 'You must be very careful with him, he's one of my best friends. I take the measure of a person by how they get on with Marvin.'

Gabriel placed Marvin's head in his mouth and began to chew. Rachel snatched the toy away from him. 'You bastard! I could kill you!' She stroked Marvin's head. 'There, there, baby, did the bad man hurt you? Did the bad man upset you?' Marvin was placed next to a fierce-looking tiger. 'Uncle Claws will look after you. He'll make sure the bad man doesn't come near you.' She tweaked Gabriel's ear between her forefinger and thumb. 'Men like you should be exterminated at birth,' she said, and bit his ear.

He leant away.

She continued to kiss him. 'What's wrong?'

'I'm going to leave now.'

And he did.

She poured herself a cup of coffee and wondered how their next meeting would go.

*

After buying a bottle of Bacardi, Gabriel sped about London, merrily heading nowhere. Eventually he stopped alongside the wall which ran around his mother's cemetery and, with his bottle safely tucked under his arm, he climbed the wall.

Just after midnight, constables Paul Roberts and David Blain, half way through completing their patrol, found a young adult of Afro-Caribbean origin climbing out of Wandsworth cemetery. Having determined that he was in an unfit condition and clearly a nuisance to the general public, they placed him in their car and drove him to Tooting Bec police station.

Gabriel was hauled before the desk sergeant, Andrew Deacon, and was asked to empty his pockets. Gabriel searched through his clothes and handed over his wallet and the egg.

'What's your name? Come on, hurry up.'

'I don't remember.'

'Don't mess me about, it isn't worth it. It'll only make things worse for you.'

'I don't remember.'

Roberts held up his hands. 'I told you he was a case.'

'You think you're pretty funny, don't you?'

'The thought had not occurred to me.'

'The thought had not occurred to you? Well, Lord fucking Byron, we'll see what occurs to you in the morning and you'll find yourself up on every charge I can think of.' Deacon waved at Roberts. 'Take him away before I forget my community training and thump him, will you?'

Roberts directed Gabriel into a cell and on to a tiny bench. 'You are a one, aren't you? I hope for your sake that you're as out of your head as you seem to be, 'cause that's the only hope you've got.'

Gabriel leaned back against the wall.

'Sobering up fast, eh? Good, good.' Roberts tapped him on the forehead. 'What's going on in your head, eh? Is someone in there? I think you need help, mate.'

Sergeant Evans, shirt-sleeves rolled up, entered the cell. 'I gather you profess to be unable to remember your name? That's very silly of you. I want you to make a statement, starting of course with your name and address.'

'I told you, I can't remember anything.'

'Are you saying to me that you can't remember anything?'

'That's right.'

'How about the cemetery, do you remember that?'

'I remember waking up and being brought here, that's all.'

'Have you been in hospital lately?'

'Hospital?'

'Yes, hospital.'

'I can't remember.'

'Of course not. We'll leave you alone for a while and maybe some memories will come back to you. One thing's for sure, you won't be leaving here until they do.'

Evans broke off for a quick conference with Roberts. 'What do you make of him?'

Roberts tapped his temple. 'I don't think he's all there.'

'Very good Roberts, that's just the sort of insightful brilliance that's going to see you take this division by storm.'

'Sir, I meant –'

Evans silenced him. 'In the morning, I want you to check the local divvie bins. Give them his details and see if they've released anyone like him lately. If not, check out some of the local hostels.'

'He doesn't look like one of them, Sarge. Usually they look like shit. His clothes are all right.'

'Yeah, but I can't believe someone like him hasn't had contact with any of the social agencies. This place is becoming a haven for half the idiots from every whacko hospital in town. As if we didn't have enough problems doing what we're supposed to do, we've also got to be rounding up these poor buggers and keeping them out of trouble.'

'What we going to do with him?'

'Follow procedure, but just in case he is a piss-taker, we'll sit him out. If he wants to play silly games, we can play them as well, but we can play them for longer. No one, but no one, comes in here and gets away with taking the piss. Understood?'

'Understood.'

Gabriel failed to recall anything about himself throughout the night, the next morning or indeed for the whole of the following day. Food was offered, but he politely refused it. As the hours passed, various officers stopped to look in on him. Hospitals were checked, hostels rung, but none could offer any useful information.

During the late evening of the second day of his internment, Sergeant Evans and Constable Roberts entered his cell. Evans asked him to stand up. 'Fun and games are over, give us your name.'

'I told you, I –'

Evans held up his hand. 'I know, I know, you can't remember. I don't want that answer. I want the truth. Your name, your phone number, your address, the school you went to, your job, if you have one. Everything.'

Evans and Gabriel faced off.

Roberts watched carefully. Evans's staring matches were legendary amongst the station fraternity. Bets were often taken when a new prisoner came in. So when Evans locked his hands behind his back, spread his feet wide and stared his opponent right in the eyes, he suppressed a knowing grin.

Gabriel didn't blink nervously or step away like those who had gone before, but calmly returned Evans's gaze. Time passed. Roberts looked down at his watch. Minutes ticked by as Roberts studied the two protagonists. They ignored him. Another eight minutes passed by. Traces of sweat built up on Evans's face and Roberts felt his heart begin to pound. A gasp escaped from his lips when the jaw-jutting Evans broke eye contact, but not before kneeing Gabriel in the groin.

'What's your game, eh? Do you think you can sit around here on your arse doing fuck all and laughing at us all? Do you think this is some sort of game? What's your name?'

Gabriel looked up at Evans with utter contempt. 'You don't scare me.'

That proved he was truly gone, and for his lip Evans dug his thumb into Gabriel's neck. 'Don't I? Don't I?'

Despite his evident pain he refused to cry out. Evans's face turned red with his effort. 'How long do you think you can keep this up? I've got men lined up out there to give you a kicking. You think we haven't got better things to do than play games with you? Do you honestly think I've got the time to mess about with you? Whatever you've got going on in your brain, forget it! I can keep you in here for ever if I want!'

Evans dropped on to his knee and twisted Gabriel's ear. Gabriel looked him straight in the eye and, as if he were trying to put a child to sleep, said, 'I'm not afraid of you. I've experienced worse.'

Evans twisted the ear again. 'You'll still be in here when you're old and grey if I say so.'

'Well you won't see it.'

Evans leant forward. 'What did you say?'

'I said you won't see it.'

'Oh, I won't see it. Did you hear that, Roberts? He says I won't see it. Why won't I see it? Are you going to do something to me? Is that it, boy? You're going to do me in?'

Gabriel shook his head, then lightly tapped his throat. At first Evans didn't understand, then his entire face and neck flushed a deep pink. Roberts reached out for him. 'Sarge, what is it?'

Evans slapped Roberts's hand away as goose bumps began to pucker along his skin. All strength and certainty began to leak from him.

'Sarge, Sarge, what is it?'

Evans could hardly speak. 'How did you know?'

Gabriel sniffed haughtily, laying down upon the bench as if he were on the beach. 'You won't see out the year.'

Evans exploded and lunged at him. 'How did you know?!' Roberts grabbed hold of Evans, pushing himself between his colleague and the prisoner, taking several kicks in the stomach as Evans screamed, 'Let me go!'

The cell door opened and two policemen rushed into the cell. Roberts implored them to get the sergeant out before he killed the lunatic. Despite his fury, Evans was hauled away from the cell. Deacon and a number of stunned officers arrived as Evans wailed, 'How did he know? Nobody knew, not even my wife.'

Deacon tried to comfort him, but Evans was inconsolable and collapsed into a heap on the floor.

'What the hell is going on?' demanded Deacon of Roberts. 'What did he do to him?'

Roberts blocked the doorway. 'Leave him, he didn't do nothing! Leave him.'

Deacon was losing it. 'You telling me this happened over nothing?'

'Yeah,' answered a flustered Roberts as Evans wept uncontrollably. 'That's what happened.'

Forty-five minutes later, Chief Inspector Brown held court in his office along with Evans, Roberts and the welfare officer, Bryant. Evans sipped from a mug filled with coffee. Brown, a heavily built Welshman, asked, 'You all right now, Kevin?'

'Yes,' answered Evans, 'thank you, Sir.'

'Well it would be best if you told us what happened.'

Evans looked at Roberts. 'We were talking to him, you know, trying to clear up a few things. I was giving him a bit of verbal, you know, playing it hard to try and get him to talk. And I told him that he would be in this cell till he was an old man if I wanted it to be that way.'

Brown lit up a pipe. 'And?'

'And he said some things to me, and I said some things to him.'

'Speak up Kevin, please.'

'He said that I wouldn't see him in the cell for as long as I was threatening. When I asked him why, he said that I wouldn't see the year out because of my cancer.'

'Why the hell should something silly like that bother you?'

'Because it's true. I do have cancer. My doctor's given me less than ten months.'

Brown took some time to respond. 'Why haven't you said anything? When were you going to say something?'

'I dunno. Soon, maybe.'

'I'm sorry, Kevin, I don't know what to say.'

'There's nothing to say, is there? Words don't change anything, really.'

'How is Eve taking it?'

'I haven't told her yet.'

'You haven't?'

'No, no, I've only had the news for a few weeks. I've asked our GP not to say anything to her. Not yet. I need some time.'

'You've only known for a few weeks, and haven't said anything to anyone. Then how can this lad have known?'

'I've no idea, Sir, none. It's impossible. That's what freaked me out.'

'All right, all right. You'd better go now, Kev. There's not much good to be done here. John will go with you and talk a few things through.'

Evans left the room, shadowed by Bryant.

Brown turned to Roberts. 'What do you make of him?'

'Do you mean, is he a villain, Sir?'

'Yes, is he a villain?'

'No, Sir, I wouldn't say so. A bit weird, but he didn't give us any hassle, no attitude. He's obviously just a bit mixed up.'

'You believe him, about his mother being buried there?'

'We checked with the caretaker, Sir. He mentioned that a young man who fits the lad's description had called to see him about a woman who is buried there.'

'And did he give a name?'

'No, Sir. The caretaker said that the name of the woman was wrong.'

'Wrong? How can it be wrong?'

'It seems he had misunderstood the husband of the deceased, what with him being from overseas and all, the West Indies I presume. So we know that his mother is buried there – the grave is unmarked – but we don't know his correct name.'

Brown examined some notes before him. 'But this caretaker has come in and made a positive identification?'

'Yes, Sir. The guy said that the lad had never been there before. Our guess is that he got a bit upset and went for a bit of a drink.'

'A bit of a drink? Hm. We haven't really got anything to charge him with, have we?'

'No, Sir.'

'I mean it's all very interesting, but do we really want all of this coming up? I think we would all agree that we might find this episode a bit embarrassing, to say the least, if all of this nonsense was to get out.'

'Is it right to let him walk the streets, Sir? I mean he hasn't given us his name or anything.'

'Perhaps it's best if we section him. At least that would keep him off the streets.'

'He's obviously quite ill – best he's somewhere where he can receive help.'

'Pity is, he'll probably end up drugged up to his eyebrows, no trouble to anyone, but getting bugger-all help. But I don't see what else we can do, and as the saying goes, we're policemen, not social workers.'

Brown's phone rang. He answered it and listened before replacing the handset. 'Well, well. It seems we have someone who has identified our friend.'

A few moments later, Rupert Wills walked into the office, carrying a light briefcase. Brown offered his hand. 'Reverend, it is always a pleasure to see you. What can I do for you?'

Roberts left the two men alone.

'Well, Inspectah, me come to find out about me daughtah and instead find yu have me nephew.'

'You've identified him?'

'Mos' definitely.'

'Your nephew? Well, that is a mighty coincidence.'

'So tell me de story.'

'A few days ago, he was found drunk and disorderly. He resisted arrest –'

'Nonsense.'

'Not at all.'

'Doan' start wid dis pohlice rubbish, please.'

'Come on, Rupert, you know me better than that. We go too far back for such talk. I was walking the beat when you didn't have space to preach to your own family, let alone anybody else. Let's not get into any of that, please. Now, I've studied the reports of the two arresting officers and the evidence would seem to indicate that he had consumed a large quantity of alcohol.'

'Me caan' comment on dat.'

'Perhaps there are some things you could comment on. Though I'd like to stress that I wouldn't want this conversation to be repeated outside this room.'

'Eif yu seh so.'

Brown raised his pipe again. 'Your nephew seems to be an interesting boy. He has said a few things which have upset some of my men.'

'Wa kine a' tings?'

'Perhaps you could throw some light on them. It seems your nephew had a lapse of memory, and was unable to remember who he was.'

'He do dat. It like a cramp, you knoh – it tighten up, den go.'

'That's hard to believe.'

'Everathing me seh be true.'

'Why hasn't he received help? Surely something can be done?'

'Me is a man of God, not medicine.'

'When another officer questioned him, he mentioned this officer's cancer –'

'Cancah?'

'A cancer that he had only become aware of recently. A cancer that he had not even mentioned to his wife, or any colleague. A cancer that your nephew should have been completely unaware of, and yet –'

'– he knoh.'

'Yes, but how?'

'Me caan' tell yu.'

'So where does that leave us?'

The smoke from Brown's pipe caused Rupert's eyes to water. 'Wen me was a bwoy, deh was dis woman. Eif yu got a graze or a bad cut, she fix it jus' by layin' her hand 'pon yu. Back home, dis kine a' ting ain' so special. Ovah heah, yu mek a fuss, put it on television, ride it hard on de news, but back home anyone who knoh anyting, knoh weh to fin' dem.'

'I'm not sure I understand everything you say. In fact I know I don't.'

'Wud yu like me to start again?'

'No, no. Look, this is what I'll do. I don't want to put a blot on this young man's record if he is, as you say, normally well-behaved. I will insist, though, on your personally having words with him about his drink problem. This time, as I said, it can go, but if it leads to another incident then I will come down hard on him.'

'Tank yu, Inspectah.'

Brown pushed back his chair and stood up. 'I'll take you to him. If, as you say, this is a phase he goes through, then it might be over by now. I must insist again that you take him to a doctor.'

The two men shook hands.

'Would you like to leave your case here?'

'Not reahlly.'

The two men left the office for the cells.

Brown stood aside as a constable opened the cell. Rupert went in, noticing the peeling paint, patches of damp and growing mildew. A breeze cooled his skin as flies circled the bare light-bulb. Gabriel, eyes shut, ignored his arrival and carried on braiding his hair.

Rupert placed his briefcase on the floor. 'Gabriel? Gabriel, me come fe yu. Yu ready to come wi' me?'

'Gabriel calmly finished off his hair before answering, 'I don't know you.'

Rupert placed a photograph before his nephew. 'Me is ya uncle, Rupert. Look at it. It woan' do no good eif yu doan' look. Tek it.'

Gabriel looked the picture over with bloodshot eyes. 'Wa' wrong, bwoy? Deh mess yu up wid some kine a' chemical shit, or someting?'

'Go away.'

'Listen, bwoy, wise up, oddahwise yu sleepin' rough tonight. Yu wan' dat? Yu really wan' dat?'

'Leave me alone.'

Rupert pulled out a portable mirror from his wallet. 'Heah, look.'

The mirror was taken from him.

'Now look at de piccha.'

Gabriel's eyes flickered from the glass to the picture and back again. 'You know me?'

Rupert chuckled. 'Yes, bwoy, yes. Me is blood to yu.'

Gabriel's strength left him and he collapsed. Rupert caught him. 'Easy youngstah, me here, me here.' Rupert held him close and mumbled, 'Josie, Josie, me doan' knoh. Tell me wat yu bring to me, tell me.'

Uncomfortable with the weight, Rupert eased Gabriel down on to the bench. A quick sweep over his own hair to press down any curls that may have been ruffled, then he got up to stretch. Behind him came, 'Rupert, how many times do I have to tell you not to do that?'

Stunned by the impossible familiarity of the voice, Rupert spun round. Everything was as it should have been. He was alone with Gabriel. His heart still beating, he mopped his mouth and reassured himself with, 'Me mus' be losin' me mind.'

Gabriel chuckled and said in that old voice, 'How many times me got to tell yu not to talk like dem oddah children?'

Mouth dropping, lungs burning, Rupert could only stutter, 'Papa?' as his nephew sat up stiffly, crossed his legs and softly tapped his raised right heel against his left shin, and scratched his chin. Rupert, recognizing the physical mannerisms, backed away from him. 'No, no, dis caan' be happen'n'.'

His nephew bellowed, 'How many times, how many times mus' yu join de table talking like some field hand an' expect to eat? Go an' wash out ya mouth. Go!'

Rupert fell to the floor, his face wet with perspiration, panting desperately for air. 'No, no, dis caan' be. De Lord wouldn' let it be so!'

He heard a rich baritone laugh he hadn't heard for years. 'Look up, bwoy, look up! Yu got nuttin' to fear fram me.'

Rupert did as he was told. He found his nephew sitting up rigidly on the bench, his head raised upwards, the muscles along his jawbone flexing powerfully, legs and feet together, hands upon his knees, thumbs slowly massaging each other. 'No, no, me doan' believe dis.' As he got to his feet, his palms made a squelching sound. 'Me caan' believe it, me woan' believe it.'

'Why?!'

'Papa?'

'Good, good.'

'No, no!'

His thumbs stopped rubbing against each other, a gesture which caused Rupert's already pounding heart to increase its fervour. 'Gabriel, wi yu do dis?'

Gabriel exploded. 'Doan' talk like dat! Does your sistah talk so silly? Look at her, sitting there having to listen to this nonsense. She is ashamed a' yu. Good people, fine people come to visit me. Do yu speak to dem, do yu listen? No, yu run out and play silly games. Wat qualification did hitting a cricket ball ever gain yu?'

Rupert lifted his hands to his face and began to weep. Through his fingers a muffled 'Oh, God,' escaped as he rolled over on to his back.

'Yu cry too easily, Rupert, far too easily. Wat tears will yu shed when yu fail to achieve creditable marks in school and ya caan' go to university? Yu tink your fadah will see evaryting right?'

Gabriel began to cough. An old, sickly cough.

Rupert placed his hands together. 'The Lord is my shepherd, I shall not want, he leadeth me into –'

The coughing was forced away by laughter. 'Rupert, yu is a grown man, stop acting like a child. Face me. Talk to me.'

Rupert got to his feet, the material of his suit soaked with the wet of his fear. 'Dis ain' right, it ain' right.'

'Start again, Rupert. Yu knoh yu can do it. I knoh yu can do it.'

Rupert glared back. 'Enuff, Papa, deh is no need fe dis.'

'No need?'

'Deh was nevah any need.'

'Wipe your face, yu sweatin' like a pig.'

Again, Rupert did as he was told.

Gabriel's shoulders dropped over his chest. At the top of his back a curve had formed, preventing him from sitting upright against the wall. 'I nevah could trust yu to do right, ongle to fail.'

'Papa –'

'An' look wat yu haf become. Did ya sistah turn out so?'

'Doan' involve her in dis.'

'Why not?'

'She got nuttin' to do wit it.'

'Rupert, yu is a man now, so why do you hide your face fram me? Face me.'

Rupert looked up. 'Wa' yu wan', Papa?'

Gabriel raised his arms for Rupert.

'No, no.'

'Come, Rupert.'

At first, as he rebelled against the truth of the meeting, Rupert's step was slow and hesitant, but as he moved in close and hands cupped the back of his head in *that* gesture, the contact brought back memories of almost forgotten touch. He closed his eyes so that vision would not interfere and allowed happiness to flower within his heart. The years fell away, the secret pains and quiet moments of despair rose, were acknowledged and shared.

Later, when he was truly sure of what had occurred, he opened his eyes and rubbed the warm hands. 'Papa.' The face before him was for the first time completely impassive, only reacting when the friction became unpleasant. 'Papa? Wi yu heah, Papa? Dis place ain' fe yu. Yu can ongle bring distress to Gabriel.'

'Forgive an old man for his selfishness. Bein' wid yu, it bring me great pleasure.'

Rupert's heart squeezed out another petal from his eyes. 'Tank yu, Papa, tank yu.' He raised the hands and kissed them.

'Dis world full a' many rotten tings, Rupert, but doan' turn ya mind against its trut's.'

'Me follah de Lord. Me knoh de trut' a' his word an' his vision.'

'An' dis trut', Rupert, do yu find dis trut' in his book?'

'Me find evaryting widdin his book, Papa, evaryting.'

A hand touched his cheek, moving as if the muscles were worn and wasted by a heavy accumulation of years. 'Doan' lose evaryting because yu place all you got in one book. Paper will burn more easily den flesh. Look to de wisdom widdin de flesh of our family.'

'Yu frighten me, Papa.'

'Did yu fear ya sistah?'

'Me knoh her, Papa, me knoh her heart.'

'Den embrace her progeny, embrace her legacy.'

'Me is afraid, Papa. Yu scare me. Me beleeve in Jesus. Me knoh he is powah. He rule ovah evaryting, but yu scare me so.'

The hand fell away from his cheek.

'Papa?'

The youth's eyes closed and he fell asleep.

Rupert ran his hands over his nephew's face, squeezing muscles, pressing into bone as if he might bring something out. It was futile. He got up and paced up and down, brought out his mirror and preened himself until his appearance was satisfactory.

Gabriel began to wake.

His uncle rushed over. 'Doan' try to stahn'. Siddun, siddun.'

Gabriel began to gag. Rupert let loose some hefty blows on his back. 'Yu all right, bwoy? Yu all right?'

A cough and a dry, strangulated, 'Yes', then a swift movement to stay the striking hand.

Rupert moved a finger before Gabriel's face. His eyes followed the digit easily enough. 'Right, right, yu seem to be fine.' With a hand over his heart, Rupert cast his gaze upwards. Tank yu, Lord, tank yu. Me knoh yu could not let dis bwoy come to any harm.'

Gabriel croaked, 'Rupert, are you all right?'

Rupert slapped Gabriel's shoulder. 'Yes, bwoy, yes, me is all right, jus' fine, me nevah felt bettah.' He bent down. 'Listen to me. Do yu remembah how yu get heah?'

'No.'

'Den how come yu so cool about all dis?'

'I am not easy about it . . . I am not alone, you are here.'

A warm honey pride flushed through Rupert's belly. 'Yes. Look, eif yu wan' ta leave dis place, listen closely to wat me seh.'

A short time later, Rupert, holding on to his briefcase, banged on the cell door. It was opened and they were escorted to Inspector Brown's office. On the way they passed a vending machine, so Rupert bought Gabriel some hot chocolate to wet his throat. As they continued on their way, Rupert could not help but notice the stares and glances directed at Gabriel. He was quite relieved to find himself within the inspector's room.

Inspector Brown, alone, stood up, 'Take a seat, please. I understand your name is Gabriel.'

Gabriel sat next to Rupert without saying anything.

'Well, I'm glad that we've managed to come to a better understanding of this situation. I don't like to go at things in a heavy-handed manner – it seldom works out for the best.'

'Me explain evaryting to Gabriel, an' he ready to accompany me to the doctah.'

'I'd like to be kept abreast of developments, if you don't mind, just in case this situation occurs again.'

'Tank yu, Inspectah, we appreciate ya undastandin'.'

'No problem, Reverend. I was born and bred on this patch; my family go way back. I've seen it change a lot, but people remain the same. I see it as part of my function to keep things on an even keel for everyone. Prisons are for filth – scum belong in there. I don't like to see –' he pauses, 'I don't like to see unfortunates in there, if at all possible.'

'Tank yu, Inspectah, tank yu.' Rupert paused, then asked, 'Well, about me daughtah?'

'I'm sorry, there has been no news. I appreciate it's been a long time for you, but it's not that long for a case like this. As I've said to you before, we can't be 100 per cent sure that it is a police matter. But with the best will in the world, without leads, well – I think all I can recommend is patience.'

Rupert bowed his head and ran his fingers over his face.

'I'm sorry, Mr Wills, but there's nothing more I can say.'

'I got someting fe yu, Inspectah.'

'Something for me?'

Rupert took a letter out of his briefcase and handed it over.

Brown slipped on his reading glasses and read out, 'Your bitch daughter is dead. All of your kind should be dead. More will follow!' After a pause he said, 'It's not very nice. I'm sure it's just the work of a crank, but I'll –'

'A crank?'

'I'm sure.'

'Dat is all yu got to say?'

'I'll look into it, of course, but I'm –'

Rupert snatched the letter back and stormed out of the office.

Gabriel followed.

*

Rupert, muttering, set a fair pace through the station. 'Deh can sit on deh bloodclat backside an' talk deh cor blimey chit chat, like dem knoh wat deh ah do. All dem ah do is kiss arse an' come up wid pure shit!' He snorted. 'De man talk shit, pure an uttah shit.'

They trotted past the reception desk, with Rupert's voice easily carrying down the whole hall. He threw his weight against a door, and bellowing, 'A lettah is a lettah is a lettah!' threw the offending paper into a bin and bounced out of the station.

Gabriel stopped at the reception area to ask for his personal belongings, which had been taken from him.

He found Rupert in the car-park, angrily revving the engine, mumbling about his time being important.

Gabriel slipped his wallet back into his pocket and took the egg out of a plastic bag the police had just given him.

'Weh did yu get dat?' asked Rupert.

Gabriel scratched absent-mindedly at the egg. 'Someone sent it to me.'

'Wen?'

'A couple of days ago.'

Gabriel looked at his uncle. Rupert was staring at the egg, distraught. 'Tell me weh yu got it fram.'

Gabriel slid the egg into his pocket. Rupert, angered, inched forward, but managed to control himself. 'Gabriel, dis na joke. Tell me wen yu get dat ting.'

'It was left on my doorstep.'

Rupert slumped forward and began to beat his head against the steering wheel, shouting, 'No, no, no,' over and over. He wept for quite some time. Eventually he wiped his face and, utterly drained, sat back in his seat. 'Gabriel,' he asked weakly, 'will yu go someweh with me?'

'Yes.'

'Good,' said Rupert, coughing to clear his throat. He slipped the car into first gear and drove away.

Rupert led Gabriel through a sprawling estate. As they approached a row of shops, they pulled over and parked. A sparsely furnished chip shop was easily dwarfed by its neighbour, an enormous newsagent's that flaunted its primary-coloured insides without a nod to taste or discretion. Next to it, a small chemist's, populated by two customers and an apathetic-looking man in a white coat and grey streaked trousers. They passed a greengrocer's, with a selection of fruit that was neither choice nor fresh. The owner sat on a stool reading a copy of the *Daily Star* as he smoked a long cigar.

Over the shops loomed a dirt-encrusted, high-rise building. Its sides had been painted a pastel green; its front was a bright Atlantic blue. The doors to its foyer were locked, so Rupert, under the gaze of a video camera with a broken lens, had to press a button on the broad signal box. A voice questioned them through the intercom. Rupert stated who he was. There was a long pause, and then a muffled chuckle followed by an electronic buzz. Rupert smiled briefly at Gabriel before pushing the door open.

As they came out of the lift Rupert examined himself in his mirror before telling Gabriel to 'Keep quiet an' follah me lead.'

He knocked on a door. Its opening released the aroma of red chicken and rice 'n' peas into the hallway. A middle-aged woman with bright brown eyes and thick artificial eyelashes stood before them, the rich brown of her ample cleavage clearly visible above the low neckline of her coal-black dress, the hips of which were sprinkled with bright, sparkling glitter. She didn't bother to hide her cool appraisal of them.

'Reverend,' she said without any warmth, 'it is lovely to see you. Come in, come in.'

Rupert entered the flat. 'Hello, Gladwin; dis be Gabriel.'

She waved them on. 'Go into the front room. No need to stand on ceremony.'

Gabriel followed Rupert through an apartment that was full of an incredible array of kitsch religious artefacts from many different cultures and ages. The main room was comparatively sparse, the chief elements being two large fish-tanks. Several framed qualifications hung on the walls, alongside portraits of literary figures such as Shakespeare, Jane Austen and T. S. Eliot.

Rupert asked about the qualifications.

'I teach,' she said.

'Teach wat?'

'Oh, Rupert, surely even you can consider people changing over time?'

'Talk straight, woman.'

'Meaning I qualified several years ago as a teacher. I teach English Literature at the adult-education college down the road.'

'Oh.'

'Oh, what?'

'Nuttin', nuttin'.'

'Aren't you going to congratulate me?'

'Of course. Well done.'

She held out her cheek. Rupert reluctantly kissed it.

'That's better. No need to be so formal.'

'And you, young man. Can I get you something? Tea, coffee, alcohol, carrot juice?'

'I will have some carrot juice, please.'

She left with a smile and returned with a tray containing a pink beverage and a china plate covered with finely chopped sticks of sugar cane. The next few minutes passed with much chewing on the cane.

'I'm sorry about your bad news, Reverend. I hope everything will work out.'

'It will, it will. I have spoke to him evary day an' I knoh dat de Lord will ansah my needs.'

Gladwin snorted. 'I always said that pride would be the cause of your fall, Reverend, and you've proved me right. Though the life of your child is at stake you're still as close-minded as ever.' She lit up a cigarette. 'Why did you bring him?'

'He is me nephew.'

'You don't travel with your, how do you say it, "picney" any more, Reverend? Or is that just when you're visiting me? Or shouldn't I speak of such things in front of your nephew?'

'Seh anyting yu like.'

'Anything?'

'Anyting.'

'The whole truth and nothing but the truth? You surprise me, Reverend. You truly surprise. I didn't think that was possible any more.' Her eyes flicked over to Gabriel. 'Tell me, does he have your devil in him? Is he unclean and full of sin?'

'Gladwin –'

'Is he full of the devil's intent?'

Rupert turned away.

Gladwin shouted, causing Rupert to jump visibly, 'Don't ever, ever turn your back on me. Especially not here.'

Rupert bit his lip as Gladwin turned her attention upon Gabriel. 'Who's child are you?'

Rupert answered for him. 'Gabriel belong to Josie.'

Gladwin's face softened. 'I thought so, but I didn't want to raise my hopes. I thought you were lost to us, child. What age are you now, child?'

'I am in my eighteenth year.'

'What a funny thing to say. When is your birthday?'

'My father didn't believe in celebrating birthdays. I go by the year.'

'No? What about school records?'

'He gave them a date; it satisfied them. The point was we knew it was false.'

'Your father was always a bit eccentric. He always did his own thing. You sound just like him.'

'So everyone tells me.'

'You must tell him to visit me, it has been too long. He disappeared out of sight after your dear mother passed away.'

She slapped his thigh playfully. 'It is good to meet you. Your mother was my best friend. England was a new place for both of us. She warmed it for me. He was a fine-looking man – well-read. They made a fine couple. We were all shocked by her death. It was so sudden.

'People like your uncle would tell us that the Christian God poached her to cheer himself up. Like all men, he must be selfish, to sadden us all.'

Rupert asked if he could open the window.

'No one is stopping you.'

'Gladwin, please.'

'Alright, we won't argue. Last time we argued it was at Jocelynne's burial. Last time I passed by, there was still nothing to mark her. Maybe you should explain to Gabriel why his mother lies in an unmarked grave.'

Rupert struggled to contain his anger as Gladwin smiled sweetly at his nephew. 'Your father and your uncle had a fall out. For some reason, Matthew never got round to putting up a stone. Rupert screamed and shouted, but did nothing. He said it was your father's responsibility. I begged him to do something, but he only complained and sulked and, to my mind, enjoyed making your father look bad. Time went by. He swore and cussed your father's name everywhere, but he never took the situation into his hands, and he stopped everybody else doing something constructive. Isn't that true, Reverend?'

'Doan' nuttin' get to change round heah?'

'Some things.'

Rupert pointed at Gabriel. 'Not evaryting. Yu sey he remind yu a' Josie. In wat way?'

'In every way,' she said gently.

'How yu knoh?'

Her voice rose sharply. 'I know. I don't need to pick up some stupid book to help me.'

Rupert chuckled, 'Or check out de bone?'

'How do you open your Bible to the exact page you want, just by letting it fall open? You know because you've carried and studied that book every day of your life. I am the same. My gift has been with me since I could walk. I can see it as clearly as I can see lust in a man's eyes.'

She ignored Rupert for Gabriel. 'I saw it in your mother. I saw it in you as soon as I opened the door. And so does your uncle, otherwise he wouldn't have brought you here.'

'Eif yu doan' wan' to help me –'

'What else do you deserve?'

'Tings need resolvin'. Me daughtah gone. She might be dead for all we knoh.'

'And you think I could find her?'

Rupert loosened his collar as his gaze fell to the floor. 'Me knoh yu do some strange tings. Me knoh yu talk to peopal hu gone befoh.'

'My ancestors.'

'Watevah yu call dem.'

'My ancestors – say it.'

'As yu call dem.'

Her laughter scolded Rupert. 'You want silver found in lead, or bread in the desert, then go somewhere else. I can't help you.'

'Me knoh yu caan' do it,' hissed Rupert, 'but me feel like Gabriel can help.'

'How? Tell me how.'

Rupert walked over to the window, rubbing his wet palms against his trousers. 'Me go to de pohlice station fe news. Me get nuttin'. But deh 'ave Gabriel lock up deh. Wen me visit ihm, strange tings 'appen.'

'Like what, exactly?'

'Look, Gabriel, me doan' mean to shock yu, but wen yu speak to me, me fadah speak thru yu.'

Rupert was pleased to see that Gabriel seemed to take this news with a measure of calm. 'Me fadah seh we can ongle resolve me problem thru family.'

'Has this kind of thing happened to you before?'

Gabriel nodded.

Gladwin's sigh was gentle and caressing. 'A few times?'

'A few times. When I was younger.'

'When?'

'I won't answer that.'

'So you didn't want this to happen?'

'Of course not. Would you?'

Rupert patted his hand. 'No, no. But yu caan' deny de good we might bring about.'

Gladwin burst out laughing. 'I never thought I would see this, but it's happened! It's actually happened!' She leapt to her feet, slapping her hands together. 'You believe, Rupert Wills! After all these years, you believe!' She raced across the floor and jabbed a finger into his chest. 'Don't give me that look! Whenever I spoke of my ancestors, you mocked me, called me a heathen like a white man. You always knew better, always listened to your books and the white voices within them!'

'Gladwin, me nevah deny de existence a' –'

'Quiet! Not a word, Rupert Wills! Not a damn word.'

As Rupert threw up his hands, she joined Gabriel. 'Let me tell you a story. It is an old story of a boy and a girl. The boy was a nice boy, of his age and of his time. The girl was a simple girl; she didn't want much from life. She had no lust for gold or glory. Just a good home with running water and, who knows, perhaps a toilet inside the house.

'The boy had a sister, a fine, good-lookin' girl who was with a good, strong man. They had a child who looked like the sister from the earth. The first girl and the sister got on fine. The first girl always played with the sister's child, because – who knows – perhaps she thought the brother, who she loved, would take inspiration and create a child with her.

'One time, since they liked those things, the girls went off to see a fortune teller. When it came to it, the sister lost her nerve, so the first girl went in all alone. She was given bad news. She was told things wouldn't work out with the man she loved. Worse, she was told that her friend would never return home – that she would die young.

'Naturally, the girl didn't take kindly to this news and sought out another person. She found this woman, her place was small, had a lot of decorations up. Now this woman had a cat, the most wicked-looking cat you could ever see. A big cat with a wicked eye. Because she was nervous she walked about the house while she waited for the woman to get ready. She was sensitive to things and the house made her feel uncomfortable. She came to a kitchen. It had a long sheet spread across its door.

'The kitchen was dark, filled with shadows. She walked about it, not bothering about anything. On the table was a cloth with nothing on it – no flowers, nothing. Suddenly, out of the dark came a deep, deep voice. It said, "Her life is over." ' Gladwin slapped her hands together.

'Well, she leaped back like a jackass on fire, shouting, "Who's there? Who's there?" Again the voice, "Her life be ovah, it ovah." She looked down and she saw the table move. Well, she was scared, but she was tough, she knew about things. She walked over to the table and lifted up the cloth and there was the cat, looking right up at her. Its eyes were red and puffed up. Its back was arched and its claws –' She shaped her hands like claws and held them up before Gabriel's face. 'Its claws dug deep into the floor and its mouth opened and it said, "Her life is ovah." And I knew in that moment that a demon was inside that cat. Well, somehow I got away from that cat, even though it tried to hold me in its power, and I ran out of the room. I ran home screaming, screaming all the way to your uncle here. I told him what had happened. I told him that we had to take steps to protect her, but he wouldn't listen. He called me everything under the sun. He said I was a witch, that I was scum. That I should go back to Africa and practise my filthy habits there. He left me then. Even though I called him and called him for months and months on end, he never returned my calls. Within twelve months he was married to her, then began raising nice Jamaican children.

'And you know the worst of it. Within four years of that cat speaking to me, your mother passed away, just like the beast said. You got the same eye, Gabriel. The same eye as that cat.'

'Enough, Gladwin.'

'It is the truth.'

Gabriel got to his feet. 'Is there anything more you two want to talk about?'

'We got a few tings to discuss.'

Gabriel shook hands with Gladwin and went into the kitchen.

Images of flying birds surrounded him. Steam rose from a pot on the cooker that contained stewing apple. As he dipped a finger into the boiling apple, a moan came from the other room, accompanied by the creaking of a chair leg. The sounds of pleasure and quickening breath reached him all too easily so he closed the kitchen door.

Eventually, Rupert, without a fold of material where it shouldn't be, joined him. 'Shall we be off?'

Gabriel went to leave, but Rupert stopped him. 'How do I look?'

'Fine. Though I think it would be best if you had a wash before you returned home.'

Rupert invited his nephew to smell him. 'See, ya caan' smell anyting.'

'You reek of semen.'

Rupert's smile froze.

'Particularly here.' Gabriel touched Rupert on the eye and on the left side of his neck.

Rupert rushed over to the sink and patted·water about his face. 'Me neck, how de Ras it get 'pon me neck?' Flustered and breathing quickly, he disappeared into the bathroom. Gladwin, perspiring a touch, joined Gabriel in the hallway.

They waited in silence for Rupert to emerge from the bathroom. Ignoring Gladwin, he headed straight for the door. 'Come, Gabriel, we bes' hurry.'

Gladwin waved them goodbye and told Gabriel not to become a stranger.

They were unable to park in Rupert's driveway since it was filled with several cars. Marianne and Ruth came out of the house and took Rupert to one side. They were upset and threw a flurry of questions at him. Rupert told them he had everything in hand, but this didn't seem enough. Ruth walked away as Rupert and Marianne, struggling to keep their voices down, argued in the driveway. Rupert held her and kissed her. She pushed him away and walked off down the street. He called after her, but she kept on walking. 'Doan' worry,' he said to Gabriel, then took him into the house.

A group of four middle-aged men stood up as they entered the lounge. They were smartly attired, but clearly uneasy. Rupert strode confidently into the centre of the room, placed his briefcase down on the floor and warmly shook every hand that was offered him.

'Clarence, good to see yu. Richard, yu is lookin' fine. Madely, Harvey, good to see yu.'

All of the men turned to face Gabriel as Rupert called him over. Clarence, a short man with a protruding stomach and a jet-black curly perm that fell to his shoulders, wrapped both of his hands about Gabriel's hand and pumped it energetically. The softness of his skin was only marginally less striking than the many gold rings which encircled his fingers. Harvey was easily the most seductive in his greetings. The others didn't bother to hide an aloofness which bordered on the arrogant. Clarence asked, with elderly condescension, 'Shouldn't he be in the other room while we talk, Rupert?'

Rupert opened his briefcase. 'No.' He produced the letter that he had shown earlier at the police station.

Clarence was stunned. 'It is too early to give up, Rupert.'

Harvey said, 'We shud not be talkin' so openly.'

Clarence backed him up. 'It is what we agreed. Too much has been said already.'

Rupert's eyes blazed. 'He has as much right as anywun to be here.'

Clarence tried to raise a smile. 'All right, Rupert, all right. You know that you have my trust. I welcome Gabriel to this meeting. But I would like to know more of your reasons for bringing him.'

Rupert, with a touch of theatre, let out a long sigh. 'I go to the police station today. I get no joy on Mary, but me meet Gabriel deh. He was in a special way. His mind was – somewun speak thru ihm, tell me tings we got to do.' He cleared his throat. 'Clarence, yu knoh me sistah well, so yu got some understandin' of wat I talkin' about. Gabriel is jus' like Josie. He got gifts we need.'

Rupert quickly hushed the shocked murmurs of the men. 'Gabriel can see tings, speak wid voices long gone. I swear it on de name of all a' me family an' tek evahlasting damnation as me course, eif wat me say is no more den a lie. I mus' speak de trut', oddahwise all dat gowan, is fe nuttin'. An' me caan' let it be so. As de eternal, everlastin' Lord be me master an' guide, I swear dat my fadah reach out fram Gabriel an' speak to me.

'Some peopal can sing like a bird fram de cradle. Some can do math like deh born to computation and calculation. Some get tings deh na' wan', but a gift is a gift. Me fadah tell me we must resolve dis problem fram widdin, dat de bwoy is here to help us. Fe ihm to help us, he must knoh wat we knoh.'

The men studied Gabriel carefully. 'Doan' look pon ihm like he got horn pon his head.'

Harvey, restless, said, 'Such tings doan' come fram God, Rupert. De lord got no need to possess. He speak openly.'

'De devil got nuttin' to do wit Gabriel. De devil grab my chile. God has shown me wat to do. He give us de tools to end de madness.'

'De devil is de mastah a' disguise, Rupert.'

'Enough a' ya nonsense, we ain' children.'

'Me doan' knoh about dis. It doan' smell right.'

'Yu all knoh Gladwin.'

Harvey spat out, 'Dat witch!'

Despite the situation, a wry smile touched Rupert's lips. 'Maybe, maybe. De point is, me tek Gabriel to see her an' she also say he can deal wit de situation.'

Gabriel spoke up. 'What is the situation?'

Madely said, 'A recommendation fram dat girl ain' good enough.'

'We all sympathize with you, Rupert,' said Clarence, 'but we all agreed on a certain course. You aren't the only one who has suffered a loss. Remember that, Rupert, and remember your reaction to that loss. Am I only to see action now that you have suffered?'

'Me nevah seh dat.'

'Then what did you mean? You convene us and tell us incredible things. How are we to know the truth of what you say? Is this some desperate attempt to make us go to the police? Is it?'

'Yu knoh me bettah.'

'Do we?'

Rupert snapped, 'Gabriel, show dem ya egg.'

Gabriel took the egg out of his pocket. Rupert snatched it from his nephew's hand and held it out to his friends. One by one they read Gabriel's name. None was able to look the younger man in the eye.

'All right then,' said Rupert. 'No more of dis devil business.'

Harvey, struggling to think clearly, said, 'But de bwoy here. De egg always come aftah. Why now, Rupert? Why now?'

Rupert was unable to answer. Gabriel watched him walk over to a wall safe and open it. Inside were a few packages. Rupert, deep in thought, fingered them absent-mindedly.

Gabriel waited a few moments and then asked, 'What does this mean?'

Rupert nodded towards Clarence for the answer.

Clarence, still avoiding eye contact with Gabriel, took his time answering. 'I'm sorry. I cannot give a definite answer to that. I can only tell you what I know, but sometimes a story escapes its telling.

'Sixteen – no, fifteen years ago, I served alongside my father in a small church in Battersea. It is about six minutes' walk from my present church. We had to move eventually, what with the increasing number in the congregation, but back then this place more than served its purpose. We were small, but we had a good atmosphere. At the time we were experiencing a number of racist attacks. Certain people didn't like to see such a large number of us meeting in one place, in such a public manner, and although the days could sometimes be unpleasant, our troubles brought us even closer.

'You know, even now, looking back, I can't remember a time quite like it. It was a special time; friendships were forged that have stood the test of time. There was a family, the Watsons. A young family, a fine couple who had a boy, James. One day I received a call from Sandra Watson, the wife. It was incredible – she had literally awoken to find her child missing. Obviously the police were contacted and they had arrived before I reached the Watsons' home. I tried to console her, but it was pretty hopeless, she was beside herself. The entire church joined in regularly to pray for James's return, but it was no use, he never came back. The couple drifted apart. The father grew quite unpleasant, if I remember. Sandra is still with me. She never remarried.' He shifted his weight to increase the circulation in his buttocks.

'Although the child was not returned – the police gave up more quickly than I thought to be right, by the way, but still, we were who we were and those were the times we lived in – anyways, something quite unusual happened. About four weeks into the disappearance, William Watson came to see me. He brought a small box with him that had been left outside his house. Inside the box was an egg.

'I was surprised, of course. It seemed an unusual thing to be left on one's doorstep. Even more unusual was the fact that it carried a small number on it. No name, just a number. Two. Will was extremely agitated and convinced that the egg was connected to his child. I told him that he was talking nonsense, of course, that it was just a prank. I think that at the time I believed it to be some superstitious object, sent by some of the less enlightened members of our community. He wanted to take it to the police, but I talked him out of it. He was distraught about the object and didn't want to take it back with him. I obliged him and took it – placed it in the basement of the church, actually. And that was that. As I said, the child didn't return. Our prayers went unanswered. Life went on. The incident was forgotten until about seven months later.

'At the time, Harvey was the head of a church in the Dulwich area. He called me to ask for my advice. It seemed that a young girl, Roberta Brown, had gone missing –'

Gabriel cut in, 'Excuse me?'

'Yes?'

'What number was on the egg?'

'Two, as I said; two. Anyway, to continue. The parent of the next missing child was a single mother and a member of his congregation. He wanted to give her some spiritual assistance and wanted to know what I had done with the Watsons.' Clarence waited for Harvey to take up the story, but Harvey remained silent, with his head resolutely bowed, so Clarence went on. 'I told him what I could, which wasn't much, and asked him to keep me informed. He didn't – the woman was unwilling to receive spiritual assistance. She drank, if I remember –'

'Like a fish,' growled Harvey.

'Anyway, time, as they say, moved on. I thought nothing more of it until about seven weeks after Harvey had first contacted me, when he came round to my church for a small fund-raising jumble sale. Naturally, we talked and the issue of the unfortunate woman came up. Harvey had no real news of her, but I remember him mentioning one detail which rather bemused him. The woman had received lots of condolences in the form of flowers, cards, that kind of thing. And, would you believe, an enormous egg coated in thin blue paint, which was marked with the numeral four.

'When he told me this, I immediately told him of the Watsons' egg. He was willing to dismiss the whole thing, believed it was obviously the work of some crank. I was not so sure, found out where the girl lived and went to see her. She was heavily drunk and quite hostile. When I arrived she was actually preparing to burn many of the things that had been sent her, including the egg. I managed to retrieve it, took it with me and placed it in the basement of my church with its partner, so to speak.

'Again time passed on. I had many responsibilities which ranged far beyond the confines of the church. Many of my congregation were uneasy with officialdom and I was always being called on to to deal with things. As you can imagine, I was always swamped and quickly got back into my normal swing of things. Then one day a package was given to me by a small boy.'

He wiped his wet palms on his trouser leg. 'I opened the package and, somehow, though it might seem silly now, I knew what was within it. Even now I can still remember the sinking feeling in my gut when I saw the egg. It had the number five on it and a name: Jennifer. I sent the boy away and just stood there like an ass. I couldn't think of anyone I knew who had a child called Jennifer and there hadn't been anything in the newspapers.

'The next day I collected my eggs –' A smile lit up his eyes. 'Sounds ludicrous, doesn't it? But there it was. I collected them and went to the nearest police station. But you know what? I could not go in. I felt stupid with my box and what it contained. I thought they would laugh at me and so I didn't enter. I have a good sense of humour, but have never taken to being laughed at.

'Anyway, I returned home. I was tense, irritable. I could not hide things from my wife and had to tell her what had been happening. At her prompting I returned the next morning to the police station. Again I did not enter. I stood there for quite some time, but then just returned home. My wife was disappointed, even angry with me. She felt I was letting myself down. Well, there wasn't much doubt about it, so I resolved to return to the station the next day.

'That night I ran things through my head, what I would say and do.

I didn't want to look a fool, and when I was content I fell asleep, sure that I would do as I should do, the next day.'

Clarence's voice resonated with the painful vitality of emotions undiminished by time or obstinate denial. 'My rehearsals, my imagined speeches, my authoritative gestures, my wise turns of phrase never came. There was a fire that night. I lost my home and my wife – everything.'

No one spoke.

'The next few days are a blur to me. I have little memory of them, I suppose because I was in such a daze.' He coughed into his hand. 'I think I recall spending a few days in hospital. I was even visited by some members of the police force. But I said nothing, I waited. I went to stay with Madely and his wife and contacted Harvey again. I told him why I felt my misfortune had occurred and even though he believed I was over-reacting, we decided to inform Madely. It was a good thing we did, since it turned out that he too had been sent an egg.'

Madely took up the story. 'It 'ave de numbah four 'pon it. Me got it several week befoh Clarence tell me wat was bodderin' ihm. But wen de two a' dem speak to me, tings clear up fas'.'

'What did you all do?'

'We speak to Rupert.'

'And?'

Rupert cleared his throat. 'We did nuttin'. Wat could we do?'

'The police?'

'No, no, we couldn' do dat.'

'Why not?'

'De time, Gabriel, de time. Yu doan' knoh wat it was like den. We was nuttin' to dem. Yu tink tings bad now, bwoy, yu doan' knoh nuttin'. In dem days deh treat us like we was lice or someting. Evary time yu pass dun de street, deh eye be on yu, watchin' yu, jus' waitin' fe a chance to pounce an' beat de livin' hell out a' yu. Eif yu speak to dem, deh laffe in ya face an' tell yu to speak Engalish. Den deh pass on quick, befoh yu contaminate dem or someting. We was all young den, we 'ave family to look aftah. We couldn' risk anyting.'

'Clarence was a lesson, a lesson to all,' added Harvey.

'De threat was clear.'

Gabriel said, 'You could have ignored it. All of you together could have ignored it!'

Clarence's irritation rose to the surface. 'We weren't all together at first. We didn't all know. It took time before we all came together. It was hard to speak of these things.'

Harvey's voice continued to rise. 'Befoh yu lecture us, yu mus' remembah how much time pass. It move on quick befoh we even knoh wat we knoh, an' wen we knoh –' He looked to his colleagues.

'So you did nothing?'

'A' course we do someting! We talk! We pray! We preach to ah peopal and advise dem to tek care!'

'Easy, easy,' said Rupert. 'We doan' wan' de whole street to heah.'

'Well, me doan' like de inference. We do wat we could –'

'Me knoh dat –'

'No man can seh we ain' done right.'

'How long have you done what is right?'

'Long enough.'

'And now you've received another egg.'

'Yu is nuttin', bwoy, yu not even a man yet. Yu tink yu could do bettah? Yu doan' knoh how much effort it cost just to line ya belly.'

'How many eggs have you altogether?'

Silence.

Gabriel waited with it for a moment before releasing his next question into the air, 'How many eggs have been sent so far?'

Rupert muttered, 'Me haf dem all in de safe.'

Harvey added, 'Ongle Rupert receive dem.'

'How many?'

'Let me see. Eif me remembah correctly – hm, me tink deh is about twelve.'

'Twelve? So you've been doing the right thing despite the disappearance and possibly the death of twelve people. Another egg has come, with my name on it. Do you plan to go on doing the "right thing"?'

Rupert tried his best. 'Gabriel, yu mus' see tings clearly.'

Madely followed. 'We didn' wan' to expose de community to de probin' an' destruction of de pohlice.'

Clarence held up his hand to interrupt him. 'Rupert, explain it all so he understands.'

'We are not as foolish as yu might believe. As yu knoh, me an' ya modah close. Aftah she pass on she come back an' speak to me in me sleep. She was in a dark room wen me meet her. Aftah we talk an' wat not, she tell me to wait an' lef' me fe a bit. Den she come back carryin' yu. Yu look exactly as yu do now. De same height, de same length a' hair, evaryting. She tell me yu will mek tings right.

'Lately me start to doubt her. But now, aftah today, wen yu speak wid de tongue a' me fadah, me knoh wat she seh be true.'

One by one the other men stood up and left the room.

Rupert welcomed the voice of Mahalia Jackson into the room by turning on the hi-fi. At the end of the first track he asked, 'Gabriel, yu alright?'

'Do you have to ask?'

'Yu need time to tink tings out?'

'Uncle Rupert, what else do you have to tell me?'

'Nuttin' dat caan' wait.'

'You have something else for me?'

Rupert returned to the safe. 'Me got a few tings to seh first.' He took out a book for Gabriel. 'Dis is fe yu.'

'What is it?'

'Ya fadah's journal.'

Gabriel didn't accept it.

Rupert thrust the book towards him. 'It belong to yu.'

'Why is it with you?'

Rupert placed it under Gabriel's armpit.

'Why is it with you?'

'Tek it.'

The book was three hand-spans long and two wide. Its brown leather hide was covered in rice paper and bound by two tightly wound strings. Through the rice paper, the name MATTHEW DUBOIS could be seen.

'A while back, ya fadah bring it to me. He ask me to hand it ovah wen yu ready fe it. So tek it as a late birtday present.'

'It isn't important.'

'Look, me knoh dis evenin' hard on yu, but go home, get some sleep. Tings will look bettah in de mornin'. Come, me walk yu to de door.'

Gabriel waited.

'Wat now?'

'Before I go, is there anything else you have to tell me?'

'No. Nuttin'.'

'Uncle Rupert?'

'Gabriel, it is time fe yu to go home.'

'No. It's time for you to tell me everything.'

'Gabriel, enough, enough.'

'No more secrets. You have too many of my secrets.'

'All right, no more secrets. You got a question fe me?'

'It's about the first egg you received.'

'Wat about it?'

'Rupert, you said there would be no more secrets.'

'Deh is no secret about it. It got two 'pon it.'

'You also told me that you and the other ministers have received twelve of these eggs over the years.'

'Yes.'

'And each has been numbered or had a name?'

'Yes.'

'And the numbers are chronological. Two, three, four, upwards?'

'Yes, unless deh was a name instead.'

'So instead of seven, you might get a name?'

'Yes.'

'But if the next egg came, it would be numbered in sequence – it would be eight?'

'Yes.'

Gabriel picked up the egg with his name on it. 'So where is the first egg?'

'Me doan' undastan'.'

'Yes, you do. Clarence received an egg with the number two. It doesn't follow that he received the first egg. You are the caretaker for the collection. Why?'

'Gabriel –'

'Where is the egg with the number one on it?'

'Enough, no moah.'

'Show me the egg.'

'No.'

'Please? Let me see it.'

Rupert pulled out another egg from the safe. A hardening agent had been applied to it. 'De first egg did come to me.'

As he turned the egg over the name JOCELYNNE revealed itself. The printing was bright against the background and didn't blur when he ran his fingers over it.

'How yu tink me feel wen dis ting start to come clear? Me tell yu, bwoy, a mind can ongle tek so much befoh it threaten to burst open an' split or someting. Yu doan' knoh, yu doan' knoh. It is a messy business.' He produced a plastic bag as if from thin air. 'A messy business.'

'I have one more question.'

'Wat?'

'I understood that my mother died from a blood clot.'

'Blast it, dat is wat me caan' undastan'. Me swear to yu, me was at de hospital, me see de X-ray an' evaryting. Me swear to yu, as God is my witness, she die fram a natural cause.'

'Then why the egg?'

'Me doan' knoh.'

'That isn't good enough.'

'Me knoh wat me see. Deh was no way someting unnatural an' bad could 'ave affect her, no way.'

As Gabriel placed the eggs and his father's journal into the bag, Rupert said, 'Ya modah ain' had much reason to visit me in de las' yeah or so, but me remembah wat she seh befoh an' me hold it in good fait.'

'You didn't say anything to the police when I showed them this egg.'

Rupert shrugged his shoulders.

Gabriel turned away from his uncle.

'Doan' look at me like dat.'

'How do you expect me to look?'

Rupert looked pained. 'Not like dat. Me doan' deserve de look yu give.'

Gabriel left the room. Rupert followed him to the door, remaining there, despite the cold, long after his nephew had left.

Upon his return home, Gabriel's sole desire was to rest. He went to bed without examining the journal. In spite of his exhaustion, sleep evaded him for hours, though eventually, as it must, it came.

Early morning.

Gabriel watched the man study the design for his mother's headstone.

'It's very good,' said the stone cutter, 'but it will cost you.'

'Name your price.'

'It will be about £500.'

'How about if I agree to pay you £450 in cash?'

'Cash?' A moment passed in consideration of the offer.

'OK. Fine.'

Gabriel handed him a series of £50 notes. 'When will it be ready?'

'Oh, about three weeks, no more. I know the bloke, Martin Bagshore, who looks after the cemetery. We'll arrange everything with him and make sure things are done smoothly.'

'All right, I'll come back in a little under four weeks. I'll expect everything to be in order.'

'Sure, leave it to me.'

Gabriel hurried to his car. The sunlight was so bright that even a few minutes' exposure threatened to burn his skin. Although he had drunk a few pints of water, the high alcohol level in his blood caused him periods of uncertainty and ill being, forcing him to concentrate upon maintaining a dignified gait.

Once home, he headed straight for the kitchen. On the table the eggs, a bottle of wine, a slim drinking glass, his father's journal, a pad of A4 writing paper and a fountain pen waited. He spent some time idling about the room without doing anything specific, before pouring out some wine. Then, finally, he opened the journal. Throughout the book had been placed a series of letters and envelopes. The first page was blank except for a record of the year, 1958. A turn of the page, then entries began. Some were marked solely by the day, some by a date, and many by a single number.

Thursday, 18 January 1958

Jocelynne is on my mind. She is sister to every thought, no matter how trivial, cousin to every deed, no matter how slight.

I am giddy. Exultant. My body is alive with much expectation and, yes, fear. I have her picture. I have replicated that self-same picture with my own hand. Given her unknown contours and clothed her in the finest material until my fingers have grown sore and my pencils have worn away. I know her. I am here. I have set down in England. Father has arranged work for me at the Commonwealth Institute. Much is expected of me. But I have no interest in these matters. The world of politics and diplomacy seems utterly irrelevant.

Jocelynne is on my mind. I must see her.

I am not a religious man. I reject utterly the corrupt myth that the Anglo-

Saxons have woven from the blurred truth of the great Rabbi's death and life. I leave the two races to quarrel over their theological and racial differences and only hope that they will not drag any more of my own people into accepting their ludicrous fantasies. A futile hope. In truth, I do not care. The plane taxis along. My fellow passengers grow restless and some ignore the advice of the stewards and stand. I do not care. Jocelynne is on my mind.

Gabriel paused before flicking through the journal again. A sip of wine, and then back to the second entry.

2

It is so cold. No wonder the English are all so reserved. Their personalities are obviously preserved under a deep and pervasive chill. They walk around, hands in pockets, heads bowed, their skin covered in red patches. They are quite appalling and have absolutely no manners at all. I asked a man for directions and he seemed to take fright. Did I do something wrong? Did I break form? Does one have to give some kind of strange Masonic signal before one approaches an Englishman with whom one is not on intimate terms?

It may seem impolite of me to mention this, but many of them smell quite strongly and clearly do not wash enough. Perhaps this is one of the drawbacks of living in a cold country. In Jamaica, I am used to washing at least twice, often three times a day. I cannot imagine any circumstances in which I would allow myself to stand before another human being reeking of sweat and exertion. I understand that Elizabeth the First was infamous amongst visiting courtiers for the strength of her body odour. Could it be that I have arrived at a time in the year when her latter-day subjects choose to honour her by leaving their homes with unwashed armpits and dirty necks? Or perhaps the government is recruiting so many of my countrymen to wash their backs, and not as we have been told, to man their hospitals and railways?

Still, this is the country which has produced the magnificent Busby Babes whose exploits are followed by my entire family, as well as the likes of Hutton and Compton. Disappointment must be moderated by the inevitable pleasures that I will take from the playing fields of this island.

January 20th

Penny Windsor, as arranged, collects me from my hotel. She is a few inches over five feet, quite plump, blonde, and heavily freckled. When she smiles it is as if a colony of bright brown ants suddenly went on the march. She is extremely perky and oozes energy. We attracted many stares. I don't believe she was ignorant of the attention, but appeared to be completely unconcerned. She interests me. I sense no malice in her, no bigotry.

She hails from Sussex and has always wanted to work for the Institute. When the chance came, she leapt at it. She has an appetite for life, an appetite for people. A natural anthropologist, she has a desire – almost a need – to meet 'other' people. People who are quantifiably different from her, whether the difference be of religion, colour or nationality.

As we drove, she pointed out places that might be of interest to me. Hounslow, Isleworth, Brentford – the names were reeled off. She was charming. I am never bored with her or stressed. I may well have found a friend. As for England? It is too early to form conclusions that will need further revision, but my first impressions are far from edifying.

This is a grey land: the buildings are grey, the sky is grey, the mood is grey, the pallor of the people, which should be a white-pink, is grey. As a child, I can still recall my parents talking about the end of the World War and the dawning of a new age. They believed that Jamaica's brave efforts in the war would be rewarded and the entire Caribbean attain a new respect and freedom, along with greater economic growth and prosperity. These hopes were unfulfilled.

The hopes of blacks who fight for their colonial masters have always been dashed. The Americans used their blacks as front-line fodder and, upon their return home, reassigned them to the cutting edge of the welfare system. In Britain, the working class gained great momentum during the War and the women, especially, broke through new barriers. I sense already that in this land many dreams and promises have been broken.

How long before these people have the guts and humility to drop the 'Great' which precedes 'Britain'? If ever a nation proclaimed its own arrogance with more bluster and insensitivity then I pray that I never come across it. Can you imagine? 'Hello, I'm from Great Britain, where are you from? Insignificant France? Dainty Portugal? Insipid Belgium? Irrelevant Hungary? Minuscule Switzerland?

Did I say that the buildings are grey? They are ugly. The city planners should be shot. People are not meant to live like this. Where are the parks, the trees? Where is the sun? Still, my stay here will be short. I have come to learn. And learn we must. Even if this country is collapsing under the weight of its history and undeniable former glory, it has much to teach me. Hundreds of other men and women have come, like me, to learn, and then to take our knowledge back with us to our beloved country. Jamaica, I have not left you for more than a day and already I miss you. But I am here to learn. And more, so much more. Tonight I meet with Jocelynne's brother, who has offered me a place to stay.

Gabriel inscribed the Christian name of his father on the A4 pad before writing on the first page:

It is a petty detail, but the prefix 'Great' before 'Britain' is a geographical clause, so that the larger island mass shall not be confused with that of – no matter.

My father speaks, as ever, eloquently, if a touch too formally, and with every word coated with the confidence which more often than not became arrogance. It is a voice I know all too well. But it is modulated by a factor I have never heard before. Youth. This Matthew is optimistic, hopeful. His love for my mother seems akin to a sickness. If I did not have this evidence before me, then I would not have believed it possible that he could have been so consumed and empowered by an emotion he always vilified and despised in others.

How old is this Matthew? He is probably my senior by three or five years at the most. But I see nothing within these passages to identify the process by which this man evolved . . .

He hesitated before writing:

. . . in truth, degenerated into the man I knew. The process may well be detailed within these pages. But already I feel a sense of –

Gabriel placed his pen down and read on.

4

I am furious. Today has been a disaster. My wishes and instructions have been cast aside and ignored, as if I were a child without common sense or purpose. I had specifically asked Papa that no mention be made of our relationship by his former colleagues and friends. And what happens? Within minutes of meeting my new colleagues I find myself being introduced to no less a personage than the director of the Institute. It was galling, for everything had been going so well.

I admit to a certain amount of trepidation as I entered the main building. I could not help but wonder, as Penny introduced me to the security guards, how Papa felt on first entering the building. As we progressed through its halls,

I wondered what exhibits Moma and Papa had gazed upon and enjoyed together. Imagine my shock upon discovering a carving of a Masai warrior along a gangway. It is the same carving that I watched my father create in his workplace many summers ago as a form of relaxation from preparing a report for the Jamaican High Commission. It stood in our garden for many weeks, along with his other works, and then was gone. Gone to greet me here all these years later and emphasize once again just how great his presence is within this building.

The initial meeting with my colleagues went well. Pride of place on one of the walls went to a printing of the principles of the NAACP of America, from which the Institute drew much of its inspiration.

NATIONAL ASSOCIATION FOR THE ADVANCEMENT OF COLORED PEOPLE. Organized February 1910. Incorporated May 1911.
1. To abolish legal injustice against Negros.
2. To stamp out race discrimination.
3. To prevent lynching, burning and torturing of black people.
4. To assure every citizen of color the common rights of American citizenship.
5. To compel equal accommodations in rail-road travel, irrespective of color.
6. To secure for colored children an equal opportunity to public-school education through a fair apportionment of public-education funds.
7. To emancipate, in fact as well as in name, a race of nearly 12,000,000 American-born citizens.

The only means we can employ are education, organization, agitation, publicity, the force of enlightened public opinion.

There are four of them: Penny; John Mills, a beefy chap who Penny says is the current man in her life; Cedric Portsmouth, a Jamaican originally from Port Elizabeth, who has worked for the Institute for over eleven years; Claire Wheelson, an attractive girl with extremely thin bones.

As we talked and shared the inevitable pot of tea, my apprehension evaporated. I became sure that I had found a group of people whose friendship and respect, won on my own merits, would be well worth achieving.

My hopes were dashed by the arrival of the director of the Institute, who brought several luminaries with him. It was clear from the shocked faces of my colleagues that the director hardly, if ever, sets foot within the office, especially not with such a high-powered delegation.

He called out my name, reprimanding me with, 'You don't remember me, do you?' I replied in the negative. 'Why should you, indeed? You weren't even three when I visited your father. I played a few games with you out in the garden. You know, out where your grandfather's tree is planted.'

My face must have revealed my confusion, for the director and his companions all began to laugh merrily as he introduced me. 'This is Anthony's son. He's here to oversee the implementation of the new exhibition on the early Caribbean slave rebellions that we'll have here for about six weeks. He's also agreed to redesign some of our models and write up new accompanying information texts.'

My sense of embarrassment increased as a bright-eyed fellow grabbed my hand and spouted, 'I'm pleased to meet you. I never had the pleasure of meeting your father, but I'm only too glad to meet one of the famous DuBois clan. Many people who work here have been inspired by your family's achievements.' And so it continued. How was it possible for so few people to mention my grandfather, my great-grandfather, my great-grandmother and so on, so often in such a short space of time? By the time the group had left, I had assured each of them that I would be only too glad to lunch with them and meet their families. The director made it clear that he was to be first on my list of priorities and that I had to meet his wife as soon as possible, especially since she had spoon-fed me at some point in my second year of life.

When I turned to face my colleagues, I could see that I was no longer Matthew Stevens, my assumed name; I was, once and for all, a DuBois. Before I could speak, Cedric was pumping my hand. 'You're a DuBois? I didn't realize. My father often talked of your grandfather and of the schools and colleges he built. My father attended one of his rallies; he said it changed his life. Even then, it was said that he was the greatest Prime Minister Jamaica never had.'

Even though I had already been introduced, my colleagues shook my hand again as if we had never met before, re-evaluating me with every passing moment and gesture. I will not try to describe the sense of claustrophobia that assailed me, nor the sense of disappointment. I had almost made it. But that foolish man, so desperate to parade his relationship with my father, had ruined everything and forced me once again to reassume the stultifying heraldry that cloaks my family, with all that means in terms of life-style and tradition. Must I have an answer for everything? Must I always have an opinion? Must every stroke of my pen be perfect? Must I lead without pause or hesitation?

Gabriel read on quickly as his father described the passing of his first day at the Institute and his impressions of the building and its staff. He slowed down when he reached the next passage:

At my first opportunity I called the number that Jocelynne's eldest brother, Maurice, had given me. A fellow answered and informed me that Rupert, Jocelynne's senior by two years, will not be returning until the early evening. I asked him to inform Rupert of my arrival and say that I would contact him that evening.

Our conversation ended, I sat and pondered the reality of my situation. It seemed clear to me that I must appear to Jocelynne and her family as slightly mad. Who knows? I recalled the first moment I saw her – it was not madness or confusion that filled my senses, only clarity. It was less than eight months ago.

My cousin Annette was holding court as she often did in our garden. Her own mother was fed up with the endless parade of men who constantly fêted and salivated over her, and Annette was forced to use our home as her own little theatre. My mother never seemed to grow bored of watching Annette flirt with these hapless admirers, who seemed blind to her obvious indifference to their humiliations and pique. Her interest was not in their glowing eyes or sustained smiles, just in their weight upon the chairs she set for them, whereupon she could indulge in her favourite pastime: performing.

It was common knowledge within the family that Annette believed herself to be the actual embodiment of Margaret Mitchell's fictional character Scarlett O'Hara. I cannot remember a month going by without seeing that abominable tome in my cousin's hands. She could repeat whole passages from that fantastical garbage verbatim, as easily as my father could run off endless quotations from Plato, Aristotle, Rousseau and Wisden.

Nothing pleased her more than reading out to her admirers letters from members of our family who had fought in 'socially just' campaigns around the globe. The DuBois clan was famous for running off to war to support the cause of the black man and the oppressed everywhere. A tradition which had started back in the earliest days of the transportation of Africans to the Caribbean. I had learned from my earliest days to recount the tale of my great, great – have I missed out a great? – grandfather, who died in a failed escape from such-and-such a plantation, whose surviving wife and child prospered, and how they in turn – I digress.

Annette was reading a letter composed by Charles Wendall DuBois. She had no need to hold the letter, for she knew the contents of it, as I did, by heart – Uncle Charles, my father's father's brother, had left the Caribbean to fight on the side of the Union in the great American Civil War. A move which would be echoed by his nephew, Edward Alphonso, who fought on the side of the Communists in the Spanish Civil War. Some of Charles's letters have been reproduced in a book, *Stories from the Front Line*. A reasonable book on the American Civil War, which fails to do justice to the material within it, an achievement matched by many comparable works on the subject. Several libraries and museums have approached the family for the letters he sent to us, but we have not cooperated with them. We DuBois have a strong sense of history and remember and cherish our own.

As I have mentioned, we (my cousin, her slavish admirer and I) were in the garden, but we were not alone. The gardener – a local man, Maurice Wills – was carrying out his professional duties. My mother, who in truth was possessed of truly green fingers, was working on her own private plot, several yards from him. The whole garden was Mother's. Father liked to potter around every fourth or fifth Sunday, prodding with his toe, 'testing' with a bony finger, before retiring to write out a small note to Maurice with his instructions.

In truth, every seed was bedded, every plant uprooted by Maurice according to the plans that he and my mother had discussed before the onset of each new season. Plans which were merely the execution of a great design. Each of her children had been left in no doubt that we were meant to contribute, both physically and imaginatively, to the creation of her vision. A vision which she always made clear would only truly begin to take shape after several generations.

I once heard her shout at my father, who never ceased to complain about the amount of time she spent in her garden, 'You may think that I have guaranteed my immortality by having your children, but I think that I can actually leave something worthwhile by other means!'

Though Father was moved to laughter, I was unimpressed by her lack of appreciation for my presence. In looks, I took after my father. My older brother William, her first-born, clearly shared more of my mother's Asian attributes in tone of skin, quality of hair and bone structure.

I had always believed, throughout my childhood, that Mother was happier with William than with those who followed. She never seemed so physically carefree with us as she was with him. She never seemed to take as much time to encourage us, or to express dismay or disappointment. I could always tell that in his face she saw her former home, her own family.

Many times over the years, when she caught his face at a specific angle, or saw him in a particular garment, she would cry out that he looked just like this person or that person. This exclamation of joy would always be followed by a warm embrace. Often I would find her in the garden, swinging gently on her hammock, content to watch William at play. Her love for him was without limit. The entire family was aware of this imbalance in Mother's feelings, but it was something we all accepted.

That is not true.

William and I fought many times over the years. These fights went beyond the natural explorative rites of manhood. They were vicious and violent. When I was eight, I smashed a frying-pan over his head. This act of cowardice was compounded by the pounding I gave him as he lay dazed on the ground. I would like to write that I was immediately ashamed and contrite as I studied his injured form, but the truth was I felt only satisfaction. This was momentarily suspended by a mighty blow I received from my father. But not once – not as he continued to beat me, nor later on, though I bowed my head in mock shame throughout his lecture – did I experience anything approaching brotherly affiliation for William. I was elated; the truth was out between us. We need not pretend anymore.

Three days later I was taken to see him in hospital. As we walked along the corridors to his ward, I promised my mother to let him know how bad I felt. But all the time, as we passed the injured and the elderly, I could only hope that his nose, which was slimmer than mine, though not by much, had been bent out of shape. That his lips, which were as slim as any white's, but to my mind always dry and chapped, were now puffy and swollen. Fortunately for me, or my punishment would have been even greater, William was, but for a distinct lump on his skull, perfectly fine. But as my mother embraced him and our eyes met as he returned her hug, I knew, as did he, that there would never again be any illusion of trust or friendship between us. I hated him. He knew the reasons why. They would never change. So there we were.

I cannot say that my own jealousy never caused me despair or shame. There was a time throughout my boyhood when I was filled with a deep self-loathing, which may well have stemmed from an awareness of my shortcomings. I believe, strangely enough, that it was this lack of esteem for the person who faced me in the mirror each morning that originally caused me to doubt the truth of the Bible that my father had passed on to me; an artefact that his father had handed over to him on his eighteenth birthday.

When I received it on my eighteenth, I was already an ardent atheist. Since William was the first-born, he should have received it, and my mother told him so in no uncertain terms. But Father insisted that my lack of faith meant that I needed the – OH HOW I PRAY TO BE FREE OF GOD, GODS AND

GODLY ONES – illogical tome even more than my brother. Though the humanist in me rebelled as my father handed the Bible to me, the second son rejoiced.

I know, through talking to many of my friends who share the same numerical lineage, that to follow the eldest male in a family which overemphasizes the position and worthiness of the first-born is a deeply unhappy position. If you try to improve on precedent, then you are accused of over-ambition and being 'competitive'. If you fail, then reminders of the first-born's glories are constantly repeated in Napoleonic terms.

I shall never forget when William performed, for an invited group of family and friends, a piece he had composed for the cornet. Mother left us in no doubt that if the archangel appeared and blew his horn, he would suffer by comparison with my brother's playing.

I set out the next day to acquire a cornet for myself, and immediately began to learn the instrument. Within just under two years I was playing to a higher standard than William, who had been practising for over five. Within fifteen months of my surpassing his standard he had finished with the cornet. Needless to say, my mother never arranged for her friends to watch me.

I was not disappointed. That had not been the point of the exercise. And besides, my mother had long been aware of the conflict that took place within her house. She chose her side. The denial of acclaim from those same friends who had applauded William was merely her expression of support for her champion. She fought her corner well. Too well. For there came a time when I ceased to compete with William for her attention and respect.

It came to me one day on my way home from school, shortly before my fifteenth birthday, that if anyone should try to earn love and respect, it was her. I did not cease to love her, far from it. Our battles did not blind me to how magnificent she was. The love I had for her and the joy I experienced in her presence never diminished. No. I simply declared to myself, and consequently to the world, that I was worthy of complete respect and love and that my respect was worthy of being won. I know that my mother realized this, and indeed respected my stance. But she felt that I had no right to question her love and ask for even more proof.

It was many years before I realized the truth of her position and the petty inadequacy of mine, and I will always regret the years when I continually erected barricades of aggression between us.

But I digress. I was telling you, imaginary reader – What a silly concept you are! What a chameleon you are! How your form changes by the dictate of my mood! – Do you recall that I was in a garden? That my cousin was reading out a letter, composed by a Charles Wendall DuBois, to a suitor as I approached Maurice, our gardener? I am sure you do. Charles's letter was brief, composed shortly before he died of bronchitis. A death which occurred two weeks before the North triumphed over the South.

Gabriel picked up the envelope that lay upon the facing page. It was stained with age and fingerprints and was addressed to a Jacque Henri DuBois of Clarendon, Jamaica. With much care, he opened the envelope and brought out a sheet of paper that contained line after line of the most beautiful hand writing.

Dearest Father,

Too many of my friends and allies praise Lincoln. They say that he is a good man, a man of destiny. I disagree. There are some men, like Mr John Brown, whose character is beyond reproach and whose greatness shines effortlessly through the filthy caricature that the slavers and their friends try to perpetuate of him. Such is the evil and sickness that fills the minds of the slavers and their supporters that they create a fantasy of Mr Brown, portraying him as some sort of rabid lunatic who can only fight for the emancipation of the black man because of an over-heated fanaticism which blinds him to the true animal nature of the Negro.

History will show the truth of Mr Brown's fight, and no doubt the Good Lord will call him on to His table at speed, when He departs the mortal web which holds us all within its furious embrace.

Mr Lincoln, on the contrary, is a man who has been handed down by history a great role. The weight of this role has proven too much for a man whose stoutness of limb has caused him to vanquish, by all accounts, a sizeable number of men in wrestling bouts. Examples of his 'legendary' wit are constantly replicated in the newspapers, but wit is no substitute for wisdom and foresight, qualities which to the great are as much part of their constitutions as the liver and heart, that are manifestly lacking in Lincoln.

He uses the issue of slavery to weaken the South. The Negro is merely a balancing weight for Lincoln. By emancipating the Negro he merely seeks to undermine the economic power of the South. There is no moral authority in his judgement. Indeed, it is said by many that Lincoln favours repatriation of the Negro to the land of Africa. Though he has veered and hedged as politicians always do, I have read enough of his statements to be sure that this is his actual position. Though the blood of the Negro provides so many of the dollars and gold bars that Lincoln buys his precious arms with, he still believes that America is essentially for the white man. The Union which Lincoln seeks to save is a Union of white peoples. I, for one, expect that when this dreadful war ends, the American Negro will still find himself outside the parameters of the Constitution.

But such beliefs are unwelcome here. As I write, it is raining heavily outside my tent. Yes, today I actually have shelter. I share this space with white men, as well as Negroes. We are all equal before the cannon. We die just as quickly and as painfully. I have seen white soldiers staring in wonderment at various wounds that have been inflicted upon my body. Some of them cannot believe that my blood is the same as theirs.

My fellow Negroes, fighting for what they believe to be a new destiny, do not want to hear my gloomy predictions. They fight for freedom. I am a free man and come from a free family. I have eaten well all my life. Shakespeare and Chaucer are my constant companions here. Many are the hours I have spent reading out my favourite poems to my comrades. The level of illiteracy I have encountered amongst my Negro comrades has confounded me. Many of them, if truth be told, have the intelligence of children. But this is not their fault: they have been bred like this, and their nature is set. I do not blame them. I would say that to see men who have spent their entire lives being trained not to think, not to take responsibility, now rise up, take arms and fight for the destiny of their children is an experience of such religiousness that I am often struck dumb by the magnitude of it. For all my learning and airs, I am as they. We share the same skin, the same hearts. And even though differences of class and education always separate men, they can never break the holy bond that exists between men of a single tribe.

I believe that this war was always inscribed in the halls of destiny for the Negro. Who knows what dreadful sins we committed in those glorious centuries when the Greeks came and sat at the feet of our scholars to learn from us; for what else could have caused us to fall from so mighty a position other than some capital sin against God? Were we, as a race, some awful echo of Milton's Lucifer? Angels thrown out of heaven because of some effrontery against the Almighty? Perhaps slavery is the price we must pay for our sins, and the way we confront it and fight it our measure of penance. If so, it is a mighty test. It is a cruel test. But the God of the Old Testament is a cruel God, given to whimsy and spite and, I believe, more than capable of punishing us so. So we must prove ourselves to the Almighty and overcome this cruel fate we now endure all around the world, from the Caribbean to Asia and throughout the Americas. If greatness was our lot, then it will be again.

We know how history will judge Lincoln? Perhaps the fairy-tale will prevail *and he will continue to be seen as the champion of the Negro. Perhaps the truth will out, and it will be seen that the greatest champion of the Negro was in fact the Negro himself. It is this role which most befits him, far more than the role of chattel, of property, of political pawn. I do not know if I will live to have children, but I know that if I do, their father will not have been a fraud or a coward. That he will have played the part that the time demanded, and that he will not have fought at the behest of blood lust, nor have taken arms for the Whites because of their propaganda. No, they will know that he was his own man, that he was a man of his race and for his race. They will know that he was proud and capable and that he lived by the provocation of his own will.*

Gabriel read the letter several times, noting the doodles along the margins of the page. Doodles that formed chains and rifles and a series of tents. He sat with it for some time before returning to his father's narrative.

Charles was a fine man. I believe that towards the end he was slightly mad: no objective reading of his letters can lead to any other conclusion. But it was a wonderful madness. A madness that belongs to poets and warriors. He was fortunate to be both. Our family is large in size and is swollen with over-achievers. But I believe that Charles was the best of us all. I hope that when I have a son Charles's spirit visits him in the womb and takes residence there. I would be proud of such a child.

But such thoughts were not on my mind that day. It was a trite, boring summer's day, which by Jamaican standards means that you could fry an egg on the ground, and that if you decided to paint the sky and the local environment a foreigner would think you had captured paradise on your canvas. This was, of course, if you lived in our suburb.

I confess, I approached Maurice only through sheer boredom. Maurice was a walking stereotype, short on words, only happy with the language of plants. As I neared him, I saw an object fall from his back pocket. It was an envelope. I could see immediately from its postage stamp that it was from England. As I said before, Maurice was the most taciturn of men, but as he picked the letter up he volunteered, with no encouragement, the fact that the letter was from his younger brother Rupert, who had left Jamaica for England a few months before. I knew nothing of his family – he had never talked about anything personal with me before – but, my curiosity stirred (on this day I would have found ant shit falling to the ground interesting), I made further enquiries.

It seemed that Rupert had qualified as an accountant and had left for England to find a new life, along with the thousands of other aspirants who were departing from our shores in a blaze of hope and expectation. I think at some point that I asked if any other members of his family intended to join Rupert. He mentioned a younger sister and produced a photograph of her.

That was the first time I ever saw Jocelynne. I will not embarrass myself by detailing my reaction to that particular photograph, but will only say that it was profound. I said nothing to Maurice of any consequence and left him to his flowers. A few days passed, and no one who knew me would have detected a change or that anything of substance was preying on my mind, but within the week I decided to visit Maurice at home.

He was surprised – more than surprised to see me, but quickly invited me into his home. His wife was absent, along with his two sons, and over a glass of chilled carrot juice I came quickly to the point. I let him know that I was mightily impressed by the image of Jocelynne and that I would, with his permission, like to meet her. I give him credit, he treated my request respectfully. He said that he had no objection to me writing, but dashed my immediate hopes by telling me that she was currently on an inter-island tour, performing in a dance, theatre and poetry company, and that she would be gone for at least two months. Furthermore, she would subsequently be leaving for England. He would, though, write to her, inform her of my interest and secure her permission for me to begin a correspondence.

I agreed, of course, and, happy with my lot, prepared to leave. He gave me pause and left the room for a few moments. When he returned, he was carrying a small bundle of papers. He removed a sheet and handed it to me. It was a poem. One of Jocelynne's poems.

With his encouragement I read the piece, and was delighted by the humour and character displayed so vividly before me. Maurice, gladdened by my reaction, handed me some more poems, and I read them all with growing admiration and respect. As I finished, the picture of Jocelynne that I had first seen in the garden lay on the table before me. With the knowledge of her talent adding shape to the mystery of her features, I confess that my admiration for her, which I realize must have been primarily based on a physical reaction, grew even deeper.

That meeting with Maurice was five months ago. I am here in England now, having taken inspiration from Jocelynne and her brother, to explore my horizons. This time has been filled with a constant stream of communication, by which we have probed and explored each other. From my first sighting of her picture, I had known that such a relationship would occur.

The door bell broke Gabriel's concentration.

Rachel waited for him on the doorstep. Her hair had been woven into a long pony tail. She wore a faded blue jean-jacket over a light black top, tucked into tight black leggings. Grey leather strips had been wrapped about her legs. She tapped his foot with a ballet shoe and said, 'It's me.'

'Rupert?'

She picked up a plastic bag. 'What about him?'

'He gave you my address?'

'Right the first time.'

'What can I do for you?'

'How about inviting me in, for a start?'

Gabriel stepped to one side, and Rachel strode over to the kitchen.

'There's only one chair,' she complained as she sat down. 'This house is beautiful, you've fixed it up nicely. Weird but beautiful.'

'Weird?'

'Yeah, different. Slightly Gothic.'

'Gothic?'

'Yeah, Gothic. Reclusive. Very different. This table is fantastic, where did you get it from?'

'I made it myself.'

'You're kidding! Wow! And the chair?'

'That too.'

Gabriel removed some food from the refrigerator and heated it up for her.

'Very traditional,' she said as he laid out plates with chicken, yam, dumplings and sweet bread. 'Have you got any tomato sauce?'

He was visibly startled and left the kitchen for a minute or two, before returning with a chair. She tried again. 'I like tomato sauce. Is that a crime?'

He placed a generous portion of green pepper and sweetcorn rice and steaming chicken on her plate. 'This has been marinating for over thirty-six hours in six different spices, in a marinade made from beer, ginger and orange peel. What do you think?'

'OK, forget the sauce.'

She began to eat at speed. The food was shovelled from plate to mouth as quickly as possible. 'This is great, I'm starving. After a workout, I could eat a horse. Trouble is, I've got this quick metabolism, burns up everything. Give it an hour and I'll be ready to pig out again.'

He removed her plate and tipped the food back on to the serving dish.

'What are you doing?'

'There's a McDonald's down the road.'

Stunned, cheeks burning, she watched him clear away the meal and pour some beer into two glasses. He offered her a drink and she swallowed it in one go. 'Do you like being rude?'

He swallowed some beer. 'Why are you here?'

'I wanted to see you. It wasn't nice, the way things ended. I wanted to say I was sorry.'

'There was no need.'

'Yes, there was.'

He poured some more beer for her.

'I mean it's not every day that a girl picks on a virgin. I didn't know how to take it. I'd like to think I was attractive enough to break the habit. But I accept it.'

She held out her glass. 'Friends?'

'Friends.'

They touched glasses.

She picked up her bag. 'Can I put a tape on?'

'Of what?'

She slid a cassette into the hi-fi unit in the lounge, removing her jacket as the voice of Donna Summer lifted out of the speakers.

'No reason why I can't give you a private performance in return for spoiling me, is there?'

Gabriel's voice faltered slightly. 'No, none at all.'

Rachel began a series of gentle stretching exercises, her movements composed and gentle as she began to lose herself within the twists and turns of her improvisation, achieving total unison with the music and lyrics. As he looked on, Gabriel began to dream.

When the dance was over she came and stood over him and looked into his unfocused eyes. A hand passed before his gaze. Nothing. With barely a pause, she began to strip him.

Her fingers spread over his chest and the soft skin of his nipples.

Then a thump in her chest as she found burn scars about his ribs. A gentle tweak of his dark nipples before moving over the flat of his belly and the curving bone of his hips, before massaging the rise of his buttocks. A kick in her belly as she found a series of scars there and along his thighs. 'Who did this to you?' she asked.

With pursed lips she blew on to his face, her arms wrapping themselves under and about him, the beat of his heart strong against her cheek. As the minutes climbed on to each other, the warm syrup from his pores eased into her flesh until she, too, was wet with sweat. Their wet expanded, separated and broke on the air before she wiped it away with her palm.

At some point he began to stir. In the flutter of his eyelids she recalled a wasp that had recently slid and fallen into her sink. She pictured its slow climb out of the soapy water, its progress across the basin and the futile beating of its wings before she turned the tap on.

Suddenly Gabriel sat up and retched.

She lowered his head to one side to prevent him swallowing his chuck, before getting a cloth from the kitchen. As she wiped him down his eyes filled with questioning.

'I'm wiping you off,' she said. 'You've thrown up all over yourself.'

There, beyond the debilitating ignorance, grew the knowledge of his nakedness. His hands came up in a curiously weak gesture of resistance and he tried to squirm away, wrapping the towel about himself and heading for the stairs. She caught up with him and pulled him back, aware of her greater strength.

'Let me go!'

She felt as if she could crush him with a determined embrace if she wanted to. 'I'm trying to help.' It came out more angrily than she had intended.

'Rachel, I'm not strong enough to ask you again. Just leave me – let me be.'

She dropped his wrist. He moved on. Bird-still, as if she were hunting in pond water, she watched him go, waiting until he had entered the bathroom before following.

In the bathroom, Gabriel leant against a wall. Shame overwhelmed him as he found his nakedness in the mirror, causing him to slump to the floor and muffle his anguish with his hands.

Rachel knocked on the door. He drew the bolt across. She called out his name as he slid over to the toilet roll, pulled down a few sheets of paper and tried to masturbate the growing nausea away. But the hardness of the floor beneath him and the spiky fear in his chest undermined him, so he only achieved a soft unfulfilling erection. Head down, chin upon chest, eyes squeezed together, he continued until he ejaculated into the folded sheets, the minimal pleasure causing his frustration to grow.

Rachel knocked again.

The door opened and Gabriel stood before her in a blue gown. She smiled a delicate, reassuring smile without guile or artifice.

He joined her in the hallway. 'Will you accept my apologies?'

'You don't owe me an apology for anything.'

'I'll walk you to the door.'

'I don't want to go.'

'After witnessing my display, I would have thought that you would be only too pleased to leave here.'

Rachel waited before placing her arms around him. She was ready for the sag and held on as his knees buckled. 'It's all right. I've got you, I've got you.' She lowered him to the floor. 'Stay with me. Stay awake.'

'I don't want this.'

The weakness of his voice threatened to break something inside her, but she went on. 'I want this. Stay with me. Stay. I want you here this time.'

Once more her fingers explored the architecture of his body: the unyielding hardness of his bones and the pliability of his skin as it stretched with her pulling. She retraced the original passage of her nails with her mouth, leaving new markings of moisture and indentation that faithfully recorded the indulgence of her teeth.

She grasped his penis and squeezed it hard. The central vein that ran along it swelled, its colour darkening, growing richer. A deep breath and then she gripped him with both hands as hard as she could, bringing forth every secret pattern of his muscle, forcing the blood to the tip. In her mind's eye, his penis burst open and material erupted forth over her hands, splattered her face and covered their bodies.

Her vagina slid over his face as she licked her fingers and slipped a nail into her anus; her wet splashed his cheek and she screamed something unintelligible and imperfect, beyond the words she spoke in church when she was called to the altar and the spirit of God filled her and she spoke in tongues, something that filled her as she separated his lips with her nails and allowed her wet to drip inside his mouth.

Rachel slid over his lips, his cheeks and eyes. She grabbed the back of his head and rubbed herself against him until she came so hard that she urinated all over him, over his chest, his stomach and on to the floor. She held him there as her muscles did their own thing and the tears rolled freely down her face.

Eventually she fell backwards and took his cock into her mouth, the knowledge that she was the first to hold him so warming her stomach like freshly boiled Horlicks. Cupping her hand over him, she caught his semen and spread it over their bodies, the drying fluid bonding them as they went their separate ways into sleep.

Gabriel opened his eyes and, startled by Rachel's close proximity, pulled away. The smell of her breath was on his lips and something else. Looking down he found the white of his own semen and the trace of Rachel's own secretions about his penis.

He took a long bath.

Afterwards, drying himself down, listening to her sounds in the kitchen, he guessed which pots and pans she was using. When he joined her she was wearing the shirt that he had left on the floor. She greeted him with the words, 'Hi, I thought I'd put something together.'

Gabriel eyed a pile of chopped vegetables on a board, some bubbling rice and frying chicken. He sat himself down at the table. 'I had some reading material here.'

'Yeah, I put it all under the table. Don't worry, I don't read other people's things.'

A quick glance under the table confirmed that Matthew's journal was indeed there. He began to tilt her remains into the rubbish bin and clean the surfaces.

'Why do that? I'm not finished.'

'I believe in cleaning as I go.'

'What a waste of time.'

'He stared at her.

'What's the matter?'

'You've come to my home. I did not invite you. You have – you have abused me.'

Her voice fell away. 'Abused you?'

'I lived according to my choice.' He advanced on her and she was sure he was going to throw a punch. 'It was my choice, not yours.' He stopped and wiped away some tears.

'I'm sorry. I didn't – I –'

He launched into the washing-up.

'You'll break something if you carry on like that.'

'You are a guest here. While you stay here, would you please try to be aware that this is my home and that I live to my own standards, not yours.'

'Can I ask you something?'

'Whatever you like.'

'Am I really your guest?'

'Unfortunately, yes.'

'Because if I am your guest, if only for a while, I should leave and get some clothes.'

'I haven't asked you to stay.'

'Then I'll ask you.'

'No, no. Absolutely not.'

'Why not? I want to stay for a while.'

'And what you want, you take?'

'No.'

'You can't stay.'

'Why not? I'd really like to stay with you for a while. You haven't given me a reason why I shouldn't.'

'I don't have to.'

'I can't believe that I scare you so much.'

He sat down. 'Why would I be frightened of you?'

'You tell me.'

'Why should you listen? You ignore everything else I say to you.'

She dipped a finger in the pot. 'Mm, you'll like this. It's very good. I'm a very good cook.'

'I am not exactly unskilled in that department myself.'

She burst out laughing and repeated his words back to him.

'Yes, yes,' he sighed, 'you are an excellent mimic. I'm sure your lovers have found it most enchanting.'

The metal in her nose glistened as it caught the light. 'You really are something, aren't you? I don't think I have ever met a more pompous human being in my life.'

'So you want to stay just for the pleasure of insulting me?'

'Not at all.'

'Then why?'

'Because, strange as it might seem, I like being with you.'

Gabriel clasped his hands together under the table out of her sight. 'Why do you make this claim?'

'What kind of question is that?'

'It stands.'

' "It stands." What are you, a fucking lawyer? And don't give me that look, either!'

'What look is that?'

'That look you gave me, like I'm shit beneath your feet.'

'I have no such look.'

'You just gave it to me.'

'I do not have any thoughts like that about any human being.'

'Why? Because you love the human race or because you think you're worse than everybody else?'

'You cannot stay. I can't trust you.'

'You can trust me.'

'No, I can't. You've proved that already.' He headed for the front door. 'Eat your food and then leave.'

She caught up with him and slapped his face.

He looked at her as if she was lower than anything he could think of. 'You don't know anything about hurting another person.'

She went to slap him again, but his eyes stopped her. Just like that it was out between them, something ugly and dangerous that had been buttoned up tight and neatly folded away. It occurred to her that she should have seen this person before. Should have spotted him hiding underneath the choice words and the careful delivery. 'I'm not scared of you,' she said.

'That's irrelevant.'

She knew it to be true. She could be quick and brave and it wouldn't be enough.

He stood there waiting to give expression to his other self. She didn't accept the challenge. He looked her over again, as though she was rotting meat, before opening the door. 'Get out.'

'I'm not dressed.'

'Dress, then please leave. This isn't for me.'

'Yeah, well don't think I like this either.'

'It's not a question of like, it's what you know.'

Rachel dressed and headed for the street, but not before spitting in his face. 'Rachel,' he said without bothering to wipe the saliva away, 'Rachel, you have no idea just how ugly and repellent you seem to me right now.'

As she leaned forward to spit again, he slammed the door in her face.

An hour passed before he made a pot of coffee. A few minutes were spent preparing a selection of cakes and biscuits, then he picked up the journal and returned to the fire in the lounge.

Sunday, 24th February 1958

We have met.

The meeting went extremely well. I lie. It was exceptional. She is truly an extraordinary woman, with exceptional emotional depth, possessed of a keen, fluid intelligence which loses nothing to the formally educated mind in analysis and thought. Indeed, during our conversation, I began to see for the first time in my life the limitations of my learning traditions.

This woman sees and creates pictures in shapes that to my own eye are bare and nondescript. Hears exciting new sounds in hinterlands whose existence I am completely ignorant of.

Could it be that all these many particles of self – personality, mind, inclination, penchant and disposition, elements that form *en masse* the entire summation of a human being, in short the cardinal constituent, the soul – can be captured by celluloid, silver gel and dye? If such an occurrence is possible, then even someone as rational and cynical as myself is vulnerable to such a phenomenon. For I was not misled by my interpretation of Jocelynne's picture. She is as I saw her and yet beyond any fevered, adolescent conjuration. She is far more.

12

Jocelynne has been interviewed in the local press. It seems that someone of note had attended a theatrical evening at which Jocelynne had recited and performed. This person has lavished praise on Jocelynne in the local paper and she has received encouragement to perform her work at a local theatre. Her family are extremely excited, as indeed they should be.

Since my time here, I have seen no Negro performer of note. The English have a few Negro comedians on the radio, but I have not heard one whose hand I would readily embrace. They are, without exception, a disgrace to their people. Their only purpose seems to be to act as the butt of a joke or confirm notions that their white audiences have of sub-standard Negro intellectual capacity.

I am quite sure that the 'true' personalities of these performers are radically different to their stage personas; at least I hope so. I only wish that they did not have to fulfil their desire to tread the boards by the use of wholly inappropriate gestures and mannerisms.

Paul Robeson has clearly demonstrated that the Negro can claim roles which increase his stature, or at the very least invest inadequate roles with dignity and charm. Not that I suppose unequivocally the Negro representation of dignity and reserve. It is not the prerogative of the performer always to be stoical in the face of racism and bigotry. We should not have to be constantly showing these people how civilized and cultivated we are – for that we need only listen to the works of Duke Ellington, an artist whose work compares to the heavenly Wolfgang Mozart. We do not need to demonstrate that we can act as well as, if not better than them. I like anger and impatience. Theatre and film should, in my opinion, reflect our irascibility and our dwindling faith in the dictum 'turn the other cheek'.

Jocelynne's poetry reflects her Creator. Her poems are full of humour as well as insight. How I wish these dreadful, melodramatic films that the Americans are beginning to produce around the issues of race contained more of our laughter. We do laugh. We are not always bound up in issues that the white creates for us. These movies fail miserably to capture our private lives.

I can see, when Jocelynne is in company, that she is a recorder; that tones and inflections, movements and tread are all being noted. I watch her watching friends as they cook, as they chat, as they laugh, as they holler, as they clean, as they try to make space for themselves in the day. I have become her shadow of late. Whenever I can be, I am with her.

My most secret friend and confidant, I confess that my circle of friends has widened dramatically, and, dare I say it, I am more at ease with people than before. My accent, my enunciation still elicit much humour, but that joke is growing weary upon the lips of those who favour it the most. Only Rupert still seems to draw pleasure from mimicking me, however badly. I am not sure why since, amongst the islands, there are many who have been educated at private schools. Still, the base elements of class humour are always good for a chuckle, especially after alcohol has been consumed, and Rupert, without equivocation, likes a drink.

I have received my free ticket for the poetry evening in which Jocelynne will take part, and look forward to it with great anticipation. There is something special between us. A great passion exists between us, but I have not attempted anything untoward. It is completely unnecessary to rush things. I know that she will be mine. We both enjoy our friendship so much. I am sure that this will stand us in good stead in the time to come when we are properly together.

Rupert, like many others in his family I am sure, believes that we have consummated our relationship, even though they believe Jocelynne to be a disciplined and Christian individual. Our closeness and physical ease with each other would indicate only one thing to certain people. But such thoughts are their own. I have mine and they are pleasant and comforting enough. *Time. They do not understand time.* Those who have so much to look forward to do not feel the need to rush.

Tuesday, 2nd February

An interesting development today.

I have been at the Institute for seven weeks now. In that time I have often heard the name Arthur Kembo mentioned. Arthur, it seems, is what the English would describe as a 'character'. Stories abound concerning Arthur, to the extent that he has become part of staff folklore.

Arthur, it seems, is extremely attractive to the opposite sex. Having now met him, the reason is not immediately obvious to me. He is very slim, has enormous hands, with bony wrists that jut out of his shirt-sleeves. His hair is cut extremely short and his eyes – his eyes to my mind bulge out of their sockets, beneath eyebrows which are unnaturally thin, due to the fact that he plucks them. He is highly intelligent, has a keen sense of humour and seems always ready to laugh at himself: something that occurs quite often since most of his colleagues seem to look forward to jousting verbally with him at lunch-time, where the topic of conversation will more than likely be his 'appalling' behaviour.

He is truly larger than life. I had observed him, prior to our first actual meeting, fairly bouncing along the corridors. We had exchanged cursory greetings and polite goodbyes, but had never really entered into any sort of dialogue. The porters and cleaners all adore him. I have never seen him without a smile or a contented look in his eye, and I cannot put this down solely to his sex life.

I will not mention here the many accounts I have heard about Arthur's sexual capabilities, nor the inordinate amount of time that is spent by my colleagues discussing the length of Arthur's penis. By all accounts, Arthur is extravagantly endowed. A fact that cannot really be escaped even by someone not yet on speaking terms with Arthur, since he wears trousers that cling to his skin like glue on paper.

I should mention here the many betrayed boyfriends who have come seeking retribution from Arthur after their girlfriends have broken down and told them how badly he treated them during their 'mistake'. But their anger is surely increased by the notion that their women could:

a) Actually be attracted to a Negro;

b) Have shamed themselves, their families, their partners, their partners' families, society as a whole, the English race abroad, the white race, and God's will;

c) Have dared to expose their bodies to the devil's penis and placed themselves beyond the ability of all white men to satisfy their lusty urges and bring them back into the white, Christian fold.

These are not intelligent times. My dear friend Penny has been verbally and physically abused (spitting seems to be the number-one choice) when she has been in my company in shops and restaurants. Not that we would be foolish enough to enter most shops or restaurants in this city of Neanderthals, but enough shopkeepers on High Street Ken are aware of the nature of the Institute and the make-up of the staff, and they cater for our business. After all, money is money, whatever the hue of the person who passes it across the counter. Ultimately, pubs and shops in this area recognize that they do not want their profits going to other high street competitors.

The points of danger remain, however, and most of us keep to the invisible lines that mustn't be crossed or recklessly challenged. But Arthur doesn't seem to give a damn. He seems to exult in situations that carry the possibility of reproof or embarrassment.

Our first true meeting took place in the Milford Arms, the drinking place that is frequented by most who work at the Institute. It is quite cosmopolitan, filled with many black and brown faces from work, as well as diplomats, businessmen, visitors, and French and Italians who also work in the area. The place is run by an enormous Irishman, John Callaghan – Catholic, straight out of the myths and poetry which tell of rolling hills, foggy moors and glorious rebellions against the British. Callaghan, for some odd reason, is extremely fond of black people. I do not know how to explain it properly, With whites, even the Irish, he is his normal, fulsome, extrovert self, but something is missing. I have watched him visibly brighten as the Arms fills up with darker faces. The tension falls away from his enormous shoulders and a warmer tone enters his heavy brogue. I cannot explain it. I have certain friends who, let us say, are over-enthusiastic admirers of the works of Oscar Wilde, who have spoken to me of being born in the wrong body. I can accept this explanation for their sexual preference, and sometimes when I observe Callaghan I wonder if the same theory might be applied to him in an ethnic sense.

Callaghan is no crusader when it comes to the cause of the Negro. Indeed, his lack of racism, I think, sometimes blinds him to the true problems that confront many of his customers. I have often seen him disparaging members of the Institute as they describe some petty incident of discrimination. He will tell them volubly that, as far as the English are concerned, he is a 'white nigger', that he is in exactly the same boat when it comes to housing and work, and that we must stop complaining and get on with our lives. The English are the scum of the earth and always will be. Callaghan loathes the English, and only allows English people into his 'home' whom he considers 'honorary human beings'. Next on his hate list are Germans, then Arabs. I do not know why, but it is so.

Back to my meeting with Arthur. Penny and I were locked in an intense debate over the comparative merits of Garfield Sobers and Keith Miller. Penny was an avid cricket follower, having a father and brother who had both played with distinction for Cambridge University, and had little time for anyone who disagreed with her contention that Keith Miller was the finest all-rounder who ever lived. Her beer was splashing over her glass as she thumped the table and declared, 'No one in the modern game compares to Miller. He was the most exciting attacking batsman in the world, and as for his bowling, well, it is recognized by even Lindwall himself that Miller with a full head of steam was even more deadly with the new ball.'

Before I could reply, someone laid a hand on my shoulder and said, in an accent that matched royalty, 'Excuse me, old chap, but I couldn't help overhearing your conversation, and I would like to say that you are both wrong. Neither Sobers or Miller can claim at this moment to be the greatest all-rounder.'

I turned and looked into the smiling eyes of Arthur Kembo, whilst Penny snapped, 'Oh, for God's sake, Arthur! Can't you keep your nose out of anything?'

Arthur proceeded to sit down at our table, though we had not invited him. 'Of course I can, darling, but not when I hear two people making such basic errors about a game that is dearer to me than life itself.'

Penny was outraged. ' "Basic errors" – don't be ridiculous! I do not make basic errors in any part of my life, particularly not cricket.'

Arthur took Penny's hand, inspiring a slight blush to spread across her cheeks, and patted it gently. Penny's eyes flickered over to mine, and in that moment of contact I was left with no doubt that Penny and Arthur had enjoyed a closeness beyond that of friendly colleagues. 'My dear girl –'

'I am not your dear girl.'

Arthur kissed her hand. 'And my life is poorer for that. Nevertheless, you are wrong on the matter of Miller.'

'Will you let go of my hand?'

'Of course I will.' His hand remained where it was. 'As I said, you are mistaken.' He turned to me with a huge grin that bared all his teeth and bright gums. 'As are you. By the way, my name is Arthur Kembo.' I shook his hand and was about to reply when he continued, 'Matthew DuBois. How could I not know you? Your family are well known in Nigeria. I believe my father once had the pleasure of presenting an award to your father.' I said that I was unaware of this. 'Why should you be? I'm sure that you lose count of all the honours your father collects. Anyway, it is a pleasure to meet you. It's quite amazing that we haven't met before, actually.'

Penny ordered fresh drinks and tartly asked, 'Why is that, Arthur?'

'Well, it's obvious isn't it? We both come from families of achievers, though my own little tree cannot compare to the DuBois's, but then whose can? We both come from families that have amassed fortunes in countries where blacks have been extremely oppressed. We both are working for an Institute that seems to cater for the idle offspring of such dynasties. So, it is odd that we should have taken so long to meet. Or is it, DuBois?' he said, fixing me with those glistening pools of his.

'I am not sure I understand.'

He leaned forward, like a Great Dane about to suck the marrow out of a bone. 'Don't you, old man? I have often observed how certain kinds of black people, having climbed their way up particular kinds of ladders, where they enjoy a rarefied standing, are extremely wary of others of their kind who wish to join them.'

I managed to raise an eyebrow to what I knew to be an extremely impressive position, and replied with a note of boredom, 'How interesting.' I am not sure what I expected, but the deep, fulsome, rich baritone explosion of laughter that erupted from Kembo was most certainly not it.

'Oh, DuBois, really, really.'

And, truth to tell, I could not suppress a smile from creasing my lips. Nor, as he proceeded to light up two cigarettes in his mouth, could I help but feel a liking for Kembo that was much deeper than the shortness of our acquaintance.

As he handed Penny one of the cigarettes, she said, 'Arthur, really, what are you talking about?' He stretched out and kissed her on the cheek. 'Have no fear, my dear. This is black man's talk.'

'Arthur, must you talk like that? It really is silly talk.'

'What is silly about it?' he boomed. 'Do you deny that there are race-specific topics that entail a certain level of experience? Or can the experience of slavery be achieved by angst-driven empathy? Can the upper-class débutante understand the pains of an Indian untouchable just by reading an E. M. Forster novel?'

'What has this got to do with cricket, Arthur? What has a Keith Miller bouncer got to do with the bloody Taj Mahal?'

Callaghan brought over more drinks.

'Nothing exactly.'

'Well then?'

'But it is hardly surprising that someone who is unable to understand, and therefore respect, essential differences of culture and heritage cannot filter out impressions of personality and charisma from the cold, hard, cricketing facts, which in this case deny Keith Miller the pre-eminence you give him.'

'These facts are?'

Arthur laid his glass on the table, licked his lips and folded his hands together. 'I need only mention Rhodes, Grace and Constantine to force you to re-examine your position.' This roll-call infuriated Penny even further. 'And, of course, I need only invoke the name of the immortal Walter Hammond to silence such nonsense for ever.'

Penny barked, 'Walter Hammond? Don't be ridiculous!'

Arthur's eyes blazed, and I could see that cricket was indeed an extremely serious subject for him, not to be taken lightly. 'Ridiculous?' he bellowed. 'My dear girl, be very careful before you expose yourself. I am talking about W. R. Hammond, indisputably, along with Jack Hobbs, Donald Bradman, George Headley, Ranji and the immortal Victor Trumper, one of the finest batsmen to ever walk the earth.'

'No one is denying that, Arthur!'

'Do you deny his claim to be one of the finest slip catchers of all time?'

'Bowling, Arthur, let us talk about bowling!'

Arthur's hand came to rest upon the deep blue of Penny's skirt. I would have had to be blind not to notice the sexual chemistry between them. As I watched the two of them argue, a warm glow spread through my heart and for the first time I began to feel comfortable in this foreign land.

Yes, my passion for Jocelynne roots me here, but the very nature of my desire for her has excluded much else. I take very little pleasure in other things, for they seem to pale before my main focus. But with these two friends I am aware that I have managed to make other bonds, that I have created, am creating a new life.

I caught familiar faces also listening and enjoying the argument, in truth the entertainment that Penny and Arthur were providing. I gave and received nods of recognition from work colleagues, who, I realized at that moment, are not bosom friends and perhaps never will be, but who are still people with whom I have forged something concrete and tangible. It was when my attention returned to our own table that I realized we had been joined by someone else.

A man of average height but stocky build, with red hair and a suit of indistinctive taste, was standing over our table. Arthur and Penny broke off their conversation. Penny asked him if she could help him. Ignoring her, he turned to Arthur and said in a low voice, as if he did not want to embarrass anyone, 'Excuse me, but would you mind removing your hand from this lady's knee?'

Arthur did not move his hand and replied, 'I'm not sure I understand.'

The stranger cast a short glance towards Penny's skirt and turned to face two men, his companions I suspected, who were seated on a table about eight yards from our own. He brought himself even closer to Arthur and continued in a manner that adults usually reserve for stubborn young children.

'Look, I don't want to make anything here, we all just want to enjoy our lunch-break. So why don't you do what you're asked – what is right – and take your hand off the lady's knee. There's no need to embarrass everyone.'

The situation was potentially difficult: the man had other friends. I had just began to speak the necessary conciliatory words when Arthur picked up his glass and poured the contents over the man's shoe.

Silence descended throughout the pub, only being broken by Arthur when he said, 'Why don't we settle this outside?' The man's face turned as bright as his hair. I believe he had expected Arthur meekly to do as he had been asked. While he was still deliberating, Arthur walked briskly over to the door. The red-haired man snapped at Callaghan, 'You saw what was going on. Is that the sort of thing you allow in here? There are laws against that kind of behaviour.'

Callaghan merely pointed to the door and said, 'He's waiting.' The man looked to his friends. It was clear that no one else was going to fight for him or with him. So he left the pub whilst I, along with Penny, Callaghan and a large percentage of those present, rushed over to the windows. Penny whispered to me in a concerned, agitated manner, 'I do hope Arthur will be all right. I hate it when he gets involved like this.'

I saw the man say something to Arthur, who answered by spitting in his adversary's face. The man was naturally enraged and aimed a punch at Arthur's head. To my amazement, Arthur ducked smoothly under the arc of the man's swing, delivered a punch to his solar plexus and followed this up with a short hook to the chin. As his opponent staggered backwards, Arthur followed up quickly, and knocked him out before calmly returning to us.

The red-haired man's friends went back to their table without showing much concern and resumed drinking. Penny asked Arthur rather unnecessarily if he was all right. He was quite dismissive of her attentions and said all too loudly, 'Of course I'm all right. The day a foppish whitey can take me is the day I go home.' To my surprise the Milford Arms erupted with laughter and people came forward to pat Arthur on the back and congratulate him.

As I took in this remarkable scene, Callaghan's voice rose above the noise. 'Arthur, you'd best have a drink and prepare yourself. The police will be along soon and they'll want to take you with them. They must be getting fed up with your beating up the white locals.'

Penny dragged him off to the toilet, saying, 'Come on, you had better tidy yourself up before they get here.' Again she had mystified me, since Arthur had not been touched. A complete stranger whispered to me, 'She'll be fucking his brains out in there; she likes a bit of blood, does that one.'

Although I could not comment on Penny's reaction to blood, something told me that Arthur and Penny were indeed 'busy' in the toilets. When they returned, Arthur just had time for a drink before the police came for him.

Callaghan, Penny and I accompanied him to the police station. Three other people from the Milford Arms came along as witnesses for Arthur, all of them Irish, and spoke on his behalf.

While we were at the station, a police constable offered the advice that our friend should stay away from white women, if he knew what was best for him.

Arthur came out of his cell three hours after we arrived at the police station. He was not going to face charges: enough people were willing to say he had acted in self-defence, and the red-haired man did not want to pursue the matter.

Later, in the car, Arthur declared, 'Nothing will deter me from enjoying the crunch of my black fist on white jaws.' Penny and Callaghan found this highly amusing, and although he was appalling, I too could not help but shed tears of laughter.

Thursday, 4th February

I am attending Jocelynne's poetry evening tomorrow. She asked me to bring some friends from work, so I have asked Arthur to come, as well as Penny and her boyfriend and Callaghan. I am aware that, of the four people I have invited, three of them are white. I cannot honestly claim to have had many white friends before now – if any. It is odd, but England, despite her damnable cold and ever-present rain, is presenting me with new possibilities. I must keep up with them.

Friday, 5th February

The theatre is in an area called Clapham Junction, on Lavender Hill. Some theatres have resonances from previous performances; the quality passes on. This theatre, immediately upon entering, gives off a warm, positive glow. As we stepped through the doors, I felt already that the evening would go well.

I was accompanied by a small contingent of Jocelynne's family. Rupert brought his girlfriend, Gladwin, with him. A lively Kenyan, she seems far too bright for Rupert, who spends his whole time listening to a chorus of disapproval from his family about romancing an African woman. I know she is aware of the comments from these 'proud West Indians', but soldiers on. An extrovert personality given to touching everyone, her flirting clearly unsettled Rupert; and to tell the truth, I am certain that, given the chance, she would have seduced me. Rupert was enraged and could barely look me in the eye. For that, I was more than happy with her company.

What bores Jocelynne's family are! As we stood in the auditorium they never stopped talking about the number of 'classy' and 'fine' white people who were present, and how proud they were of Jocelynne for bringing such distinguished people to the theatre, and how wonderful she was for mixing with such famous English poets. You would think she was a pet monkey performing with a higher breed of circus performers the way they carried on. Mercifully, I have and shall continue to have little to do with them.

Arthur turned up and created quite a stir. He was accompanied by a white woman called Beth Daniels. They made no attempt to disguise this or hide the fact that they had already drunk too much. Another couple accompanied them – two people from Barbados, John Sweet and Brenda Soft. My heart sank as they opened their mouths; one Barbadian in a room is bad enough, but two? Arthur's loudness of voice and general manner were enough to capture attention by himself, but the presence of his companion ensured that when he joined us we were all the centre of attention. We all talked as if nothing were untoward, but we would have to be blind to be unaware of the many baleful glances that were directed at us. I, for one, was extremely amused by the sight of so many whites, after turning up to see an evening of poetry that consisted mainly of West Indian performers, unsettled out of their liberal niceties by Arthur.

Jocelynne did not appear for the first half of the performance, but this did not dim my enjoyment. It was a pleasure to hear voices giving life to characters and situations that I knew so well. The gusto and conviction of the performers was tremendous, as was their stage skill. At least five of the six were first-time performers, but a lifetime of enthralling their families had prepared them well. The applause at the end was generous and, if slightly too long, more than deserved.

In the interval, we all discussed what we had seen. Arthur's companion John was, to be frank, tiresome. He was too forward. It seemed to me that he was mimicking Arthur's persona. His jokes were echoes of Arthur's; even his movements and the ham-handed way he put his arms about people were an imitation of Arthur. But whereas Arthur's touch is accepted, even wanted by people – Arthur has such charm that people feel excluded if it is not directed at them – John's over-familiarity was offensive. But not as much as his rather boorish attempts to seduce some of the white women who were present. He seemed determined to leave the theatre with a woman – it would have been immaterial if she were ugly, obese, thin or blighted by dwarfism, as long as she was white. This need of his was transparent to all, especially his supposed companion, Brenda. I have no love for the people from her island: I find them to be almost without exception obnoxious and convinced of their superiority to every Negro who was not born into their island heritage. But I would not wish such racial shaming upon anyone. To watch John insult a woman who was cut from the same wood as his mother or his sister was quite sickening. He shamed himself, and by the same process every other Negro in the room.

The performance continued, and two more performers were presented to the audience before Jocelynne was introduced. As the compère did so, my heart skipped a beat and I turned instinctively towards Rupert, to find him, along with Gladwin, beaming in my direction. I found myself rather sheepishly bowing my head to hide the grin that spread across my face, for it contained an undeserved pride. My pride was in association, not in action. The gifts that Jocelynne possessed were her own.

The applause she received as she stepped on to the stage grew as she made her way to the microphone. The stage area was in truth a floor, about which we sat in a circle of chairs. I noticed immediately that, as she began to speak, the distance between herself and the spot where I was seated seemed to shrink and become more intimate. Her voice as she introduced herself and gave a short autobiography was soft and gentle. I was completely surprised when she put the microphone to one side and continued to speak to us, her voice easily reaching past us to the walls. She was indeed a practised artist. Observation of these qualities did not however stop my heart from beating rapidly. I could not bear the thought of her failing in some manner or other. My fears were groundless, for as she launched into her first poem – a poem about her mother and her mother's world – it was clear that she had the audience, as the saying goes, in the palm of her hand.

This Jocelynne was so much like the woman I had come to know, but qualitatively different. She demonstrated a confidence, almost an arrogance, that I had never encountered before. It was not an arrogance of ego, but an arrogance that comes from those who take comfort in their own excellence and proceed without fear of failure or derision. This confidence caused the audience itself to relax, for we knew with certainty that we were going to be entertained, and so we were.

The poem was alive with reality: the mother of the poem was at once real and yet completely comical, like a strip-cartoon character who immediately causes you to think of someone you are intimate with. The laughter that the mother drew from Rupert and the other West Indians present confirmed the truth of the character, though the laughter was never mocking, always affectionate. My background prevented me from sharing the same sort of connection as many in the hall, but I had met this persona many times, and as Jocelynne brought her to life, home drew closer towards me through the walls of the building and warmed me with its own special life.

For Jocelynne had become the characters of her pieces. Her mimicry was accurate and at times bordered on the cruel, so unsparing was she with her renditions, but always, always there was something that could only be described as love. I experienced that strange process of revelation which occurs when one human being recognizes another to be that rare creature, separate from the pseudo impostor and shallow aspirant, an artist; and more, an artist of note.

The show over, I stood with her family and waited for her to finish giving an interview for a local paper. She posed happily with the other performers and acknowledged passers-by who stopped to compliment her.

As we waited, Arthur led me to one side. 'DuBois, old chap,' he began, 'you know that I find you to be a fine chap.' I shrugged my shoulders and tried to respond modestly. There was something about Arthur that always caused me to shrug my shoulders. 'You know that, despite our disagreements about cricket, world politics and your quaint notions of honour and chivalry –' He held up his hand to silent my intended response. Out of the corner of my eye I could see Penny scowling at Arthur. Through the course of the evening I had witnessed Penny whisper several harsh words into Arthur's ear. Despite the presence of her boyfriend and Arthur's companion, she had not made the greatest of efforts to hide the jealousy and irritation that Beth's presence had caused her. 'Why bother to hide it, old man? You are what you are. No, no, let me finish. You are a fine human being, which leads me to the meat of our impending discussion. This woman of yours is quite something, eh?'

'I think so.'

'Yes, old man, she is, she really is.' He slipped an arm around me and patted my shoulder. 'I want you to know something.' He laid his free hand upon his chest and patted it gently. 'I am an African. I am a proud African. I am proud to be an African. You may not think that because you see me spending all my time with these dreadful white women.'

'Arthur?'

'No, no, don't deny it. That's what you think. That's what you all think. But let me tell you something: I love black women. I lay myself before the shrine of the woman who is black. No, no, hush, let me speak. The simple truth is I have never found a black woman who could meet my standards. I am cursed.

The European has filled my mind with certain expectations, so I — ' his hand drew a small circle in the air, 'I pass my time with these women. I hate them, really. No, I love them, I hate them, I love them. It's a curse, you see.'

And with that he turned and made his way over to his companion of the evening. I watched him until Jocelynne came over to me and took my hand. It was quite delightful being the companion of the star turn.

Monday, 8th January

I have been summoned home. When I arrived for work this morning, I was handed a letter. The sender was my sister, Meredith.

Gabriel opened the envelope and read the letter contained within it.

Dear Brother,

Father is unwell. He has been poorly for over two weeks now. At first we feared that it was another stroke, but the doctors assure us that this is not so. They suggest that he may have overworked himself; the heart is, after all, a muscle. He refuses to slow down and Mother is growing frantic. He will not listen to any of us. He continues to insist that 'everything is controlled by the mind' and that he will solve everything by maintaining the 'correct attitude'.

If only you could see him — his face grows more gaunt with every passing day. There is a constant parade of selfish fools through the house who will not leave him in peace.

A massive conference is being held; several leading dignitaries from the United States are attending. A leading representative of the American Southern Christian Leadership Conference and a close friend of the organization's principal leader, Dr Martin Luther King, will be attending. We hope to gain more insight from him not only about the organization's affiliate bodies and strategies, but also more about the personality and philosophies of Dr King.

King's employment of civil disobedience and creative resistance has wonderful echoes of Harold Moody, founder of the League of Coloured Peoples in England, whose efforts and organizational drive inspired many of the founders of the Institute where you now work. Perhaps you might consider the background of the two men and the impetus and direction that their Christian faith gave them. Many of King's utterances could have come directly from the mouth of Moody. I hope that analysis of these two men will help you to come to an understanding of my own faith and how it empowers me, something I could never achieve.

Please come home. We all miss you. Father would never admit it, but he would give a lot to have you back. Your departure was so sudden. I know that your arguments with Papa and Mama had grown even more heated of late, but I cannot accept that something was said that could make you wish to be away from us for so long. You are our parents' sounding-board – the rebellious, less tolerant part of themselves that they have never really given expression to. Their fight with you is a fight with their impatience and potential intransigence. Deep down, they know this as we all do. Come back to us, little brother. You know that, besides needing you, we ultimately trust you. Come as soon as you can.

All my love,

M.

Before he replaced the envelope, Gabriel lifted the paper to his nose and caught the faintest of scents. On with the journal.

Meredith's words moved me greatly. Any child likes to be told of their worth and value, but the simple truth is that, for all my sister's entreaties, the words come from the wrong source. There has been no split with my parents; I have documented my reasons for leaving already. Let us say instead that I had no great reason for staying. If my parents want me to return, then they will have to cast aside their pride and write to me directly.

16

My dear friend, privy to every thought and deed, you know me best. I brought you to life when I came to this country and you have grown along with me, flourished with every stroke of my pen. I am sure, such is our intimacy and shared knowledge, that you are already aware of my intentions.

Jocelynne and I are happy together and will continue to be happy together – we have no doubt of that. I want to marry her. I suppose I have always wanted it. I am meeting her tonight. The usual crowd will be in attendance, but we will have time alone together and I will ask her to marry me. There is no need for an engagement. The time has come to dispense with our trite independent existences and get on with living together.

17

My friend, I am sure that you expected me, upon my return, to continue my narrative with a flourish of romantic rhetoric and confirm the things that I hinted at before. I will come to those issues, but before that I must tell you of events which preceded my 'evening' with Jocelynne that have necessitated a temporary pause in any important declaration.

I realize now that I have been profligate with my energies, pampered and insensitive. My life will change from tonight. Tonight I will lower my head on to the pillow as my old self, but when I awake in the morning and lift it from that self-same pillow, I will have broken contract with the man who closed his eyes the night before.

Gabriel swallowed his glass of wine in one swoop, before refilling and gulping down the next. Something gave him pause and he left the kitchen to peep through the spy hole of his door. Rachel sat on the doorstep with her back to him. He thought things over, then opened the door, picked up her bags and carried them into the kitchen. When she joined him he apologized.

'There's no need.'

'There is. All you've done, admittedly in a rather eccentric manner, is to offer me friendship. I'm not very good at all this bonding business and perhaps I misunderstood a few things.' Her mouth dropped. 'I admire your courage. I could not have stayed if someone had behaved as badly towards me. I appreciate the gesture.'

'Go on.'

'You're an extremely attractive person. I should be flattered that you would spend so much time and effort on me.'

'Oh . . . Good.'

'I'd like to offer my home to you.'

'Pardon?'

'You can stay.'

'Right. OK then, I'd like to take a bath, then go to bed.'

'I only have one bed.'

'I don't mind sharing.'

'I will share with you as long as you behave yourself.'

'I promise to behave myself.'

'Good then, as long as we understand each other. Do we understand each other?'

'To be honest, I don't understand you at all. But I hope that you understand me a little.'

'I'm not sure that I do.'

'It's OK, I'm used to it.'

She picked up her bag and left the room. Gabriel listened to her progress up the stairs and into his bedroom, before continuing with his reading.

19

It seems that I will have to leave the Institute if it will not alter its present role. It is true that I have not been over-excited by my work there. Much of that which it is founded upon irks me. Its very title irritates me.

Why should we designate ourselves as coloured? White is a colour, but these people are not even singularly that. They are often pink, sometimes yellow, sometimes blue and their bruises can turn a bright purple. In the sun, they can turn various shades of brown, and when they are deprived of light for too long, they become alabaster. They are the true people of 'colour'. I do not understand why a nation, indeed many nations – for the white race is outnumbered when counted alongside the black, the brown and the yellow – should define a body of peoples and cultures in relation to something outside of themselves.

It is also true that the Institute has on its board of trustees a number of agencies with whom I disagree. We are associated with a number of Christian groups who have a long history of anti-racist activity, but I find the moral, biblical base of their arguments feeble and intellectually silly. The Institute, moreover, like all such formations – the original Pan African Conference of 1900, the American National Association for the Advancement of Colored People, my father's own Negro Liberation Movement, Moody's League of Coloured Peoples – is composed essentially of the black intelligentsia.

These organizations exist, to my mind, primarily because certain gifted individuals cannot accept intellectually or egotistically that their path through life should be diminished or restrained because of the colour of their skin. The leaders of these organizations have spent most of their lives on hustings and in debates, proving to the white man how erudite and verbose they are. They fight for recognition as equals, and their organizations are dedicated to the production of Negro men and women who talk and walk like them, and who will be just as acceptable as they are.

They speak constantly of recognition, equality, and the understanding nature of the white man. They never seem prepared to agitate forcefully, to step outside the bounds of respectability, lest, like Shakespeare's Othello, they reveal the savage heart that beats beneath the civil brow. Let me record here my reserved contempt for the bard of Avon for creating such a magnificent edifice to racial conformity. But these thoughts are not new to me; only the vehemence with which I now feel them. If I am to continue working at the Institute, I will try to make profound changes in its outlook and manner of operation within the public domain.

Thursday, 11th February

Yesterday was a day for which I had such plans. It turned out to be one of the most important days of my life. It turned out to be most interesting, primarily for two reasons.

I spent much of the day with Byron Constantine, the main speaker at functions, lectures and media events for the Institute. As the most public member of the Institute he has attracted quite a following in the press and media, so it is not surprising that his stays here are considered something of a star turn. I found him to be a highly attractive person; gifted in the extreme and most personable. We got on remarkably well, and he invited me to attend a series of lectures that he would be giving in Brixton. I assured him that I would bring along some interested parties, primarily Jocelynne, who is an admirer of Byron's work and has been pestering me for weeks to arrange a meeting with him.

After leaving Byron, I made my way to Penny's office to confer with her about the possibility of sending a letter of support to Doctor King and his associates. I found her engaged in an argument with a clearly distressed individual. I immediately recognized the stranger by his accent and appearance as an Indian Trinidadian. He continued shouting. 'You say this is the Institute for the Negro. What would you know about the struggle of the so-called Negro?'

Penny, having been thrown this poisoned dart before, retorted, 'It is the belief of this Institute that the fight for the emancipation of the black man is the fight of everyone, and that there will always be a quota of staff who are drawn from races other than –'

'You know nothing! Nothing! None of you know nothing!'

Penny, never one to be dictated to in an argument, shouted back, 'I follow Karl Marx's belief that white labour cannot be free until black labour, which means the vast majority of the black race, is freed.'

'Talk, talk! That's all you are, talk, and more fancy talk.'

Penny tried to include me in the 'conversation'. 'Mr Williams, if you feel that, because of my colour, I am unqualified to answer your admittedly sincere but, if I may say so, misguided comments –'

'Misguided?'

'Then maybe my colleague here can help you?'

He turned to me and looked me over with unveiled contempt. 'I don't need to speak to Uncle Tom here.'

'Mr Williams, I suggest that you get your facts right before you come in here and abuse people.'

'No, no. I've come in here for you to get your facts right.' They exchanged more words, until Penny lost her patience and left the room. I took more abuse from Mr Williams, until I made it quite clear that I would not allow him to malign my character or my racial consciousness any further. And I was not bluffing. Although I cannot claim to share Arthur's relish of fighting, I will not allow any man to label me with terms that insult even the lowliest of us. And perhaps it was just as well I did; certain men – and I would include Mr Williams amongst them – only respond well to men who bark back at them and make the right sort of manly gestures of aggression and bluff. Once I had displayed these qualities sufficiently, we were able to begin to converse in a manner that enabled me to see what had brought our visitor to us in such a highly emotional state.

Sonny Williams had arrived in Liverpool two weeks ago on a boat from Trinidad. He had come to join his brother, Alfred, who had arrived in July 1948 on the *Empire Windrush* as part of a group of skilled and semi-skilled labour. Alfred had managed to find work quite quickly and had settled down in Liverpool. Sonny had been a young boy when his brother had left, but now an adult and a qualified electrician, had taken up his brother's entreaties to join him in England. What he found had devastated him.

Alfred had not been at the Liverpool docks to meet him, as arranged, and had not been contactable by phone. When he made his way to Alfred's house, it was to find that his brother had been missing for over five days. Three days after Sonny's arrival, the body of his brother was discovered in an empty garage about three miles from where he lived. An investigation was carried out and it transpired that an unemployed white man had set on Alfred after leaving a pub in a drunken state, and had kicked him to death. Traumatic as this news was, the events which followed had done little to settle his mind.

The area where Alfred had lived was teeming with teddy boys. They were constantly harassing the local black community, and put extreme pressure on landlords and bosses to kick blacks out of their homes and remove them from their jobs, so that whites could replace them. In despair, Sonny had decided to come to London, pinpointing Brixton as an area with a growing number of

West Indians settling there, who enjoyed good relations with the local white community. He had been in Brixton for more than two weeks and had so far failed to find accommodation. He had spent most of his nights on park benches and in doorways, and had been harassed by members of the local police force, who had several times threatened to report him to the Home Office. It seemed that if he was without a job or a home he was a prime candidate for enforced repatriation.

While searching through a paper for housing opportunities – the local black grapevine had proved fruitless – he had come across the name and address of the Institute. In desperation he had turned to us, only to find a collection of people who, for all their fine words, had nothing as far as he was concerned, 'in common with the ordinary black man'.

I was in a difficult position. I explained to him that the Institute did not seek housing for people, but assured him that I would do all I could to help him, and that he was free to use the phone in my own office if he so wished. He asked me to call up potential landlords for him. I failed to see why, since he was perfectly capable of dialling a number, but he was quite insistent.

Although I was extremely busy, his attitude offended me. He clearly blamed the whole world for his own shortcomings, and it occurred to me that I might be doing him a favour if I showed, by my own success, where the actual fault lay. After fifteen minutes on the phone I had four confirmations of available space for him and handed him a list of the relevant addresses and landlords. He asked me to go with him.

I was less than impressed by his request. I was not ignorant – I knew that discrimination of white landlords against blacks was widespread and manifest. But Sonny Williams was well-dressed, well-spoken and quite clearly had the skills to pay his way. I could not believe that out there, in the great metropolis of London, he could not find accommodation. So again I took up his challenge. It was eleven in the morning when we left the Institute.

I had called landlords in Brixton and nearby areas, since it seemed logical to try and find him housing where he could be near an emerging black population. The first address was in Coldharbour Lane. I had confirmed a meeting with the landlord at 11.45 a.m. and arrived more or less on the dot. The house looked pleasant, with three floors and a garden. After I had rung the door, the curtains at the window to my right parted and a woman in her early fifties looked out at us. I smiled at her and stepped back from the door. She waved us away. I approached the window, and as she pulled back I could see her apprehension.

I called out to her, 'Mrs Thompson, my name is Matthew DuBois. I spoke to you on the phone a while ago.' I watched her absorb my name, and a mixture of confusion and uncertainty took hold of her. Behind me, Sonny whispered, 'Let's go, man, we're scaring her. We don't want any hassle.' I held out my hand to calm him and repeated my name to Mrs Thompson. She edged forward and pulled the window up slightly. Her voice, when it came, was tense and high. 'I spoke to you?'

'Yes, on the phone. I asked you about a room you had advertised in the *Express*.'

'The *Express*?'

'Yes. You said you would be happy to give it to me, that I was the first caller.'

At these words, her eyes lit up. 'Oh, it's you.'

'Yes,' I replied, my heart rising now that our communication problems were at an end, 'it is me.'

'You don't sound nigger,' she said.

'Excuse me?'

'You don't sound nigger.'

'How do I sound?'

'Like a white man. You sound like a white man. That's what I thought you were on the phone.' She waved me away again. 'The room isn't for you – it's gone.' And with that she shut the window and retreated back into her room as if she were withdrawing from a bad smell.

Our second landlord was polite but firm in his refusal to let us view the room. I was by now quite angry, as well as slightly tired, but refused to give Sonny the satisfaction of seeing my irritation. We set off again.

Our journey took a severe turn for the worse as we made our way down the High Street. Outside the local Woolworth's, a number of men and women were holding up placards and banners proclaiming that white labour should not be undermined by cheap black labour. As Sonny and I approached, a man pointed to us, shouting, 'See, look at 'em! Come for our jobs, boys?! Come for our jobs? This place isn't for the likes of you! We have good white staff here!'

Someone shouted, 'The train station's down there, mate!'

Another voice, angry and unpleasant, rang out, 'Go home – we don't want you here!'

Had I not come across that line before? Only now I wasn't sitting in the

Institute reading, with lofty disapproval, statements of whites about the 'influx' of blacks from the West Indies into the Mother Country. I was standing in a street having those words hurled in my direction.

The crowd was small, and my way through it clear, but my legs seemed to suffer from an awful stiffness. I turned to Sonny, and was gladdened to see him right behind me. A man leant forward and spat in my face. As he stepped back, a woman reached out and patted him on the back. I raised my fist and punched him full in the face.

As I wiped this Neanderthal's spittle off my face, there was a moment's grace, which broke suddenly as a number of men attacked us. Sonny was magnificent and my abiding memory of him will be of his brightly polished boots flying out randomly into the air, making heavy contact with whatever was in their way. At one point we were fighting together, then we were moved apart. An opening occurred and we instinctively ran for it.

Oh, how I ran. Heedless of direction, aware only of flight. Whenever I turned my head to see who was pursuing me, it was always the same two men.

My pursuers, with their more intimate knowledge of the area, must have split up, for as I turned a corner one of them appeared right in front of me. He crashed into me and we fell into a heap on the ground. As we rolled about, the other one joined in and kicked me in the face. There was a moment of darkness and complete loss of coherent thought as I fell backwards.

I watched the two of them begin to punch and kick my body as if from a distance, before my senses returned to me and the force of their blows began to register. Their language was unimaginative – they seemed stuck on 'you black bastard', 'nigger' and 'fucking coon', and repeated these phrases chant-like with every blow. The assault ended only when they had exhausted themselves. One of these anthropoids, after swearing at me again, walked away. The other kicked me one last time, spluttering, 'Don't let me ever see your black arse here again. Do you understand? This place ain't for the likes of you.' His noble speech concluded, he staggered away to catch up with his brother in bestiality.

No matter how hard I tried, I could not move. A couple looked at me through their window. I called out to them for help, but they turned away and hurried into another room. So I cast my eye over the houses before me with their curtains and blinds and wondered how many people stood there, watching.

Except for my bloodied presence, this street had nothing to distinguish it from hundreds of thousands of other streets throughout this city and indeed throughout England. This is indeed a nation of cowards and bloodless, down-trodden souls. Only a nation of the defeated could stand by idly while a man is subjected to the type of beating I received.

Somehow I managed to get up and stagger away. I felt proud of my body's ability to endure such an attack and even prouder of my mental ability: the blows could not affect my intellect or my imagination. Even after the attack, I was still an intelligent, thinking person. My attackers were still, after all, morons.

A police car came to a halt beside me, so I eagerly began to tell my story. I might as well not have spoken, for they were only interested in arresting me for disturbing the peace. I was taken to Brixton police station and marched to the cells, with no regard to the attack on my person or my stated desire to call a friend, or even any effort to summon a doctor.

I will not bother to record in detail the number of visits I received from men who spoke to me in language that made my assailants seem civilized. An animal is of its kind, whatever pattern its fur takes. The uniforms that these men wore failed to induce in them any attempts at civilized behaviour.

The worst of these people visited me some time after his companions had left. As he opened the cell, I instinctively straightened up on my bench. He locked the door behind him and asked, 'Hurtin', are you?'

I asked, as I had asked before, for a doctor to be called. 'My name is Matthew DuBois,' I said. 'I have been attacked by two men. I think you should apprehend them, before they hurt anybody else.'

He lashed out and struck me on the right kneecap. As I fell to the ground, his hand came down over my mouth to silence me. As I crumpled, I felt the impact of a new series of punches. These blows, upon my already bruised flesh, were absolutely unbearable.

My secret friend, I would not confess this to anyone else, but tears flowed freely from my eyes. I tried to stop them, but they came at their own behest, oblivious to the entreaties of my pride and useless anger, and but for his hand, clamped as it was over my mouth, I am sure that I would have cried out as a young child stung by a wasp for the first time.

I remember looking up at him as he towered over me. His lips seemed to be moving, but I was not interested in what he had to say. I think my contempt for him must have been readily apparent, for even though he was in a position of strength, something in my eye seemed to disturb him, and he resorted to kicking me again. I tried to move away from him. It was an utterly silly thing to do, for I had nowhere to go and was incapable of getting there. But instinct is a law which the body always seems to obey under duress. This same principle caused me to force my eyes open – so it was that I saw him take out his penis and urinate on me. Horrified, I kicked pathetically out at him. He was oblivious to my feeble efforts at retaliation, and concentrated on this humiliation until he was finished.

As he closed his zipper, our eyes met once again. 'I don't like you people. You're no good. You shouldn't be over here. If you know what's good for you, you'll get on one of those banana boats and fuck off home.' And with this he left the cell, the smell of his effusion filling my nostrils. Many thoughts went through my head. Absurdly, an old song, which I had not thought of for years but which my father had often recited, played through my mind and I found myself mumbling it over and over, until I fell asleep. It was said to be a song for the king of the Eboes, and it went like this:

Oh me good friend, Mr Wilberforce, make we free! God Almighty, thank ye! God Almighty, thank ye! God Almighty, make we free! Buckra in this country no make we free: what Negro for to do? What Negro for to do? Take force by force. Take force by force. To be sure, to be sure, to be sure.

This morning I was allowed to leave the police station, but not before I received the most incredible lecture from the station's senior officer. They had decided not to press charges against me. I was to thank my 'lucky stars' and go home. Incredulous, I demanded that the men who had abused me be brought to book. It was a complete waste of time. The senior officer made no attempt to hide his disinterest in my claims and behaved as if he was a direct descendant of that dullard, Bottom. I now imagine the same applies for the overwhelming number of people deemed worthy of wearing this nation's police uniforms.

I headed straight for the Institute, where my appearance caused much consternation. As I told my tale, the looks of outrage and disbelief only served to increase my own fury, and I am afraid that by the time the director of the Institute arrived (Penny had called him), my voice was raised to its full pitch. When I finished, there was uproar. Penny was incandescent, as were many of my colleagues. I had expected Arthur's response to be the most dynamic, but he was strangely silent.

The director called for calm in the gentle manner that was his hallmark. Though originally from Trinidad, he had been raised in Edinburgh and his accent was unmistakable, as was his lawyer's background: he was not a man to respond emotionally to any situation. He explained what his response would be and advised everyone to remain calm. He was quite sure that, once the police were informed who I was, the matter would be dealt with. His words struck me as completely inappropriate and I made my opinion known to him. Perhaps I should not have been so forthright, for my disagreement with him, before such a gathering, might have been interpreted as a challenge to his authority, but such thoughts did not occur to me, and neither did petty considerations of ego and status.

'Mr Pettington,' I began, for we were not allowed to use first names to senior personnel during work hours, 'I cannot accept that.'

'Matthew,' he said, 'I think the course I have outlined is for the best.'

I continued, 'These men assaulted me because of what they saw before them. As far as they were concerned, I was of no importance purely because of my skin. You want to call whoever it is you think will listen to you, and make it plain that they must not abuse a black man of my background and supposed status?' I did not bother to keep a heavy sneer out of my voice.

'But surely that is the case. Or would you be happier if members of this Institute were attacked on a regular basis with no recourse to the law?'

'I would prefer it if no black person, whether they worked in this Institute or not, was subject to attacks from mindless thugs. If we are to admonish the men who did this to me –'

'We cannot admonish anyone; that is for the senior officers to decide.'

A colleague – and in this moment I was acutely aware of the true meaning of the word – said, 'They won't admonish anybody. You know it and we all know it.'

The director was not enjoying this situation. I could not blame him; he was far more suited to the debates that took place in the gentlemen's clubs of which he was an honourary 'white' member.

'Matthew, you are upset, rightly so, but this situation does not call for anger.'

'Then what does it call for? Are you saying that I should not be angry? What do you want me to do: compose a letter and make a list of complaints that will be thrown in the bin, or more likely framed and shown off?'

'You're proving my point by making such ridiculous statements. Go home and rest.'

'No! No! That will not do! This Institute should not have to go running to outside bodies for support. We should be able to stand and fight for ourselves.'

'What fight? This is not a fight! We do not fight! This is a research organization; we publish information and agitate through specific routes for the betterment of our people. We will not achieve that goal by losing our heads whenever an unfortunate situation occurs. Calm is what is required here, calm.'

'Why should we be calm? Who asks us to be calm in the face of such behaviour? Who asks us to be rational and sensible while they deny our people jobs and accommodation? This is an unacceptable situation which demands a positive response, not posturing and pomposity.'

'Matthew, I respect you enormously. You have done the Institute proud and carried the name of your family with grace, so I will ignore those words. I suggest you allow me to deal with this my way. Come with me and give me all the details you can.'

I strode over to Penny's desk and sat on it.

He muttered, 'So be it,' and left the room.

Such was my anger that I did not notice my colleagues leave the office and barely heard their words of sympathy – my mind was racing too hard, too fast. Why was he so useless?

I was left alone with Arthur and Penny. I was shocked when Arthur ventured, 'You and I should wait for the men who beat you up, follow them, and sort them out when we can.'

I asked him what he meant.

'Exactly what I said. If you really want to do something about this, then we take it into our own hands.'

Penny exploded. I have never seen her more furious. 'Are you mad? We are responsible people, we have responsible jobs, we represent a responsible organization. We do not behave like thugs.'

'It's your problem, DuBois, as is the solution. I am merely offering you another course. You know that the police will do nothing. This organization is clearly run by bourgeois reformists who lack the stomach for any sort of direct confrontation. I do not believe in allowing any man, of any class, persuasion or colour, to lay a hand on me. That is my code. I have offered to help you; the decision is yours.'

I was stunned by Arthur's offer, but more by what it revealed of his inner self. His offer was made not because of friendship, but because of creed. I thanked him, but made it plain that such a course was not for me, and that I would find a solution which I was happy with and which would not bring the Institute into disrepute. Penny and Arthur left me alone in the office, no doubt to continue their own debate, while I attended to my own business.

Before I headed home to clean myself up and get some rest, I drafted a letter and placed several copies up on the Institute walls. The letter read as follows:

An Open Letter to My Working Colleagues.

On Wednesday 10th February I was assaulted by a number of policemen from Brixton police station. I intend to picket the station and demand that action be taken against the offending officers. I hope that you will support me in this cause. This is a private matter, and those who join me will be acting as private citizens. Those of you who seek further information and discussion can meet me on Friday 12th February at Flat 3, Cornwall Road, Battersea.

I would like to quote a piece on agitation from the journal Crisis, *the mouthpiece of the NAACP, an organization the Institute professes to admire:*

Agitation is a necessary evil to tell of the ills of suffering. Without it, many a nation has been lulled to a false sense of security and preened itself on account of virtues it does not possess. The function of this association is to tell this nation of the crying evil of race prejudice. It is a hard but necessary one – a divine one. It is pain; pain is not good but pain is necessary. Pain does not aggravate disease – disease causes pain. Agitation does not mean aggravation – aggravation calls for agitation in order that remedy may be found.

Yours with much respect and hope
Matthew DuBois

Tonight I have returned to my own company. Rupert is out, as are all the others. I tried phoning Jocelynne, but there was no answer, which is unusual since, like myself, she shares a house with several people. Perhaps it is for the best, for I am able to sit alone in the kitchen and ponder the events of the last few days. It is clear that I have reached an important moment in my life. I have been insulted and mistreated, but more importantly I have the abilities to rectify the situation and bring these unfortunate events to a satisfactory conclusion.

Friday, 12th February

I have met with the director and a number of the trustees of the Institute. We discussed the situation amicably and with a genuine concern for all the reputations involved. It was decided that I should embark on a leave of absence, during which time I would be free to act as my conscience dictated. The director decided to explain to the entire staff what had occurred between us. Much to my surprise, Arthur, Penny and two other colleagues, Cecil Banks and William Espedair, announced that they would also like to take a leave of absence so that they might help me. I cannot say who was more taken aback, the trustees or myself, but I was only too grateful to accept their offer – a gratitude that extended to the director when he accepted their wishes with grace and bestowed his good wishes on us all.

I accepted Penny's offer to head for her home, since she had space and a phone, and agreed that it would become our operational base. Once there, we began to discuss our intentions and strategy. Penny suggested that we should involve the trade unions, and actively engage the leadership in discussions that would result in education of the workers, so that they would not fear the arrival of black labour. Arthur wanted to deal with the press and media. Cecil put forward the case for liaising with the local churches, especially those which had strong connections with people from the Caribbean. Their suggestions took me by surprise: I had only foreseen a small-scale activity by ourselves, and did not want to blow the situation out of all proportion. But Cecil was adamant: he believed that the civil rights movement taking place in America demonstrated clearly that blacks needed coherent strategies when responding to incidents of institutionalized racism.

An impassioned debate took place, which I felt in all honesty was worthy of a greater stage in response to a cause more relevant than mine, but the intellectual contributions and emotional support were more than welcome. As the afternoon unfolded, I grew more and more relaxed, sure that I was amongst friends of such good character and worth that whatever trials lay ahead would be overcome.

Again I tried to contact Jocelynne at home, but to no avail. My troubles were made clear to me when I returned home to find my kitchen crammed full with Rupert, Gladwin and a number of people I had never seen before. Several of the men were bruised and had cuts about their faces and necks. It transpired that all but two of them are tenants from Jocelynne's home in the nearby borough of Wandsworth. Since they numbered fifteen in all, they must have been living in extremely cramped conditions.

I learnt that several white neighbours, outraged by the presence of blacks next door, had indulged in behaviour which was at first merely offensive and intimidatory, but which had recently escalated into acts of violence. Interestingly enough, the landlord was also a Negro, but this fact did not seem to prevent him from packing his house unduly and consistently raising his rent to a wholly disproportionate level.

The remaining two strangers were white, and intrigued me greatly. Their names are Michael Cole and Andrew Miller. Both men are students at a local college, and share a basement flat on the same street as Jocelynne. Having witnessed some of the unpleasantness that my fellow Caribbeans had been subjected to, they are committed to stopping any more outrages. Both men are young and burned brightly with the faith of what I found later to be deep-seated communist convictions.

Their discussion was passionate and angry, but filled with confusion and lack of confidence. Anger was balanced by a sense of hesitancy and fear of deportation if too much 'trouble' was caused. The plot thickened when Cole made it clear that he believed the real problem lay not with the neighbouring whites or the black landlord, but with the owner of the property. He is a white man, Peter Sledgley, who specializes in attaining black tenants, and then using them to drive down the values of nearby properties, so that he can acquire buildings cheaply. Cole believes that the best way to tackle this problem is to educate the angry whites, who, after all, are of the same class as the black tenants, and form bonds of solidarity between the warring parties.

I was intrigued by the similarities between the experiences of this group of tenants and my own experience, and explained my case to the group and the routes which we were exploring. It seems clear to me that our mutual problems are symptomatic of a whole series of events, and that people who are suffering similar problems of race and hostility should be put in contact with each other, so that our troubles might be shared and jointly tackled.

Saturday, 13th February

Last night, Jocelynne and I finally talked, swapping stories about our recent experiences and comparing notes. I was upset by her lack of communication and even more by her declaration that she had not wanted to bother me with her problems. We both raised our voices and said a number of unpleasant things, but what matters is that we managed to get on to lighter matters, having determined to communicate about any matters that affected us in the future. Having overcome our differences, we resolved, once this dreadful business is behind us, to marry.

Wednesday, 17th February

Much has happened in the last few days. I shall attempt to recount here as much as I can of what has passed.

On Saturday, I was standing outside Brixton police station, with a placard that complained in bold letters about police brutality and called for justice, for about twenty minutes before the trouble began. In that time, a small crowd had gathered about me – some had been abusive; many had enquired about the purpose of my one-man demonstration. I had noticed several policemen looking at me through their station windows, laughing and joking amongst themselves. It seemed I was a figure of ridicule. Not for all, though – one constable came out of the station and warned me that I would be arrested if I did not 'clear off'. I reminded him of my right to protest and continued to hold my ground. The conversation only served to attract more viewers. About ten minutes after this, I was arrested and escorted into the police station. The time was 2 p.m.

At 2.10 p.m. I met the booking officer, Storey, who had dealt with me before. He had had an unpleasant day, was extremely tired and didn't need some 'fucking coon with a fancy accent' messing up his day. To underline his message further he brought with him the lout who had urinated on me during my last visit. I informed him of the reasons for my protest and said that all would be resolved when and if the officer was dealt with in an appropriate manner. I was quickly thrown into a cell.

I sat there hoping that all would go well. Fifteen minutes passed before Storey returned again. This time he brought with him Michael Cole and a young woman, both of whom he marched into my cell. Storey, red-faced and angry, began to yell at us. We all remained silent and refused to answer any of his questions. He left, promising to 'sort out any trouble-makers'. After his departure, Michael introduced me to the young woman – she was his girlfriend, Sharon, and it was with some amusement that I watched her berate the officers who stood watching us.

In the early evening Michael and Sharon were allowed to leave. They promised to return the next day and start where they had left off. Storey warned them to leave before he gave them a 'good thumping' and advised them to grow up. He informed me that I, too, could leave if I promised to 'behave' myself. After I had made it clear to him that I intended to continue my protest he hissed 'Sod you,' and left me alone.

A few hours later I received a curious visit from the officer who had urinated on me. He was totally confused by my behaviour and demanded to know what I was 'playing at'. I had been 'out of order', and he had tried to put me right. That was 'how things worked around here'. A series of questions followed: Did I know what I was getting myself into? Did I want to go to court? We began to talk and I could see that he was not a bad person by any means; he was simply of his time and of his culture. He had acted as he had believed he should, and I think he understood that the same held true for me. When he left, the gulf that had existed between us had not closed, but his import-ance – scale, if you like – had been significantly reduced in my mind. My anger faded and was replaced by a mute sadness. I did not bother to analyse it.

On the next day – Sunday – things began to warm up. I was joined by Jocelynne, Michael and Sharon, and a number of the tenants I met recently. We learned that Michael had made a speech which had attracted a large crowd. A policeman came in and demanded a statement from me. I left with him and filled out several pages of a form, which we then both studiously went over. He found it hard to believe that I had been attacked in the manner which I described. His opinion was of no consequence. Despite the unpleasantness of my environment, I was beginning to feel more confident. I was in the right. That fact would see me through.

Jocelynne and Sharon left the cells later on Sunday, only to return again the next day. The officers who escorted them were clearly losing their patience, but, more importantly, they obviously did not know how to deal with the developing situation.

Due to our circumstances, I grew much closer to Michael over the next few days. Michael is full of the fire and brimstone of his Marxist principles. My father despised Marxists: he found it hard to believe in a movement that was founded by a man who, in his words, 'lived off the sweat and blood of his wife and children'. Michael believes that Britain stands on the threshold of a social revolution, that the failures of the labour and conservative governments since the war will result in action which will usher in a new dawn for the common man. He is quite set in his opinions and dismisses middle-class lefties with no real experience of the common man. I prayed that Penny would not be locked up with us. Michael kept promising me that something interesting was going to happen.

This afternoon – Wednesday – Michael's surprises came to visit. Four elderly though fit-looking men were escorted into our cell. It turned out that they were all relatives of my cell-mate, miners from Swansea who had taken the weekend off to come and show support for me.

I was taken aback. I would never have anticipated such a thing, but as I listened to them it emerged that Michael came from a line of committed social activists who, it seemed, never missed an opportunity to agitate and fight for their social and political beliefs. I could barely keep my eyes off these men. They were hard, strong characters with confusing accents and scatter-gun delivery, unlike anyone I had ever met before.

Soon we were joined by Jocelynne, William Espedair and virtually all of Jocelynne's house-mates. It seemed that everything was going to plan. Storey, when he visited us again, was in a state of extreme agitation. He said that I was abusing the hospitality that had been offered me as an immigrant (I paraphrase his words, of course; one gets tired of recording the same old racial slurs) and that there was a set way of doing things. The abuse he heaped on my white comrades was truly memorable.

Within hours, the police cells were full. It was clear that the police could not contain the situation. Every new person the police brought in was able to give us further information about what was happening outside the station. It seemed that all the people we had instructed to arrive and protest had come and that, unbelievably, through sheer boredom or God knows what, many passers-by had joined in the protest. Penny and Arthur were in full flow and were creating quite a stir. They had not been arrested because Penny had arranged for two journalists she was acquainted with to stand by her side and conspicuously take notes.

I stood there in the cell, surrounded by so many strangers, slightly overcome by the whole situation. Since my original arrest I had been in a tunnel of concentration. It was only as the reality of our planning hardened about me that I began to take in what was happening. I could not understand it. How was it possible for things to go so well? I overheard snatches of conversation between Michael's relatives; they, though excited, were also confused. I heard them discuss 'campaigns' and 'fights' that they had taken part in before. These were spoken of in almost reverential terms. Actual physical clashes with police officers were recounted with pride. They spoke of bricks through windows, fire bombs underneath police cars. I could not believe my ears. One of them began to laugh: a laughter that deepened when he looked into my eyes and knew immediately what was horrifying me so. He slapped me on the shoulder and shouted, 'Don't worry, lad, you'll get used to it!' I don't believe I have ever seen a group of men so clearly in their element. But still the question remained: what was going on?

Soon after this, I was called into a room where three senior officers awaited me, each with a copy of my statement. Their manner was cordial and polite, but I sensed that they were in uncharted territory, seeking to maintain control. They questioned me about my background, my work, my reasons for coming to the country, etc., etc. I answered them truthfully, if not expansively. I was asked about my reasons for causing so much 'trouble' and why I was working with 'professional trouble-makers'. I explained my case again, carefully and slowly, and we entered a long discussion which went on for over two hours. By the end, I was being offered cups of tea and cake. Two of the officers, who had constantly referred to being pressed for time and having important meetings to attend, had remained to talk to me. Our conversation covered many things: the government, sport, detective novels, gardening (oh Maurice, you would have been astonished to hear my enthusiasm for a subject for which I showed not one jot of interest throughout our relationship), and, inevitably, the joys of Manchester United. One of the officers, upon learning that I had never actually seen the great team in the flesh, even offered to take me to a match, 'once this unfortunate business is behind us.'

I was informed that my incarceration and the subsequent behaviour of my associates had attracted a certain amount of media interest and that the situation demanded 'cooling'. Much to my surprise, the police constable who had defiled me was brought into the meeting. His eyes never met mine as he was told by his senior officers that his behaviour was unacceptable and that they were prepared to press ahead with disciplinary action if I indicated my desire for punishment. As I looked at this rather pathetic figure in blue before me – no longer arrogant and unfeeling, but almost boyish in his embarrassment – much of my anger left me. I cannot say whether my decision was due to lack of faith that the police would carry out their threat, or the fact that, suddenly, the apology he was forced to make to me seemed sufficient. At that moment it was enough that he had to treat me as an equal; that, whatever his view of me as a human being, he realized that before the law I was a citizen who deserved his respect.

I am not sure what I expected on leaving the station, but it was certainly not the sight that greeted me. Outside, apparently waiting for me, was quite a crowd. A crowd that contained friends and comrades, as well as a number of reporters and, unbelievably, a television crew. I have only seen televisions in shops and they still seem to me almost alien in origin and concept. To see television cameras actually aimed at my own person was quite intimidating, as were the cheers and applause which greeted me. Sheepishly, I accompanied the two officers to what seemed to be a prearranged spot and waited as one of them read out his statement.

He made clear his regret about the attack on my person and insisted that such behaviour was the exception; that Brixton was, like England, a place that 'welcomed people from the West Indies with open arms' and that his station would work arm in arm with the local community to ensure that cordial relationships were maintained between the white community and its new neighbours. A reporter asked him about my alleged mistreatment by Brixton police. The officer declared that the matter had been resolved. He deflected subsequent questions and invited me to come forward and read out my prepared statement. My statement was brief and went as follows:

I want to thank all those who have supported me throughout these past few difficult days. I came here because I believe in values such as justice and fairness – qualities which reflect the nature of the British people more accurately than the unpleasantness which has brought me to this present situation. I took my stance, as did my friends, because we are unwilling to settle for less than we expected from the British. My hope is that this incident will clarify the expectations of all those who now have the great pleasure of calling England their home. Thank you.

I received much applause after I finished speaking, more than I felt was due, and attempted to walk away. But I was not allowed to. Questions were fired at me – some serious, a few humorous, some shocking. How was I? Had I been mistreated? Was I happy to be in England? Was I surprised by the level of support that I had received? Did I believe that Britain had as much racism as America? Was my aim to create disturbances such as those that had become commonplace in America? Was I a supporter of Martin Luther King? I stayed for longer than I expected and answered the questions as best I could until Arthur and some friends brought me home.

Thursday, 18th February

Last night a party was thrown by all my friends and supporters, and in truth the house was overflowing with people who I had never seen before. The atmosphere was jubilant. It seemed that those present felt that anything they set their minds to could be achieved. Some of the talk almost took my breath away, but I trusted that these wild statements would soon be grounded by hard reality and logic.

So many people came forward to pat me on the back, rub my arm, squeeze my wrist. I knew that their praise was not just for me personally, but for the deed. Amongst the joy and pleasure, arguments raged. Michael was shouting heatedly to William that the next fight would be with the landlord who was terrorizing his friends; that we could build on this success and go forward. 'We can take on all the Sledgleys and the Rachmans. If we all band together, we have nothing to fear!' William was dismissive. He had given his services to a colleague, he was not a 'social campaigner'. Similar conversations were taking place all around the house. I myself felt that it would be only right to reciprocate the efforts that the tenants association had made on my behalf.

141

But, like William, I did not see myself embarking on some sort of crusade.

Today I had a long meeting with the director of the Institute. It seems that they have been flooded with letters addressed to me from many parts of England. He directed my attention to the many letters on his desk requesting interviews for magazines and radio programmes.

'I am wasting my time reminding you that you acted in a private capacity, and that we are primarily and essentially involved in research, not social engineering.' Thankfully, these words were accompanied by a tiny smile, which assured me that he was not altogether unhappy about the publicity. 'I would appreciate it if you could provide a full report to the board so that we can be completely up-to-date with everything. We don't want to look like complete dunces.'

I assured him that the reputation of the Institute would remain unimpaired by my actions. He advised me to answer my letters, and not to worry about my work. It was important that I should respond to all those who had written to me, and perhaps take advantage of their initial interest to spread the word about my 'real' work and make new contacts.

26

My correspondence has proved to be extremely distressing. Letter after letter details situations of extreme distress endured by individuals and groups which provide a composite representation of rampant prejudice that I find quite unsettling.

Gabriel opened a few of the letters that had been attached to the page.

Dear Mr DuBois,

I have read of your plight and wish to communicate to you my sincerest sympathy and best wishes in your brave stand. I am a hard-working man who has fought hard to get where he is. I own a small café in Shepherd's Bush, which caters mainly for blacks, but which I hope one day will serve everyone. Recently, five white youths attacked and wrecked my shop. It was as if an earthquake had descended upon me. I have received little help from the police and the magistrate's court ordered them to pay the piffling sum of £10 each. Where is the justice for a black man in this white country?

I wish you well.

E. Adams

Dear Mr DuBois,

I am an economics student. My parents worked long and hard for me to come to London and study. Last Thursday, I was making my way home when for no apparent reason a group of whites set on me, screaming at me in broad daylight that they intended to lynch me. These people chased me through the streets and I am sure that but for the kindly intervention of a shop owner, who allowed me to take refuge within his shop, I would be a dead man.

God bless you for your stand, your fight is for all of us.

J. Obiani

Dear Mr DuBois,

I am pregnant with child and scared, so very, very scared. Where I am, I can hardly walk for fear of abuse and hate. At the corner if I bump into them, they react. If I am in front of the queue, they complain. If I ask for change, they are rude. Their anger knows no bounds. I fear for my unborn child. I do not want him to have to clean up human filth from my door, as I do many a morning when I open it to face the sun. What have I done to them? I came at their invitation. Now they spit at me and my husband. For what? Are their own lives so poor, so miserable, that they must abuse us so? What gives them the right to think they can behave so? I am with you, my prayers are with you. I pray for you and my child. Stay away from them. They only mean you harm.

C. Armstrong

Gabriel folded the letters back into their former positions before reading Matthew's response to them.

And on and on. A litany of hatred that ranged from the petty to the trivial to the unbelievable. I was angered, moved and, dare I say it, even bored. Bored by the endless stupidity of it all. The examples of hatred are so ponderous and the perpetrators so often clearly imbeciles that one cannot but grow weary of their childish effects. Sadly, these are children with power, destructive power.

Monday, 22nd February

Jocelynne called me at work this morning and asked me to go around to her house this evening, since she had organized a tenants meeting. She said her landlord had agreed to come. It was the last thing I wanted to do. I wanted to sleep, just sleep, to go somewhere with her and forget about everything. But I agreed to go; how could I do otherwise?

143

I made my way to her with my mind ablaze. I could not help studying the faces of those about me, their body language, posture, everything. I wanted to be inside their heads. I wanted to see myself from their points of view. I watched black train attendants going about their business, seeing them as if for the first time. I observed them performing menial tasks, while white colleagues stood around and did nothing.

Question 1. If there was always so much racial discord about me, why am I only seeing it now?

Question 2. When the veil is ripped away, does one's vision continue to grow sharper?

I was beginning to feel uncomfortable even before I reached Jocelynne's street. My instinct was confirmed when I saw her house, for a number of unpleasant slogans had been painted on it. My entry was observed by a small gang of white youths loitering across the street.

The meeting took place in the ground-floor flat which was shared by Jocelynne and Gladwin, and it revealed much genuine fear and anger. A public phone has been installed in the hall and it rang continuously. Every call was from some poisonous individual, spewing hatred and filth down the line. It was decided at the meeting to change the telephone number and organize a trip to the local police station, asking for protection. All the tenants agreed to coordinate their trips to and from the house so that they might always travel in pairs.

I left the house late. On my way to the bus stop I was followed by the youths who had gathered earlier. They waited for the bus to come, during which time their verbal abuse was continuous. I had to sit on my hands to hide my trembling.

Thursday, 25th March

The trustees, it seems, are interested in moving me to a different department. Apparently they are quite happy for me to take on the position of liaison officer. Since this job entails acting as the organization's representative and explaining our policies and work, it would give me a great deal of responsibility and involve a lot of travel. I must learn to drive.

Friday, 26th March

Jocelynne and I shared the great pleasure of viewing a double bill of *Henry V* and *Fire over England,* two movies featuring England's leading stage and film actor, Laurence Olivier.

144

No wonder the English love him so. He seems the literal embodiment of many of the qualities which his fellow countrymen claim is a birthright. He is tall, erect, projects an air of indisputable masculinity, and seems without fear or doubt. He moves directly, in straight lines, always sure of his destination and what he should do when he arrives at the desired point. He is strong, almost athletic in appearance, and possessed of a profile that reminds one immediately of the screen idols Coleman and Barrymore. His voice rings out clearly, with perfect enunciation, and his diction is faultless, almost mechanically so. It is a tiger of a voice that seeks to dominate and lead. Effective in moments of action and conflict, one senses artifice and methodology in scenes that require stillness and tender emotion. This is an actor who comes from a nation that built an empire and lost its women to the French. A charismatic utterly rooted in narrow parameters of nationhood and culture.

Mr Olivier carries no hint of anything imported or inherited from distant shores. He is completely of his age and of his time and he is, like Van Gogh for the Dutch and Picasso for the Spanish, a marvellous national advert for his people and his era. As such he strides the world stage in much the same way as a Bradman or a Fangio. His triumphs are his nations'. On an artistic level, I was able to share in his victory, but could not help but ruminate about the England he represented and where I and others of my ilk are to find our place within it.

After we had left the cinema I tried to discuss my alienation with J. She was completely uninterested in my angst and mumbled something about the great actor's breathing. She was of the opinion that if she improved her breathing she might do anything she set her mind to. And that was her last word of the evening. I walked beside her and her silence and her reflection; the inner world of the artist is often at its most splendid when it operates in ethereal isolation. I knew then that there will be many more silences between us, when she strolls along an inner landscape to which I am not privy.

Saturday, 27th March

I joined Jocelynne and Gladwin for a walk around Clapham Common. G. is in tears for much of the time. She believes that her chances of marrying Rupert are slim. Jocelynne promised to try and sway her brother. I cannot understand the woman's attraction.

Sunday, 28th March

Jocelynne is pregnant. I am delighted and also fearful. I am delighted, as any man is, to find that the woman he loves will bear his child. But I am fearful for the child, for its future. The world is indeed an ugly place. Our battles for freedom from discrimination are outbreaks in a long-running war. What does our success really mean when placed in the even greater context of world domination? We fight for the right to move freely and live safely in our own homes, while global powers threaten to destroy whole continents. How long will it be before the black race can achieve global parity and influence the course of world events? It seems the white man is unwilling to share Eden with anyone else. By the time we are allowed in, all the apples will have fallen.

Gabriel took a break. The year on his father's journal was 1959: four years before his birth. When he resumed his reading, despite his attempts at relaxation, his heartbeat had quickened.

Sunday, 4th April

A trip to Oxford with W. Espedair. My, the town is enshrined in its own antiquity. No visitor to these shores should ever confuse the large metropolises of England with the towns and counties that exist beyond the borders of the big cities.

Monday, 3rd May

Lena Horne will be playing at a jazz club in London. I am under instruction from Jocelynne to obtain tickets, or else.

Wednesday, 5th May

The local newspaper reports today that a petrol bomb was thrown through the window of a home in North Kensington of a pregnant black woman. The incident mirrors several that have taken place in Nottingham lately, where, it seems, race hatred has been on the increase. Matters there have not been helped by the two Nottingham members of parliament, one conservative, one labour, who have called for a halt to immigration and urged for the introduction of deportation laws.

Saturday, 8th May

Callaghan has volunteered to give me driving lessons. I took up his offer today. What an experience! The man becomes incandescent if anyone dares to overtake him. His ranting and raving reduced me to a nervous wreck. But for the fact that I must obtain a driving licence I would never climb inside a car again.

Monday, 10th May

An amazing letter from my sister. It seems that news of recent events has reached home in quite some detail. Mother and Father are concerned about me. It seems they are also proud, if not a trifle confused.

Saturday, 15th May

Had the most extraordinary conversation with a teddy boy outside the Milford Arms. What a character! Completely bamboozled by me. Informed me that he didn't mind blacks so much, it was 'Pakis' that he really hated.

Sunday, 16th May

Despite my strong objections, Gladwin dragged myself, Jocelynne and that damnable brother of hers along to a church. I had to endure an entire service of the most irritating, pious nonsense. I almost stood up, waved my hands and started singing 'Old Man River'.

Thursday, 20th May

A real character, a vagrant, wandered into the Institute. He offered to read cards, palms, eyes, anything. He predicted that within twenty years a man would be on the moon, and that within another twenty-three the Soviet Union would have a female premier. He also foresaw that Elizabeth the Second's second son would marry a black woman. Splendid stuff.

Tuesday, 25th May

Reports in the morning newspapers and on radio of race riots in Nottingham. Most upsetting.

Wednesday, 26th May

Jocelynne called me this afternoon – there have been more incidents at her home.

I arrived there at seven o'clock to find many of the windows smashed. The kitchen was full of tense men and women. Underneath the table, several hammers and baseball bats had been laid.

It seems that Gladwin was accosted on the way home by several youths and was pushed and spat on. Although this incident had been reported to the police over an hour ago, they had not yet arrived. As these events were related to me a brick was thrown through Jocelynne's window. Despite G.'s advice not to, I left the kitchen and took a look outside.

I immediately recognized some of the youths who stood across the street as those who had harassed me last time. Only now they were accompanied by four older men, who were evidently encouraging them to new heights.

I retreated back to the kitchen. It turns out that on a nearby street is a working-men's club that regularly hosts meetings for an organization that goes by the name of the English Fascist Party. This information both saddened and infuriated me. How was it that my Jocelynne could have come to live here? As I listened to the fears that were expressed, I grew progressively more outraged. It is unacceptable that a group of people should be treated so, purely because of their colour. I also could not but be aware that the group was looking to me to take the lead. Obviously the publicity I had received had convinced everyone that I was the man to come up with some answers. As I considered what to do, the sound of more glass shattering reached my ears, and in that second I had my answer. I picked up one of the hammers from under the table and headed for the door. As one, my comrades followed me out on to the street.

We stepped outside to the sound of braying chants, but the faces of the men before us betrayed their surprise and apprehension. This, far from quieting the anger that raged within my breast, caused a deep pounding to explode between my ears. These thugs were frightened by the prospect of a fight. They were cowards.

As we stood there, some of our more aggressive opponents hurled insults and swore at us. We told them to leave us alone. They told us to leave their country alone. A confrontation followed. One big chap picked up a brick and came for me. My legs shook as he advanced, but in truth his face was obscured by memories of the policeman who had urinated on me. I know that I moved forward not with fear, but with anticipation, with a thirst for revenge. I hit him several times before he caught me a glancing blow with the brick, but I did not seem to feel it. I was filled with a mighty strength as I set into him. As he fell to the ground I felt a tremendous glee, stronger than any I had previously known.

Not satisfied with his defeat, I managed to engage myself in a number of other conflicts. I had always imagined that such things happened incredibly quickly, but it was as if people were moving slowly, as if I had all the time in the world, and in that time everything was amazingly quiet, the silence only ending when I heard the voice of one of my comrades shouting out, over and over, 'It dun, it dun!'

I found that the battle was over and that I was in fact being restrained by my friends. When I calmed down I found a number of those who had threatened us lying on the ground, bruised and bleeding. At G.'s hysterical insistence we all retreated to the house. The other men agreed to leave quickly, but I decided to stay with Jocelynne.

Prison Diary

Friday, 28th May

I am to be charged with assault and causing a public disturbance. From what I understand, no charges are to be brought against those we fought with. I am upset, but not surprised.

Sunday, 30th May

I was visited by Rupert. He disapproves of my relationship with his sister. He believes I am a trouble-maker, and that if I have any true feelings for his sister, I will leave her alone. His pomposity disgusts me and I told him so. He is a fool and I see no reason to keep that information from him. His departure brought me no sadness. The world within which he functions is tiny and has compressed his brain. Since he cannot come between Jocelynne and myself, I am not concerned with him.

Tuesday, 1st June

I have been charged. The magistrate's court was quite full and I noted that a significant number of journalists were present. The magistrate addressed me at some length and made several undeserved comments about my 'lack of gratitude towards my host country'. He was a pompous oaf and I was glad to be taken away from him.

Friday, 4th June

I have had a steady stream of visitors, including my local parliamentary representative and two of his labour colleagues. They intend to ask questions about me in the House of Commons. Much to my surprise, a photographer was brought to the cell and our picture was taken. It seems I am considered a minor celebrity by the press. Much of our conversation was taken up discussing aspects of the civil rights movement in America and its reverberations in England. Once again, I sensed a new energy is abroad that is waiting to be employed.

NOTE: Jocelynne is showing. She has told me about comments that Rupert has made. It seems he has screamed at her and abused her. The man is a pig. Still, these are conservative times. We will be married as soon as possible.

Wednesday, 9th June

The farce reached a high point today, as two of those I had fought against took to the witness stand. Although they had been clearly advised and well rehearsed, they often slipped into the language of the gutter. It was almost pitiful, the way they squandered the initial sympathy of the all-white jury. I shall never forget the lowering of several heads in the jury box as one of the men, a rather excitable fellow, began to provide a rather aberrant account of the aptly named holocaust. His explanation of a Jewish conspiracy and the role of blacks in this all-pervasive strategy provided a wonderful insight into the warped logic of a twisted fanatic. The case against me has been dropped.

Friday, 11th June

A party was thrown to celebrate my court victory. Many people, both black and white, were there, including several reporters from national papers. The organizers of the party, Penny and Michael, announced the forming of a group called People Against Racism. M. was extremely proud of the colours of a banner he had prepared, which he unfurled with a dramatic flourish. I was dragged out before everyone to make a speech. I took the opportunity to announce my forthcoming marriage to Jocelynne.

Saturday, 12th June

Just managed to see Orson Welles's *Touch of Evil*. My, what a film! Dietrich is still the greatest screen female persona after Brooks and Garbo. Still, great though they were, none of them could light up the screen as easily as my favourite actress, C. Lombard.

Sunday, 13th June

A confrontation with Rupert. The man is obsessed with making money and approached me for a loan for the most ridiculous get-rich scheme. I told him my opinion of him and his schemes. He left. We will never be friends.

Monday, 14th June

I withdrew large amounts of money from my bank account. Everything must be done properly.

Wednesday, 16th June

I had a lengthy chat with the director. I explained my situation to him. He assured me that he will be able, through his Methodist contacts, to find a suitable place for Jocelynne and myself.

Friday, 25th June

A telegram from my father has arrived expressing his dissatisfaction with my wedding plans. Intimations of lunacy and bad judgement. He will not attend and has forbidden any other member of the family to do so. Still, he has paid a cheque into my bank account, so that our first few months together will 'go smoothly'. I have written back to him. He is a hypocrite and an unrepentant snob. For all his fine talk about justice and equality, he cannot accept someone of his own ilk who lacks a 'proper' background. A sad and despicable postscript to all of this: he has sacked Maurice. It seems that, for all Maurice's hard work and support over the years, Mother did not fight to keep him on.

Sunday, 4th July

The wedding yesterday was extremely successful, even though none of my family attended. I will never forget the appearance of my bride, the simple elegance of the church surroundings or the beautiful words that Arthur spoke in an address to the congregation. I am not a religious man, but only a fool could fail to be moved by the air of, for want of a better phrase, 'spiritual godliness' that was present.

Our home is in Notting Hill, near the underground station, on the top floor of a building that is owned by the local Methodist church. We are the only Negroes in the building, but have received a wonderful reception from our fellow inhabitants, all of whom belong to the Methodist church. It seems that this particular building is generally used to house missionary workers, so our neighbours are more than used to black faces. This will be a home of love and joy. Whatever has gone before is irrelevant. My life begins anew with my wife. I shall make sure that it is splendid.

Someone was banging on Gabriel's door.

As he walked down the hallway he heard a car driving away. At his door he found a long, black bag waiting for him. The zip resisted him at first, but moved easily after a hard tug.

A rich composed filled the bag, made up of petals, chopped-up flower stems, twigs and bark. Gabriel cleared a layer away to reveal the naked corpse of a black girl. He moved some of the pieces of bark from the immature face, plucking out some of the soil that had collected in the nostrils. Her eyelids were unnaturally swollen. Gabriel opened them and found two penny coins, the kind he had used to buy liquorice with as a child. The girl's mouth was stuffed full of sliced fruit. Gabriel's fingers caressed her face, finding unseen cuts and grazes. As his palm rested on her parched lips, his tears began to fall.

Two days had passed since Gabriel had found the body.

On the afternoon of the first day he was allowed to return home. On the morning of the second he was picked up again. Late that evening, his uncle the Reverend Rupert Wills entered the police station for his appointment with Chief Inspector Brown.

The windows of the office were open and an extra fan had been brought in, but both men struggled with the humidity, made even more unpleasant by the stale air rising up from the offices below. Rupert fanned himself with a copy of the *Daily Mail* that he'd taken from Brown's desk. Brown, in turn, had asked for a glance through Rupert's edition of the *Voice*. He read in silence before complaining about the 'bias' of its editorials.

'No moah bias den dis,' said Rupert, handing back the tabloid.

'I don't know about that.'

Rupert accepted the *Voice* back.

Brown rearranged some papers on his desk. 'What good does it do, attacking the police like that?'

'Me doan' remembah comin' across anyting like dat.'

'It's right there before you, practically on every page.'

Rupert scanned the paper. 'Oh, yu mus' be referin' to dis likkle bit about de SPG breaking dun de house of –'

'No, I was not.'

'Den it mus' be dis article. De one about de yout' on Railton Road gettin' harass all de time.'

Brown shook his head despairingly. 'The police in that area do not harass – they patrol, they do their job.'

'Deh job?'

'I tell you what, I'll make you a deal.'

'On wat?'

'If you can guarantee that talk and smiles will remove all the drug dealers and the pimps and the muggers who have plagued that area, then I'll personally ask for the operation –'

'Operation Swamp?'

'Brown held up his hands. 'I'm not a politician; name games don't matter to me or to the men who implement the clean-up operation.'

'Hmph.' Rupert examined his nails. 'Can yu tell me someting?'

'Of course.'

'Why yu peopal enjoy jumpin' on me nephew all de time?'

Brown leaned back in his chair, his papers on his lap. 'That's a ridiculous thing to say. I wouldn't expect such a thing from you, Rupert.'

'De proof is in de puddin' an' I can assure yu it is a most bitter cake.'

'Need I remind you why he is here?'

'De bwoy dun nuttin' an' yu knoh it. Gabriel barely go into de world. How he gwine find time fe anyting like dis?'

'He claims to have found the body.'

'Found? Since wen peopal get lock up fe findin' anyting?'

'People don't tend to fine dead bodies on their doorsteps –'

'Deh do eif peopal put dem deh.'

'We would have been failing in our duty if we hadn't questioned him fully.'

'Hmph.'

Chief Inspector Brown handed an A4 sheet over to Rupert. It was a flyer for a gospel competition that was to be held at Earl's Court stadium. 'I see your church is going to be there.'

Rupert beamed.

'Any competition this time around?'

'None. Evary membah of me choir got de voice of an angel. Any one of dem could be a recordin' star. But we doan' wan' dem singin' all dis filt' de radio love so much.'

Brown passed a photograph of a girl across the table, and asked Rupert if he recognized her.

Rupert didn't.

'Her name is Roberta Andrews. She went missing from Tooting Common about eight years ago. We've had no leads, no information, until yesterday when she was "found" by your nephew. If I remember correctly,' said Brown after a deep breath, 'and I'm sure I do, your church became involved in the effort to find her.'

'Yes?'

'You are affiliated with a Pastor Madely?'

'Reverend Madely, yes.'

'The girl's parents were part of his congregation. He was affiliated with you, so your umbrella organization became involved.'

'Me caan' recall dat far back.'

'It was a long time ago, but even so –'

'An' me daughtah?' insisted Rupert. 'Any news?'

Brown took his time before going on. 'We are still looking for her. I'd hoped that there might be a connection between her disappearance and this body.'

'Like wat?'

Brown's voice rose for the first time. 'I don't know, I'm only a policeman, Reverend. I don't have a hot line to God or anything like that.'

'So me got no reason to hope fe de quick return of me daughtah?'

'I'm sorry.'

'Yes, right. Me suah yu is.'

Brown let him have the last word.

Gabriel was handed over to Rupert. Peter waited for them in the car park. As they pulled out into the street the questions, unlike the traffic, flowed. Rupert was insistent and repetitive. Likewise Peter, only more aggressive.

What time did he find the body?

What did the girl look like?

Why didn't he call them first?

What did he tell the police?

Rupert mopped his face with a handkerchief. 'Deh wan' to knoh wat yu like, weh ya fadah is, wat yu do, evaryting.'

'The truth is,' said Peter, 'we couldn't tell them anything.'

'Me tell dem yu is a singular man, but deh keep on pluggin' away. Deh wan' to knoh evaryting about yu.'

Peter looked pointedly over his shoulder. 'We couldn't tell them anything, because we don't know anything. I couldn't say where you were the night Mary got taken –'

'Not dat we tink it got anyting to do wid yu.'

' – because I didn't know. You turned up in my life and all this shit happened.'

'De timin' was unfortunate, to seh de least.'

'The police don't like coincidences. Coincidences don't make sense to me, either. My brain's juggling all these things, and I can't come up with anything that helps me.'

Gabriel, enjoying the motion of the vehicle, the blurring landmarks and flickering buildings so different from the monotony of his police cell, said, 'I want to go home.'

Rupert exploded. 'Wat?!'

'I want to go home.'

'Why?'

'Because I want to.'

'Yu wan' to? Nevah mind wat yu want. We need to knoh wa's goin' on heah.'

'I want to go home.'

Rupert sucked his teeth. 'Aftah yu do ya duty an' speak to me family.'

They carried on in silence until Peter came to a set of traffic lights, whereupon Gabriel opened his door, slid out of the car and headed for the nearest underground station.

Peter swung the car around and caught up with him as quickly as he could.

'Gabriel,' screamed Rupert, 'stap dis nonsense!'

Peter braked hard, throwing his father forward. Whipping his seat-belt off, he came hurtling out of the car. 'Fuck all this family shit! I don't know you from anyone, OK? I've never seen you before. You mean nothing to me. As far as I'm concerned you don't just walk into my family like you belong!' His finger jabbed heavily into Gabriel's chest. 'You want to call yourself family, then stop acting like you're something special and show some manners.' And with that he walked back to his car and leaned menacingly against the bonnet.

'I don't get it,' he shouted at Rupert. 'Why are you spending so much time on this joker? If I had my way, I'd kick his arse all the way back to our place.'

Gabriel walked away from them as Rupert called out, 'Come back heah, come back!'

He kept going.

Rachel, travel bag at her feet, waited on Gabriel's doorstep. 'You took your time,' she growled. 'Uncle Rupert told me you left him over forty minutes ago. He told me you and Peter almost had a fight.'

He walked through the dark of the house, drawing comfort from its silence, before continuing out into the garden.

Rachel called out from the kitchen, 'Come inside, it's cold.'

He took her advice so she handed out more. 'Go to bed, don't make things worse.'

'I begin my day quite early, so don't worry if you hear me moving around down here.'

'Aren't you sleeping upstairs?'

'No.'

'OK, I'll sleep downstairs, you sleep where you're supposed to.'

The matter over, Gabriel went to his room.

After washing, he laid some candles about his bed and brushed out his hair, braiding his long strands with a fluency born of hours of repetition. His task completed, he lifted up his pillow, removed his father's journal and, after opening the pages at his marker, settled down to read.

November

1

We have moved into our new home. A few days before any furniture was moved in, Jocelynne insisted on performing a small ceremony with Gladwin. I suspect that Jocelynne finds her a mine of information about African folklore and customs. Gladwin said it was to chase away bad spirits and to make our ancestors welcome. None of this religion, spiritualism, whatever sits well with me. To be frank, as Gladwin threw various powders – 'Muti', she called it – about my walls, it was as if something ancient and rather strange had been invoked, and in truth I felt slightly embarrassed.

2

All goes well. The house is taking shape. It seems I have inherited my mother's gift for interior arrangement. I cannot bear it when J. places something in a corner or on a shelf that does not fit. I have implored her to leave everything to me. She can tinker afterwards if she must, but I will not be able to sleep if I leave the look of the place to her. She really has no sense of where to put things. Something to do with the pregnancy, no doubt. Her stomach has grown enormously. It lies between us in the dark. She can hardly turn over. It really is the most incredible sensation, feeling the movement of the baby beneath Jocelynne's skin. My heart almost bursts every time I feel the baby. I had no idea that my heart could fill so. I must take care, otherwise this poor thing will be smothered by my love. God forbid I produce an over-indulged, spoiled creature like my brother! I sure this child will put me to shame and fulfil all the expectations that proved too much for me.

3

To my great embarrassment, J. has a knack for carpentry and has been eagerly putting up book shelves. I have been left in no doubt that I must not confuse my books with hers. The woman is a gluttonous reader. Still, her only interest is in literature and poetry. My own passions have, in the main, little appeal for her.

I like Notting Hill. There are many of us here. We pass each other in the street and nod at each other. As I carry on, my heart is warmer, and I am not alone. Sometimes, on a bus, I turn round and a brother catches my eye. I can feel his presence throughout my journey, and it is truly comforting.

Sometimes, in a gathering, I see one of my own, acknowledge them and get nothing in return. An immediate harsher reassessment takes place. Perhaps it is pressure or fear of standing out, a desire not to be marked as 'one of them'? Who knows?

4

I had a bad dream last night. It concerned my father. I was young. We were arguing right up to the moment of my waking. I pray that I will not repeat his mistakes.

Jocelynne's mood fluctuates. She does not seem happy with the changes her body is going through. I was unaware that vanity might affect a woman's joy in her natural role. She seems determined to get on with her life as quickly as she can. Obviously I disagree with the notion of her working. Surely it cannot be healthy for the two of us to work, once the child is born? I have money, my investments are sound, there is no need for her to work. Still, the baby is only a few weeks away. There is no need for any undue stress to be placed on my wife.

5

I like Notting Hill, despite the occasional outbreak of racist violence. It seems the local teddy boys pride themselves on their reputation. Still, we are happy here.

Yesterday, we popped into a little café, the Dominion, where many West Indians enjoy a pleasant meal. We met up with Wellington Abrahams, who has progressed from cutting hair within his own home to opening up his own modest business, Winston Graham, a trainee lawyer who wants to start up the first all-black darts team in West London, and Mercedes Williams, an interior decorator whose ambition is to decorate Buckingham Palace. We raised our voices freely, and jokes and insults filled the air alongside nostalgic memories, made obese by indulgence and self-gratification.

8

Jocelynne has taken to writing short stories: fables with a mythological bent. She writes, Gladwin draws. They seem to be collaborating on a series of stories about some mythical monkey character, a more 'African' version of the Judao-Christian serpent. She showed me one of her scripts. I don't know what I said to offend her, but she took offence. Despite my efforts to make up with her, she will not relent. It seems we are at war. An awful business, but I am not going to break first.

10

Work was boring and my mood was foul. J. refused to speak to me over breakfast and mumbled something about not being a child as she left for work. She has found a job with some Jewish woman in Clapham Junction making dolls. I gather the business is going well and her employer seems pleasant enough. I am sure that she is behaving better towards her colleagues than towards her husband.

12

It seems J. was unhappy about comments I made about her monkey character not refuting people's racist ideas about blacks. Many whites feel we are the Devil's people, so I had merely pointed out the disadvantages of writing about a black Satan. That was it – no more. But she has not forgiven me. At least I know now what irks her so.

I have meetings scheduled in Manchester, Derby and some damnable place named Rochester, wherever the hell that is. The director wants me to attend some luncheon with him at the Boys' Brigade, of all places. Penny never stops bleating about her boy-friend and whether he'll ever get up the nerve to propose to her. And Arthur has not been seen for two days. The director is furious – no contact, no letter of apology, nothing. One thing's for sure, I won't be taking care of any of his paperwork.

15

I helped J. clean up.

She went to bed, but not before spitting out, 'Matthew, me love an' respec' yu, but we bot' knoh racism was not someting yu a deal wid wen yu grow up.'

I spluttered vainly.

'So why yu carry on like Paul aftah his conversion, like de light a' trut' shine brightah fe yu den anyone else? Yu act like de holy word come fe yu an' yu alone, wen we bot' knoh de trut' lie wid de kine a' peopal yu nevah broke bread wid till yu hook up wid me.'

And with these words, her sense of timing no doubt honed by years of performance, she left me standing on my own.

17

Arthur is still absent. We have grown quite concerned. I went around to his flat, but there was no reply. She must be some woman. I hope she is worth his job.

18

Great news. We have heard that Martin Luther King is planning to visit London shortly. He intends to meet several individuals and representatives of organizations who support his goals. The director is one of them and he has promised to include me in the gathering. The news cheers Jocelynne greatly and the ice between us finally breaks. Hmph.

19

Terrible news. Arthur has been found. He is in Charing Cross hospital. He has been terribly beaten up. I will visit him a.s.a.p.

Gabriel skips on.

25

Jocelynne and I visited Arthur today. He is in an awful condition – heavily bandaged and reeking of medication. His jaw has been broken, the doctors surmised by a blow from a heavy instrument. His hands are also bandaged. Someone had repeatedly stamped on them until they were broken. His lips are stitched together, for someone had sliced them with a knife. I could hardly speak. What animal could have done this to him? According to the nurse, he had been found in the early hours of the morning on Shepherd's Bush Green. The police were making enquiries, but had no leads. We spent as long as we could with our friend.

26

Flowers and gifts have poured into Arthur's ward. Everyone who knows him at the Institute has been devastated by this. I find myself feeling vulnerable as I walk home.

27

Arthur is recovering well, but has refused to speak to anyone about the attack. Indeed he claims to have lost all memory of the event. It is not bravado. I believe him. What an appalling thought, that such a fine mind should have been damaged. But isn't that what always happens? As Hitler understood all too well, if you truly want to undermine a race, you kill off its best and brightest.

December

13

Jocelynne's belly is enormous. We lie together in the dark and take turns feeling the movements. The sounds of the street enter our room and the cool English air bites through the covers, but this embryonic life warms us. I feel for the first time, as does she, a sense of family, stronger than any I have known before. Perhaps this is what a true family is, when it begins from your own loins. What will it be? A boy? A girl? A scholar? A painter? A writer? An idiot? What a wonderful mystery.

14

Whatever next? Rupert, it seems, has discovered his calling. His is determined to become a preacher. More, he will set up his own church. How will he do this? He will borrow money.

Unbelievably, he has approached Arthur for a loan. Worse still, Arthur has given him money for the 'cause'. I am incensed. How can he have approached a friend of mine for money? Rupert was unrepentant, so I threw him out. How is it possible for a woman like Jocelynne to have such a brother?

15
Arthur has finally returned to work, but, understandably, he is not his former self. His face has been badly damaged; he will never be thought of as handsome again. The smile and the ready laugh are gone. He does not speak about the incident and resents being asked.

16
For several weeks I have bided my time. This afternoon I spent the afternoon with Arthur in the Milford Arms and tried to bring him out of his shell, but nothing I said seemed remotely to interest him.

Out of the blue, Callaghan came over and threw a copy of *The Times* down on the table, shouting, 'You see, all you two do is complain about this and that, but the Irishman is no better off.' Before us lay a photograph of a white man, standing outside a house which carried the sign, 'No Blacks or Irish.' 'But do I carry on and organize marches? Do I write letters to members of parliament and harass law-abiding citizens to fight for the cause? Do I?' And with that he stormed off and pulled himself a pint.

I was about to push the paper away, but Arthur took it from me and began to read the piece. Perhaps encouraged by this, Callaghan rejoined us and waited for a response. My friend finished reading the article before handing it back to our publican, who demanded, 'Well? Have you nothing to say?'

With a shrug and a sigh, Arthur replied, 'David Oluwale.'

'Who?'

'Exactly.'

Callaghan snapped tartly, 'If you have a point, try to make it before I fall asleep.'

'David Oluwale', said Arthur, 'is a name you won't find in *The Times*, or in any other national newspaper for that matter.'

'So?'

'Oluwale was a Nigerian tramp who lived in various alley-ways and door-ways in that great and noble city known to us all as Leeds. One day, about nine months ago, two police officers, Kenneth Kitching and Geoffrey Ellerker, came upon him, beat him, urinated on him and kicked him to death, before dumping him in the countryside. The two men were actually charged with manslaughter, but on the judge's direction Kitching received twenty-seven months and Ellerker three years for assault.'

Callaghan tapped *The Times* with his forefinger. 'OK, but what's that got to do with this?'

Arthur got to his feet. 'It means that I couldn't give a shit about your affecting little story. Go pay a brickie to let off a bomb or march upon some Protestant mayor's office. My concern is for my own.' And with that he left the pub.

Callaghan called out after him, 'And fuck you too,' before turning to me and asking, 'What's got up his arse?'

I did not know and told him so as I followed Arthur out on to the street.

I found him some distance from the Milford Arms, sitting on some steps on Kensington High Street, watching passers-by. We sat without speaking for a while as various tourists walked by, swinging their shiny handbags.

I began with, 'Callaghan was just being Callaghan. Why be so harsh?'

Arthur kept his silence.

I quoted, ' "My concern is for my own." '

His nostrils flared as if I had released some appalling odour into the air.

'Who is she?' I asked.

'Really, DuBois. Your natural aptitude for offensive rhetoric leaves you without peer.'

'What is her name?'

His sigh was that of the immortal Atlas, wearied by his eternal burden. 'Look around you, DuBois. Even a culturally blighted member of the diaspora such as yourself can only be disenchanted by the sight that faces us now.'

I looked about the High Street, with its famous stores and high-rise buildings, and the grey clouds above them.

'If a sophisticated dilettante such as yourself', he continued, 'can long for the sights and smells of your own homeland, even if it is but a diluted, cultural hand-me-down of my own African home, then you can understand the greater intensity of my own longing, since I miss a truer, more vital land.'

'Let me guess,' I said. 'She is a beautiful brunette.'

'DuBois –'

'About five foot six.'

He began to mumble to himself.

'And how has she managed to hurt your feelings?'

This ushered in a long silence. I waited, sure that it would, like the clouds above us, break.

'DuBois, you love this woman of yours?'

'I don't need to answer that.'

'True. I cannot say that I fully understand this passion of yours. She has many qualities – she is pretty, bright and possesses a wonderful smile – but I cannot say she is your equal.'

I turned sharply towards him.

He held out his hand to pacify me. 'You are easily her intellectual superior. I have listened to your conversations. I've seen you hold back when your discourse starts to become too learned; I've seen her struggle to understand you. But no matter, you love each other. Still, you cannot look me in the eye and say that she is the sort of woman that you and I were raised to marry.'

My cheeks burned.

'Nevertheless, she is a remarkable woman – a remarkable woman.'

I waited for him to go on.

'It is', he said, 'a source of some regret to me that I have not come across a suitable black woman.'

Nothing more was said for a while. I looked at all the white women walking past us, noticing the make-up on their faces, the swelling of their bellies and breasts, the skirts that fell to their knees, the panty-line on their buttocks, the swell of their calves and the curve of their ankles. I stared until my eyes stung and I had to wipe them. 'Perhaps "suitable" is the wrong word?' I ventured.

'Perhaps, perhaps. Yes, I have, after all, met many women of, let us say, colour – yes, that's a pleasant phrase – who have had fine minds. They possessed grace and were endowed with plenty of charm. I have dined with many women who my mother would be only too pleased to call daughter. Still, the simple truth is, I have yet to meet one woman – one black woman – who causes me to lose sleep, fantasize, ache and, most of all, need.'

'Arthur,' I said, 'I find that hard to believe.'

'Why?'

'Because there are so many attractive black women out there. There are many women at the Institute who are extremely attractive.'

'Yes,' he said wearily, 'I'm sure you're right.'

'I cannot imagine making love to any other woman than Jocelynne, but I'm sure that if, by some unimaginable event, I were faced with loving another woman, she would surely be black. I cannot imagine that these women who obsess you possess anything that I could not find in abundant measure in a woman of my own race.'

'Is that so?'

'I believe it to be so.'

'Tell me, DuBois, have you ever slept with a white woman?'

'No, and I have no desire to.'

'None at all?'

'None.'

'You have never wondered what it would be like to sleep with a white woman?'

'Never.'

'You've never wondered what it would be like to fuck a white woman?'

'Never.'

'Liar. Every man of colour, whether black, brown, yellow or red, wonders what it would be like to fuck a white woman.'

'According to you.'

'And I am but a foolish Hussite and easily dismissed?' He lit up a cigarette, a sure sign that battle had commenced, before pointing across the road to an advertising hoarding. 'How could it not be? The face that advertises the cigarettes I smoke is white. She sells these cigarettes because she is beautiful, because she is beautiful by white standards, and therefore is beautiful by global standards, for women like her adorn similar posters all over the world.

'Your precious women of colour the world over look at her and want to be as beautiful as she. Your mother, no doubt, judged herself by those standards. Your cousin had a fixation on a certain Scarlett O'Hara, did she not? Though I hesitate to mention this, your beloved regularly combs her hair with a hot comb, so that it will be straight.

'How is it possible, then, for the discerning man of colour such as myself not to desire that which his own women place on the highest pinnacle? But you would have me believe otherwise, and how can I doubt a man of your sterling character?'

He dropped the cigarette butt on to the ground and immediately set about lighting another.

'Sometimes', I said, 'you take yourself too seriously.'

'Probably. Then again, I take everything seriously. Including the opinion of a man who makes a judgement on a subject he knows nothing about.'

I looked away from him.

'DuBois, old chap, may I ask you another question?'

I nodded.

'Can you, for one earth-shattering moment, place your redoubtable character to one side? Having successfully managed to complete this nigh unimaginable event and survived the traumatic curtailment of ego, try to evoke the following scenario.'

I listened carefully to what followed.

'Imagine yourself lying on a bed in a room. Turn over, stretch out and look to your right. Lying beside you – now this will surely stretch your new-found heterodoxy – is a white woman. Safe and secure within the shabby recumbency of this room – it might well be a hotel room she has sneaked you into – you undress her. Perhaps you fumble as you turn the lamp off. Then, as your eyes adjust to the dark, you find yourself struck by the tone of her skin as you grasp her breast.

'You suck her nipple. Perhaps it is cool upon your tongue as it swells? Perhaps you are surprised by its hardness? You pull your head back and, as you do, a car passes by and its beam fills the room. As you look down, something catches your eye and makes your heart leap. For there, right between your fingers, caught by the passing light, spreading out from this woman's nipple in a tiny wave, is a pink flush. The light fades away but the image is still there, burned on to your cornea.

'You fuck her and play with her, but all the time you're waiting for that next car to come along. And when it does, you lift up your head and squeeze both her tits as hard as you can. And there, expanding outwards like blood from the body of a squashed beetle, is that same flush between your fingers.

'Afterwards, when all is done and you smoke a cigarette, already planning your exit from the building, that image turns over and over and over in your mind. And it is a sweet image, it tickles your belly and makes you feel good. Very good.'

I sat alongside him, unable to look at any of those who passed us without stripping them and conjuring up a series of pink flushes. I could only say to him, 'I suppose I should be happy for you?'

Having finished his cigarettes, he sauntered over to a news vendor and acquired some more, before flopping back down beside me with circles of smoke rising into the air. 'There is no need to feel happy for anyone, DuBois. No need at all. Well, that is not true. I am happy that you are happy.'

I said nothing.

'I truly am. A part of me envies you.'

'Arthur, your love life is your own. I have no right to comment on it or make any judgement.'

'Love? What has love got to do with it?'

'You tell me.'

He sucked hard on his cigarette. 'What is this thing called love? Something the ladies invented because they were tired of us rushing them from behind.'

'Nonsense.'

'What then? A need, a desire, a sickness, a euphoria, a flood of adrenalin?'

'It's all of those things.'

The cigarette butt fell between his feet and his eyes never moved from it. 'It is a sickness, an affliction that leaves the mind incapable of rational thought or clarity.'

'Thomas Mann', I told him, 'wrote, "It is love, not reason, that is stronger than death." '

He took a deep breath. ' "Love is not always blind, and there are few things that cause greater wretchedness than to love with all your heart someone you know is unworthy of love." '

'Somerset Maugham, *The Summing Up*. A wonderful book.'

'Indeed,' he said, lighting up once again. ' "When a man is in love he endures more than at other times; he submits to everything." '

'Nietzsche.'

' "There is always some madness in love. But there is always some madness in reason." '

'The German again.'

' "To be loved means to be consumed. To love is to give light with inexhaustible oil. To love is to pass away, to love is to endure." '

'True, but I am unaware of the writer's name.'

'It is obvious, love is the true author. The name of the conduit is unimportant.'

'The source would seem to be pain, perhaps bitterness?'

'Constant companions of the phenomena we invoke.'

' "Love",' I quoted to him, ' "should be a tree whose roots are deep in earth, but whose branches extend into heaven." '

'Russell had a fine mind, but some felt him to be naïve.'

'I admit to a certain naïvety, but I would point out that I am happily married, while you are single and miserable, and clearly, for all your worldly wisdom, have fallen in love with someone who has caused you much pain.'

He began to chuckle. 'DuBois, you really do have a gift for lacerating the jugular.'

'And you for the obscure.'

His laughter was most welcome and when he was done, he began to talk. He spoke of a girl who, rather predictably (he showed a hint of embarrassment),

166

fitted my description exactly. Their attraction had been immediate and passionate. She had spoken to him of her brother and his hatred of blacks. He had joked and shrugged it off. They had become lovers. One day the brother came home. A scene developed. He warned Arthur to stay away. Arthur ignored him. Shortly after this argument, Arthur was set upon by the brother and a group of friends.

The girl had come to visit him in hospital and made it clear that their relationship was over. She had seen the light and understood that couples like them weren't meant to be.

Arthur smiled and shrugged his shoulders as if he were dislodging a shower of leaves. 'There you have it, DuBois. Clichéd, boring, humdrum, but the truth.'

We sat on that bench until he stood up and said, 'Come, let me show you where she lives.'

I followed him, sure that no good would come of it.

Gabriel's attention was broken by a knock on his door. 'What do you want?'

Her irritation came through the wood. 'To come in, of course.'

'No.'

'Why not?'

'I'm reading.'

He listened to her walk down the landing, open the bathroom door and turn on the taps, until he could bear it no longer. He slipped on a robe and went to the bathroom, only to find the door locked. 'Will you open the door?'

'I'm taking a bath.'

'Open the door!'

'I respected your privacy.'

'What!' He was strengthened by his anger, but after the momentary exultation came a deep shame that caused him to walk away. The floorboards recorded the shifting of his weight, preventing him from slipping away unknown to her.

'Gabriel?'

'Yes?'

'Do you want to come in?'

He swore under his breath, the fists of his shadow clenching on the wall. 'Yes, I would like to come in.'

He heard her move towards the door. 'I'll let you in if you promise to behave yourself.'

'Behave myself?' He kicked the door. It held.

'And if you agree to respect what I say and do.'

There was a long pause before he said, 'I agree.'

Rachel unlocked the door. Gabriel entered the bathroom to find the blinds down. A packet of bath salts stood on the floor, its contents having turned the water a deep blue.

Naked, Rachel sat on the toilet, a green towel across her lap, and watched him inspect the room. A towel was rearranged, a flannel picked up, a hair removed from the bar of soap, before his attention fell on her, his eyes directed below her waist.

'Why don't you get into the bath?' she asked, as liquid dripped from her into the toilet basin. 'I can tell you want to.'

'I wash alone.'

'It doesn't bother me.'

She covered her eyes. He removed his robe and sat down in the water with his hands across his groin.

'That's better,' she said. 'By the way, you never answered my question properly the other day.'

'Which one?'

'I asked you why I frightened you. I also said you thought women were dirty.'

'I don't think that women are dirty.'

'No?'

'I think you have a heavy bladder, but that's it.'

She laughed lightly. 'I don't have a heavy bladder. I have a heavy period.'

He closed his eyes and eased himself down into the water.

She dabbed at herself with some paper, before studiously sniffing the redness on it. 'Sometimes I can tell if it's going to rain, by the smell.'

'A precious gift, I'm sure.'

She got up and the towel dropped from her hand as she stepped into the water, the muscles along her thigh tensing, her calf contracting into a firm mass. A red bead ran down her leg, colouring the water as she breathed heavily out through pursed lips. 'Sometimes it hurts, you know. My father told me once that it was Eve's punishment for eating the apple. I had my first period when I was twelve years old. My father had always held me until then. The day I had my first period is the last day that he ever picked me up. I've never really felt clean since. It was as if I was too dirty for him to hold.'

The blood eased towards him with the ripples from her movement. She ran her hands through the beetroot water, pouring it over herself, the mixture adding a luminous sheen to her skin. Water paddled over him until the whole of the bath was dyed red and their bodies submerged beneath the tincture.

It seemed as if he could smell everything: the aroma from her armpits, her breath, her skin, the scent of her vagina and the blood as she cupped a hand underneath herself, waiting for the bleeding to continue. 'I don't want you to be afraid of me.'

She dipped her mouth below the surface, sucked up water and dribbled the redness on to his face, as her hands pressed his penis into the warmth of her belly button. He pulled away and tried to climb out of the bath, but she entwined her legs about him and began to coat his penis with her blood. She blew over his face, whispering, 'Open your eyes.'

He opened his eyes and found bubbles of red forming about her fingers. As he ejaculated she rubbed the scarlet sperm over their bodies before offering it to him. As he took her finger into his mouth she stroked his hair. 'How's it taste?'

'It's not something I'd recommend.'

Unbidden, he lifted her on to him and began to lick her. She moved his head about, calling out every now and then, 'Slowly . . . faster,' then held him still, 'There – there,' until she came against him.

She thanked him. He wasn't sure what to say, so he just buried his face in her shoulder and kept silent, as she slid down to cover him.

'Gabriel, can I tell you a few things?'

He couldn't look her in the eye.

'My name is Rachel Hannah Wheeler. Hannah was my grandmother's name; my mother's best friend was called Rachel. I believe that people are essentially good. I live by my standards.' She brushed her hair away from her eyes. 'I try to live my life with what I believe to be grace.' Her hand shook as she placed it upon her chest. 'I have so much love in here – more than you or anyone will ever know.' She began to cry. 'I was the first woman to make love to you, who ever held you. When you think back to this, remember who I was. Remember that I accepted

you with love and that we came together in grace. Will you do that?'
She lifted his chin up. 'Look at me.'

He cleared his throat. 'Yes, I will remember.'

She kissed him and her tongue seemed impossibly delicate as she
guided his penis against her.

'This is my labia . . . This is my clitoris.' She guided him inside. 'This
is my vagina.'

A sound, new to him, slid from his lips. His rich pleasure called on
her own excitement, as she rocked on him, until she received his come.
And as the strength fled from him, she held him tightly and kissed him
until the fear in his eyes receded.

Early morning.

Gabriel spent some time looking at Rachel as she slept, caressing her
hair. Half awake, she muttered things that frightened her, that filled
her face with pain and worry, so he held her until she was calm again,
until he was sure she would not awake, and then joined her in slumber.
He awoke to find his penis in her mouth. Something fearful and trench-
ant twisted in his belly. She caught the change and moved away. 'What's
wrong?'

He wasn't sure, but without her touch the fear receded. Curious, she
squeezed him, drawing forth a moan that held no pleasure. 'What's
wrong? Tell me.'

He buried his face in the mattress and refused to speak to her. His
muscles, despite her careful massaging, remained tense and unyielding.
Tired of waiting, she began to stroke his pubic hair.

'Don't,' he said.

'I want to know what happened.'

'No.'

'Don't you want to know what happened?'

'I know what happened.'

'What was it, then?'

'It hurt.'

'Hurt? How?'

'It hurt.'

'Tell me where.'

He pointed to his penis, then to his stomach. 'Everywhere.'

'Here?'

'Yes.'

She massaged his penis. 'And here?'

'Yes.'

Her thumbnail ran along his stretching skin. 'Is it hurting now?'

'Not yet.'

A pungent scent lifted into the air as his muscle grew, its brown, bright and vivid. 'And now?'

The pleasure broke his focus and left him adrift and scared. From a distance he heard, 'It's OK, I'm here, I'm here.'

A sharp heat warmed the tip of her tongue as he lay on his back, unable to prevent or control the fear that welled within him, stripping him bare of any rational control. Behind the ethereal twilight of his eyelids sped an enormous roll of film. Bright stills, each containing exquisitely detailed images, began to present themselves to him.

Picture One. Gabriel climbs the stairs to his father, who swigs from a bottle of home-made cider. 'Gabriel, this is good. The best yet.'

Gabriel nods. 'I think I'm getting the hang of it.'

'And the rest, it's as good?'

'Yes. Do you want me to refill the bottle?'

'Of course.'

Gabriel heads back to the cellar, his last view, that of his father's growing pot-belly hanging over his shorts.

Picture Two. Gabriel and Matthew sit in a headmaster's office. Gabriel's eyes remain fixed on his shoes as his father lectures the grey-haired figure before them. '. . . It is my duty to correct the mis-information that your teaching staff keep feeding him . . . I won't punish him for protecting himself . . . I have taught him to look after him-self and I'm proud of it. At least in that department, he's been a fine student.'

Picture Three. Gabriel and Matthew struggle with each other in a hallway. Matthew cuffs his son several times about the head and opens a cupboard door. Gabriel kicks his father in the shin. Matthew pushes him into the cupboard then locks it. The dust begins to sting Gabriel's eyes and within seconds he is sneezing.

*

Gabriel sat up, breathing quickly as certain frames blurred and bent tantalizingly away from him. Blurred faces materialized and dissipated, leaving only the merest impressions of forgotten memories.

He eased Rachel away, got up and slid over to the coolness and solidity of the wall, ignoring her questions until she stopped asking them. In the quiet, much to his annoyance, his eyes stung and his vision blurred with moisture.

'It's all right,' she said. 'You should cry if you want to.'

He looked away from her. 'Do you have any idea how trite you sound?'

'I'm only trying to help.'

He opened the window and the breeze cooled his skin.

'I don't mind crying,' she said.

'The point being?'

'That's it. I'm not afraid to. What have you got against crying?'

He concentrated on something out on the street.

'In fact,' she said with a warm grin, 'I rather enjoy it. I used to drive Peter mad. He can't cope with women crying – confuses female tears with his mother's, you know.'

Gabriel sat down beside her and took her hand. 'Are you still in love with Peter?'

'No, not at all.' She put her hand across her heart. 'Hope to die if I tell a lie. Truth is, when I look at him now, I'm embarrassed.' She stroked his face. 'What happened when I was kissing you?'

'I'm not sure.'

'You scared me.'

'Then why didn't you stop?'

'I didn't want to. No one's ever reacted like that.' She grinned, her face flushing with the presence of a younger self. 'I'm terrible, aren't I?'

'That's not for me to say.'

'Why not? It's your body.'

'Ultimately, I consent to everything.'

'What does that mean?'

He lay down beside her. 'Why do you ask so many questions?'

Her tongue sought him out again. He tried to push her away, but she held on and took him in her mouth, murmuring, 'No.' He fell back, assaulted by another cavalcade of images.

*

Picture Four. Gabriel stands before a mirror and studies his reflection. He feels himself: the firmness of his muscles, the flexibility of his skin, the elasticity of his lips, the rigid structure of his cheek-bones. Stepping closer to the mirror he twists about, bringing into view the scar tissue on his buttocks and hips.

Picture Five. Matthew and Gabriel are boxing in a cellar. Matthew jabs at Gabriel, who blocks the thrust with his right hand. Matthew throws a left cross, Gabriel ducks and delivers three quick blows to his father's body, then covers up as his father lets rip with a series of punches. Matthew can't get through, so he stamps on his son's foot. Gabriel grunts and drops his fists. Matthew hits him with an upper-cut to the chin and follows up with a right cross. Gabriel sinks to the ground. Matthew flops on to a chair, panting, 'I won, I won.' It takes Gabriel time to collect himself. 'You cheated!' he yells. Matthew throws a glove at him. 'Of course I cheated! I fight – you do what you have to do. Don't expect life or people to play fair with you.'

Picture Six. Matthew and Gabriel stand on a street corner. Matthew points at several small boys who are walking along the street with their parents, then saunters away to a parked car. Gabriel weaves his way past a number of people until he comes to a shop-front and stands alongside an older boy. He looks over his shoulder at his father, who nods his head and moves the car forward a few feet. Gabriel studies the boy next to him, before punching him in the face. As the boy screams, Gabriel runs for his father's car. As he draws level, Matthew begins to move away. Gabriel calls out to him, but Matthew drives off into the traffic. The mother of the stricken boy advances on him. Gabriel kicks out, claws and runs.

Picture Seven. Matthew lies on a sofa drinking sherry from a bottle. Gabriel sits on the floor before him.

'You must remember', says his father, 'that women are quite unhygienic. Their vaginas secret all kinds of fluids and they cannot wash themselves as easily and as well as we can.'

Gabriel asks about his geography teacher. 'Mrs Banks – is she unhygienic?'

Matthew objects to the question. 'She is who and what she is. It is not a question of choice. They are how nature designed them. You know how meat rots in a man's stomach – well, consider how material collected in the vagina that isn't absorbed fully decomposes and putrefies.'

The boy wrinkles his nose. 'It's quite disgusting.'

Matthew offers the bottle to his son, who swigs from it.

'Does that mean Mother was dirty?'

Matthew is silent for a while. 'That is a good question. It's most interesting. It shows that you are willing to consider things logically. I couldn't do that when I was your age. I was a romantic, always getting excited about this and that.'

This brings a smile to Gabriel's cheeks.

'Yes, believe it or not, I was.' He holds out his hand. Gabriel grasps it. 'I'm glad I've freed you of that. It's the only thing that keeps me sane, the knowledge that you won't have to go through the nonsense I went through.'

'Thank you.'

'You don't have to thank me. I've only done my duty.'

'I appreciate your efforts.'

A tear falls down Matthew's cheek. 'See,' he says in a breaking voice as he wipes the moisture away, 'I'm a fraud. I haven't got to the blessed state that you enjoy.' He feels his son's fingers squeeze his hand. 'You're too kind. I'm weak. I'm weak and I hate myself for it.' Matthew weeps for a few minutes. 'In answer to your question, yes. Your mother, for all her many qualities, was as dirty as any other woman. Nature brands us as it chooses and we can't deny the blemish.'

Gabriel ponders this for some time, until his father prompts him. 'You have a question? Come on, spit it out.'

'Well, I was just wondering, how it is that if Mama –'

'Mother. You are not to say Mama. You have no right to be that familiar – you didn't know her.'

'I'm sorry.'

Matthew waves him on. 'Your question?'

'Well, if Mother was so unclean, how was it that you had sexual intercourse with her? You've often told me how you never wanted to interact with society,' Gabriel's head indicates something outside the room, 'how you wanted to find somewhere quiet and far away –'

'A retreat.'

'And lead a monastical life.'

'I should have. I try to now.'

'Then why let all those ambitions go? Why did you throw away everything on a woman? Especially since she was as dirty as you say?'

Matthew swings his legs off the sofa and sits up. 'You're on good form today.'

Gabriel blushes and looks down at the floor.

'I was a fool, that's why. I threw everything away because I was a fool. No more, no less. I held back my disgust and let myself be led astray. I'm not proud of it. I've learned from it, I've tried to teach you the profits of my lessons, but I'll never be able to take that time back and change it.' He rubs his son's hair. 'And?'

Gabriel shrugs his shoulders.

'Don't do that. Only imbeciles do that.'

'I'm sorry.'

'Don't be sorry; be correct.'

Gabriel takes note. 'All right. I was wondering –'.

'Ask, ask.'

'Well, it's not really a question – I know the answer, so –'.

'Share the answer with me, then.'

'Well, it must be that if Mother was dirty, then I was born into dirt.'

'But you've always known that. What do you think the point of original sin was? It's one of the inescapable conundrums of life. I've wasted too many years thinking about it.'

Gabriel sits by his father for a while before going to the bathroom, running a bath and scrupulously washing himself.

Picture Eight. Gabriel and Matthew stand in their garden holding several plastic bags, before a fire that has already consumed a number of possessions. Matthew drops a bundle of letters on to the fire as Gabriel hands him more. 'Do you understand what I'm doing?' he asks.

Gabriel shakes his head. 'Not quite.'

'I'm doing what is necessary. You know that a man must always do what is necessary, no matter how difficult?'

'Yes.'

Matthew drops more letters on to the growing fire. 'These are letters from my family: my father, my mother and others.'

Gabriel looks into his bag. A single letter remains. He crumples up the bag.

'I've held on to these letters for too long. Now everything has ended.'

Gabriel holds the bag to his leg as his father places a hand on his shoulder. 'When your time comes, I trust that you will act with the same strength.'

Gabriel looks his father directly in the eye. 'I will try to.'

Matthew walks back into the house.

Gabriel waits for his father to close the door behind him. When he is sure that he will not return, he takes the letter from the bag. It has been recently sent and its back is marked with a precautionary return-address. Gabriel runs his hands over it before throwing it on to the fire. He watches the flames bite into it, then grabs it back. He walks around the fire picking away the charred edges of the paper. He makes sure his father isn't looking before pocketing the letter and going into the house.

He makes it to the top of the stairs without much noise and opens the detention cupboard carefully, so that it won't squeak. The cupboard is, as ever, completely empty. Though he has washed it out many times, the faint smell of his urine and excretion remains. On the walls are scribbled in pen the names of various foods: APPLE, CHEESE and CHICKEN. A faint breeze comes through a small section of brick. It had been covered with paper that he'd designated CHOCOLATE, but last week he'd eaten all that section. He pulls out one of the bricks, places the letter underneath it, then heads for the kitchen.

Rachel wasn't shocked by the groan that came from her lover's lips. The muscular tremors had warned her, but the sound still chilled. She tried to comfort him, but with eyes bulging he pushed her away, gasping, 'I can't breathe.' She came back and held him. 'Breathe in deep,' she said, 'then breathe out slowly.' He tried to follow her instructions. 'Now breathe in for five seconds . . . breathe out for eight.'

Tears began to roll down his face. He heard her calling out his name and, shamed by her witnessing of this awful moment, gave himself up to the weeping. He felt her move alongside him and grasp his penis. It seemed that he had never been harder or more sensitive, as every motion of her hand seemed to call forth an unwelcome memory.

She sat next to him, pulling forth the tears, telling him, 'It's all right. I'm here. I'm here. I'm here.' Later, when he was calm again, she bathed his face as he dozed off. Humming her song of the moment, she kissed his hand and went to sleep.

The morning brought blazing sunshine and a clear blue sky. Rachel had brought a second chair into the kitchen, and they sat at the breakfast table with the blinds down, eating slowly, drinking leisurely. They didn't speak much, and Rachel said she liked it that way. 'I know you find that hard to believe,' she said, 'but I do.'

She launched into another slice of toast. She had already gone through half a loaf of bread. 'I don't know why. I guess I'm getting used to it. You used to freak me out, but I think I'm starting to get the hang of it.'

He offered her some more coffee.

'No thanks, I'm full.'

The doorbell rang. He didn't move.

'Aren't you going to get that?'

'I don't have visitors. It'll be a salesman or someone canvassing.'

'You don't have visitors?'

'No.'

The bell rang again and again.

'Doesn't sound like nobody to me.'

He left her and opened the door to Rupert and Peter. Rupert's jacket was folded over his arm, his shirt was stained with sweat and he was mopping his brow with a handkerchief. His son wore cycling shorts and a ripped T-shirt that showed his powerful physique to good effect. Rupert took a step forward. 'Me caan' handle dis flippin' heat. Me need a drink.'

Gabriel held out a hand to stop him. 'I don't want you inside my house.'

'Wat?'

'I don't want you in my house.'

Rupert could hardly believe his ears. 'We need to talk.'

Gabriel went to close the door. 'You need to talk. I don't.'

Peter slammed his foot in the doorway. Rupert pushed with him against Gabriel. Rachel, hearing the commotion, rushed into the hallway. 'What are you doing?' she yelled.

Gabriel stepped back and the two men came in. Peter made a grab at Gabriel, shouting, 'Who the fuck do you think you are?'

Rachel, fists clenched, stepped in between Peter and Gabriel. 'What the hell do you think you are doing, coming in here like this?'

Rupert's voice bounced off the walls. 'Enough! Enough! Stap it!'

Peter, hands trembling, eyes glaring, backed off to the door.

'Look, Gabriel,' said Rupert, 'let us all calm down!'

'You have no right to be here.'

'No right!' screamed Peter. 'My sister is missing and you say it's got nothing to do with us?!'

'That's got nothing to do with Gabriel,' shouted Rachel.

'He should tell us what he knows,' yelled Peter. 'Everything is important now! The body didn't just turn up by accident. We're all in this together and he should be listening to us!'

Gabriel turned and walked into the kitchen. Rupert told Peter to control himself and Rachel to mind her own business. As she followed Gabriel into the kitchen she hissed, 'It is my business.'

Peter bumped her with his shoulder. 'Just because you're fucking the guy doesn't make it your business.'

Gabriel was at the sink, cleaning some plates.

Rachel pointed at the table. 'You might as well sit down.'

'We'll stand,' said Peter.

His father sucked his teeth and sat down.

Peter stood by his father. 'Very nice,' he said. 'Very twee.'

'Something bugging you, Peter?' asked Rachel.

'Not at all.'

'Really?'

Rupert told them to shut up. 'Gabriel,' he began, 'we is family. We jus' wan' to talk.'

Gabriel finished his washing-up and put some forks away in a drawer.

'Could you answer my father?'

'Peter, please, ease yaself.'

Peter crossed his arms, his biceps pushing out.

Rachel covered her mouth with her hand. 'Oh Peter, you look so butch, so manly.'

'You disgust me,' said Peter, 'you really do.'

At that moment, Gabriel pulled a rolling pin out of a draw and knocked it against Peter's head, quickly following up with strikes to the knees and shins. With hardly a sound Peter collapsed to the floor. Rupert, mouth open, got to his feet. Gabriel whacked him across the knee. Rupert hopped back with a howl and almost lost his balance.

Gabriel thrust the rolling pin into Rupert's face. 'Leave.'

When Peter had regained some level of sensibility, Rachel and Rupert helped him out on to the street. The sun bit into their eyes as they sat him down in the car.

'Easy, bwoy,' said Rupert, 'easy.'

Peter wiped away blood from his nose. 'He hit me when I wasn't looking. Just give me a couple of minutes and I'll kill that fucker.'

'Doan' talk like dat.'

'No one hits me when I'm not looking.'

Rachel looked up and saw Gabriel walking towards the car. 'Just go to the hospital, Peter, you might have concussion,' she said.

Peter pushed himself out of the car. Rupert tried to restrain him. As Peter attempted to throw a punch, Gabriel pulled a fork out of his pocket and jabbed it into his face. Peter clutched his cheek and staggered back. 'My face,' he stammered, 'you cut my face.'

Rachel took his hand and helped him into the car.

After they had driven away, Rachel turned to Gabriel. 'You shouldn't have done that.'

He walked back into his house and closed the door.

Throwing back her head she let out a scream; a long, long wail that hurt her throat and made her dizzy.

Rachel found Gabriel in his back garden, shielding his eyes from the intense light, sipping a cup of coffee next to a young tree. He failed to acknowledge her, but that was no surprise. 'That was pretty vicious.'

He carried on drinking, with no apparent interest in what she was saying.

'I'm not stupid. I saw it in you the first time we met.' She took his free hand. 'That sort of thing isn't for me and you. It will never be between us.'

Later that afternoon, as Rachel worked out, Gabriel paced about her. 'This is ridiculous,' she snapped. 'I can't relax with you carrying on like this.'

He picked up some of her clothes. 'I need to work.'

'Well, I'm not stopping you.'

He dropped an empty coke can into the bin as she slid into the splits. 'Haven't you got something to do?'

'I don't have to sign on till next week, and I only work on the weekends.'

'Sign on?'

'Yes.'

'What does "sign on" mean?'

'Very funny.' As she squeezed her toes it dawned on her that he was serious. 'You really don't know what it means?'

'No.'

Her chin came to rest on the floor. 'You don't smoke. I doubt that you could roll a spliff. You don't lie and you have no idea what it means to sign on. What kind of black man are you?'

He frowned before he dipped his head and when it came up he was laughing openly. She joined in. When he was finished he excused himself.

'Where are you going?'

The smile faded, as if his cheeks had been punctured. 'Nowhere. Just into the house.'

'It's hot. Why don't you stay outside?'

He shook his head and left.

Mumbling, 'OK, OK,' Rachel lay down on the grass and began to day-dream.

Gabriel searched through a drawer until he found an old matchbox that held a single key. He took the key out and picked up a Swiss army knife before making his way up the stairs to the cupboard on the landing. The key slipped in easily and Gabriel turned the lock without difficulty, muttering, 'The architecture of necessity dictates all.'

The door opened. The air inside was dusty but bearable. As his chest tightened he flicked out a blade and ran his hands along the walls, cutting quickly into the paper. The brick amused and confused him, so perfectly did it resemble the brick of his memory which he had suddenly recalled during his time with Rachel. It was lined with paper and came free without much effort. He found nothing underneath it.

Disappointment seized him, made him feel like a fool. His hands trembled as he tried to replace the brick, causing it to slip from his grasp and break open on the floor. The brick was hollow. At its centre was an envelope wrapped in plastic. The burnt tissue flaked apart as he opened the envelope.

He found two photographs and a few wisps of curly hair. The photographs were of a sleeping infant wrapped in some blankets. Eyes closed, Gabriel sat down on the floor of the cupboard until he was ready. After a period beyond counting, he read the letter. It was a short message to Matthew warning him that she would be returning home late. Nothing more. But it was enough. He studied the curls of her writing, the rise of the 't's, the bends of the 'e's and the shape of her name, before placing the note in his back pocket.

He remained there for some time, ignoring Rachel's calls as she searched the house for him. When he was ready he emerged, washed, changed his clothes and surprised her in the garden. She lay near the tree-infant, her leotard damp with spots of sweat, reading the *Socialist Worker*. 'Where did you go to?' she asked, handing the paper to him.

The front page had a picture of a group of demonstrators protesting against the closure of a youth centre. A smaller photograph showed Sonia Richards and Edwin; their anger and commitment to preventing the closure of the youth centre was well detailed.

'Would you believe it? The council has brought forward its closing date. Today is the end,' she said.

Gabriel handed the paper back. Rachel flung it away. 'These bastards have no shame. They lock these kids up for walking the streets and close down the places where they go to escape being arrested.'

He waited until he was sure she had finished and said, 'I'm leaving.'

'Leaving? Where to?'

'I'll be gone for a few hours.'

She shrugged her shoulders. 'OK. Could you give me a lift to the youth centre?'

'Which one?'

Mumbling, 'For God's sake,' she walked away into the house.

Gabriel drove past a group of police officers and parked by the main body of demonstrators. There was not much activity: placards rested against the walls, banners lay on the ground. Several pairs of shoes had been removed; their owners stood barefoot on the hot pavement drinking cartons of fruit juice. Edwin moved about the gathering, taking photographs and offering words of encouragement. Sonia smiled and hurried over to Rachel as she got out of the Volvo. Gabriel pulled the passenger door shut and drove away.

The heat was unbearable as he approached the cemetery and he found himself sweating profusely. The stench from the rubbish dump on the nearby common was appalling. He stopped by the entrance and surprised himself by removing his shirt. Breathing quickly he wrapped it about his waist and sat down on the pavement.

The traffic passed him without slowing down.

No accidents happened, no one stopped, no one stared. No one looked away disgusted. No one threw up. No one screamed insults.

He remained there until the sense of his own exposure became too much.

The doors to the chapel were closed. A wheelbarrow filled with rubbish was parked against its walls. In the distance, Gladwin waved to him. Gabriel joined her on the earth beneath which his mother lay. She wore a light, multi-coloured summer dress. Two roses lay at her feet. She held out a hand to him and kissed him on the cheek.

'I thought you might come today. I was looking forward to sharing some time here with you.'

'It's hot – I might not have.'

Her nails gave him a reproachful bite. 'I'm an African, I don't need telephone conversations to confirm things.'

'Intuition?'

'That's a Western word. I have to slide on my Western eyeglasses when I used words like that.'

'Eyeglasses?'

Her laughter mocked him a touch. 'When I first came here, many, many things used to confuse me. The way people talked, how they acted. I realized that it wasn't just a question of language, it was a question of this,' she tapped her temple. 'I realized people looked at the same things I did, but saw different things. So I decided to imagine myself wearing different glasses at different times. When I was with Africans, I would have my African glasses on, and when I was with English people –' a shrug served as a full stop.

'And what glasses have you got on now?'

'Over the years I have developed a pair of glasses that have two different lenses. The one on the left is African, the one on the right is Western. I've got that pair on now. Sometimes they leave marks on my nose and I bump into things, but generally I can get to where I'm going in them.'

They stood together. There were damp spots beneath Gladwin's armpits, and Gabriel could feel a line of sweat developing along his back. Martin came through the cemetery gate chewing a kebab and waved briefly at Gabriel, who waved back, but his gesture went unseen as the Yorkshireman dipped his head and continued on his way.

'He's a nice man,' said Gladwin.

'He seems to enjoy his job.'

'Some people like keeping the dead company. Can you imagine how wonderful this place can be?'

He tried to imagine.

'Do you like cemeteries, Gabriel?'

'Not really.'

'Why not?'

'I don't know. I'm just uncomfortable here.'

'Why?'

'Why do you ask?'

'Because I want an answer.'

'I've never felt at ease in places like this.'

'Really? I've always loved cemeteries. There was a huge cemetery near my parents' home – one of the largest in Africa. We loved to go there, to picnic there, to talk. It was wonderful being so close to those who had passed on. My father always felt that his ancestors would respond quicker if he asked his questions near to them. I trust the dead. They've no reason to harm you.'

He picked up one of the roses.

'I got them from a shop down the road. They have beautiful roses there.'

The flower was fresh, its stem hard, almost crisp, the thorns resistant to his touch. She knelt beside him. 'I will never forgive your uncle for his disrespect towards your mother.'

'And my father?'

She took a deep breath. 'I have anger towards him. I'm sure that he must have had his reasons for this, but nothing can explain how a man can . . . I mean, she had two children for him.' A stiffness passed through her and she moved round to rub her painful calf. 'It's all these stupid buses. I don't get enough exercise. I'm old and fat now. You won't believe me, but when I was your age, no one could catch me. I could outrun anyone.'

'I believe you.'

'Trouble was, I could never catch your uncle.'

The stiffness passed and she was content to rest her hand on her leg. 'I loved him for years. Now I can hardly believe what all the fuss was about. I hope you don't make the same mistake I did and waste yourself on the wrong person. Is there anyone special in your life?'

'I'm seeing someone.'

'What's she like?'

He stared at her.

'What?' she asked.

'This is odd.'

'What's odd about it?'

'Us talking like this.'

'Why?'

'I'm not used to talking to a −'

'To what? A mad old woman?'

He was horrified. 'No, not at all. Please don't think that.'

She calmed him down. 'I'm joking.'

'I didn't mean to offe—'

'Gabriel, it's fine, really. I was joking.'

'I'm sorry. I'm not too good at humour.'

She hurt his ears with her laughter, his bemused expression causing her to bellow even harder. 'Oh, look at you, just look at you!'

When it was time for her to move on, she encouraged him to come and visit her and refused to take no for an answer. She turned down his offer to accompany her to the nearest bus stop, insisting he should stay and enjoy his visit on his own. As she brushed herself down she asked, 'How many times has your mother visited you?'

He appeared to be confused by her question.

She held out her hand and, when he took it, kissed his. 'My sweet boy, I'm not stupid. I know who you are. Answer me.' Even though his palm grew slick within her grasp she did not release it. 'Come,' she said, kneeling beside him. 'I'm an old woman with nothing to hide.

You can tell me. In the dark, when you're all alone, how many times
has she come to visit you?'

He didn't want to answer.

'How many times?'

'I – I'm not sure.'

'Yes, you are.'

'No, no, I'm not.'

'She used to come to me months after she left the hospital. Always
talking and worrying about your father. I used to try and comfort her,
but her pain was too great. It was a blessing when she sorted herself
out. I missed her, but every now and then, when I've needed advice,
she's been there.' She handed him a rose. 'Take it. Look after it until
it's ready to be thrown away.'

She kissed him and walked away. When he was ready, he took out
the journal and began to read.

16

Arthur took me for a ride in his brand new Citroën – he asked his father for
a car – and drove me over to Golders Green where his love, a Sharon Goldmeir,
lives. The house is enormous. She obviously comes from a wealthy family.
We passed the time chatting and waited and waited. Eventually she turned
up. She arrived with her parents. The parents are short and unimpressive. The
lady herself is extremely pretty and well dressed. The family seem close and,
despite Arthur's insistence on her broken heart, she clearly enjoys an intimate
and friendly relationship with her father.

9th January 1960

The baby was born last night. My God, I didn't believe in the existence of
hell, but last night at the maternity ward I discovered the error of my ways. I
have never heard such awful sounds before and hope that I never will again.
I was treated as if I were a complete simpleton by the nursing staff, who kept
reassuring me with the most banal platitudes. When I was eventually allowed
to see J., I felt as if I had been allowed into sacred territory. Still, it was only a
matter of minutes before I realized that perhaps that awful place, smelling of
disinfectant and soap, was hallowed. J. was sitting in bed looking, I must say,
an absolute wreck. But in her arms was our child. The baby is small and, dare
I say it, perfect. Her skin is flawless, her hands and fingers are perfect, her feet
and toes are perfect. A nurse told me that she is virtually blind, but I swear

that she looked at me. J. confirmed this and we were both sure that the child had recognition in her eyes. J. has constantly said over the past nine months that the baby would recognize my touch. I used to mock her, but, to be honest, it seemed to me as I held the little angel that she did indeed respond to my embrace.

Did I love my wife more yesterday evening than ever before? Probably. How could I not, when she had given me everything: her own love, incredible physical intimacy, laughter, and now a child. I doubt that any man has ever been happier. If there is such a man, then let him come forward and make his case. I would defeat him.

1

I threw a party here last night, and invited all my closest friends. I showed off a telegram from my father. It read: 'Congratulations on a job well done.' Penny was so impressed with my happiness that she decided there and then to cast away all her doubts and marry her latest boyfriend. His name is Brian, he is a pleasant fellow and seems, even though he and Penny have only been together for seven weeks, to think it is a good idea. The director turned up and wished me well. Even though we asked him to stay, he left after only a few drinks. I appreciated his visit. Unbelievably, Gladwin and Rupert turned up. My moronic toadstool of a brother-in-law made an attempt to be gracious, but I was not impressed or moved by his goodwill.

3

Jocelynne and the baby – we have been unable to agree on a name so we have decided to refer to her as 'Little One' – came home yesterday. J. took some time to fall asleep for she was determined to watch the baby for as long as possible. As they slept, I worried about touching the babe, for her skin seemed delicate enough to tear if I even rested my finger on it. J. has always seemed so capable, so strong, and yet the sheer physical stress of the birth is clear. It is terrible, this unavoidable pain that accompanies the most glorious act of all.

NB. Strange – come the early hours of the morning, I experienced a strong sense of estrangement. The unity of mother and child excluded me. Still, I am sure my time will come.

4

A fire in Golders Green was reported tonight on the radio. An Andrew Goldmeir and wife, Micha, were burnt to death. They were survived by their children Adam, Sharon and Elizabeth. The names are unfamiliar to me, but I am uncomfortable.

8

We have decided on a name for the little one. To be honest, I gave up fighting. Cuffay is the name J. has set her mind on. I take no responsibility for this. Her mother can explain her reasons to the child when she returns from school having been mercilessly attacked and humiliated.

Gabriel skipped past entries that deal with Matthew's work and his plans to travel abroad to liaise with members of the American civil rights movement, until he found a section that grabbed his attention. The normally ordered writing had changed quite dramatically. The weight on the pen was heavy and words fell over lines and were stained with ginger prints.

14

I knew that life had been too kind. I knew that I could not trust these happy times. Everything was going too well.
Pride. Pride. Pride.
My child is dead. Cuffay is dead.

Gabriel looked up. Except for Martin, tackling some weeds in the northern part of the cemetery, he was alone. The streets, too, were deserted of pedestrians. It is too hot: too hot for walking, too hot for playing, too hot for shopping. He was in need of a drink, but Cuffay's story called out and he read on.

15

I cannot make sense of it. The evening had gone well. We had talked, laughed. J. has been quite prolific recently, writing of the birth and her experiences. She enjoyed, I believe, a renaissance of faith, the life-affirming nature of the birth confirming her belief in a Creator. The truth is, as asinine as it sounds, I came close to doubting my own principles. So many times, when I looked at Cuffay's face, I sensed something so profound, so utterly poetic that I . . .

Jocelynne had placed her in her cot. Everything was as it had been the night before and the night before. We went to bed, as we had done so many times before. We slept. I awoke to screaming. Jocelynne was screaming, howling. Desperate. She scratched my face as she pulled me out of bed. The baby was in her arms. Cuffay was not breathing. She looked so peaceful, so beautiful, but she was not breathing. Her skin was the colour of – Nothing we did –

16

J. is on medication. I stay with her at the hospital for as long as I can. I am weak. I need some assistance myself.

17

My friends mean well, but they drain me. I cannot deal with their comforting and their pain any longer. I have begged them to leave me alone for a time.

18

Cot Death. Unexplainable. Unknowable. Unpredictable. Capricious. Fanciful. Malicious. A phenomenon. A culling. A whim. A lottery. A passing finger that pauses where it will. Siva, destroyer of worlds. Death in so tiny a place. So virginal a place. Unwanted. Uninvited. Bitter, bitter pill. My life is empty. I am destroyed. My wife, my darling, my love, my queen, my empress, my friend, my companion, my heart, is destroyed. She lies there. Her eyes are vacant. Her body has become a vacuum, her soul wanders. I am sure she is trying to pull our angel back. Her food is left uneaten. The doctors worry. She has not come out of the shock.

What has she to come back to? Me? I am no substitute. Her child, her love, her flesh, her joy, her investment, her fancy, her play, her toil, her anguish, her transcendence, her heart, her spleen has been taken away.

The walls crowd in on me. I am surrounded by toys, clothes, the bottle that touched our little one's lips. I hold it in my palm. I suck it. I wash with it, eat with it, lie with it. I carry her clothing – the cloth that wrapped her, the smell of her, her urine. I inhale so hard, I lick it. I need it. She was here. She gave this, left this.

Let me wake, let me wake, let me wake, let me wake. All will be well if I can only wake. My eyelids will open. I will smell Jocelynne's breath. The night sweat will be there. The breeze from that damnable window will irritate my cheek. I will stretch and yawn and turn from the light coming through the curtain and look to the cot and she will be there. If I can but wake.

I will wake. I will wake. This cannot, will not be. My reality is my own. I can control it. I can reach into the earth and shape cities. I can mould the primordial sludge into things that walk and walk. If I choose to, the easel of my imagination will paint landscapes that will outdo those of this monster who has bitten me. Jehovah, Buddha, I challenge you. The walls of Asgard will shake with my anger. The gods of sacrifice and slaughter will bow before my wrath. Abraham offered you his son. My child was not for you. Give me a chance and I will walk through the valleys. Orpheus was weak, weak, weak. I am strong. I will not look back. Though you have ignored the pleas of others for a millennium, flatter me. If shepherds and hoarders of dung could know you, why not I?

Answer me. Answer me. Give me a minute and it will seem like an hour. Give me a second and I will employ it as if it were a blessed eternity.

I am not circumcised, but my race has known pain. Your people knew slavery, as did mine. They were punished, their cultures ransacked, as was ours. I can claim to be of your tribe, for you are surely the chieftain of all peoples. Forgive me. Forgive me. Forgive my arrogance, my churlishness, my insults. Forgive me. I acknowledge your strength. You are omnipotent. You are most mighty. Your light is the purest. I have never worshipped any idols except those of my own rationality and intellect. I know that your supremacy is sovereign. I am penitent. Forgive. For- give. For- give. Forgive.

*

Can you hear me? Will you hear me? You are a bitter God! You are a spiteful, petty God.

Have I not humbled myself enough? This morning, I took a bowl into the bathroom and cut open my wrist for you. I offered up the contents to you. I know you. My wife's Bible details you well. I know what you like – sacrifice, sacrifice, sacrifice. You cannot get enough of it, can you? You demand it. You obsess over it. You crave it. Words will not appease you, for you have been lied to in a thousand tongues. Proof is what you need. Earthquakes and floods are too easy. It is the little things that you want. Like all true sadists you require the sufferer to be fully aware of their pain. Oh, little, little God, take it, drink it, spill it, shit in it for all I care. Just bring my Cuffay back to me.

You obsess over it. You crave it. You have had enough. Bring my child back.

I am waiting. I give you one more day.

I give you one more week.

Enough. You fraud. You charlatan. I will wait no more. I reject you. I renounce you. I renounce you. I renounce you.

21
I put the cot away before Jocelynne returned home yesterday, but she wished to see it. After sitting with it, she asked me to fetch Gladwin. I did so. Gladwin said that the spirit of the child would linger behind unless certain steps were taken. Jocelynne believed her. I left them and retreated to the peace of the bedroom and, as Gladwin led them into who knows what, laughed and cried myself to sleep.

22
We have passed several days in bed. The bed provides comfort – that is the main thing.

Jocelynne now writes and writes and writes. Sleep eludes her. I understand that; her imagination is far brighter than my own. I hate to think of it turned against her when she sleeps.

*

190

26

J. talks in her sleep, sings songs, shouts a lot. Says 'No,' over and over. I have given up trying to comfort her. She has no sense of me. It will go on until it is done.

27

Letters have arrived from my family. They ask us to visit. I will not. My father has had enough opportunities to play the Big Man. He will not enjoy that role because of my child. My strength returns. I – we will endure.

28

This hellish time continues. Jocelynne began to bleed during the night. I had to take her to hospital. It seems she has problems. The doctors feel she should avoid falling pregnant for a few years, so she can regain her strength. She took the news well.

29

Penny called round. She was distraught. It seems Arthur has lost his temper several times at the Institute. According to Penny, he seems incapable of discussion or any exchange of views. I told her that it was understandable, considering the beating he had received. She agreed, but felt that he was holding on to his anger for too long. I could not comment, since we had hardly spent any time together over the last few weeks. I felt she was too close to him, and that events that were actually minor might seem to her greater than they really were. She would have none of it, said Arthur was heading for a big fall and that it was our duty as his friends to do something. I was equally blunt, and told her that Arthur is my friend, but my concern is for my own well-being and Jocelynne's. Arthur will have to wait.

30

Work calls. It has served us both well, for Jocelynne and I had the great privilege of meeting the Reverend Arnold Hubert, a leading American civil rights campaigner. He spent an evening, along with a few invited guests, at the director's house. He impressed everyone greatly, including the reporters who have followed him everywhere. He is bright and humorous and enjoys company. Hubert was clearly aware that people hung on his every word, but showed no enjoyment of his celebrity status. We were all fascinated by his descriptions of marches and he was extremely candid about his fear when confronted by hate and violence.

Amazingly enough, despite all the demands on him, he spent some time with Jocelynne and said a prayer for Cuffay. The effect on J. was tremendous. We shall never forget it. My wife's faith has been untouched by our experience and I was glad for her sake that she took such comfort from the great man. As he left, we were struck by how much we had truly liked him. It is quite inspiring when your heroes fulfil expectations.

31

The autopsies and investigations are over. We buried Cuffay today. She rests in peace. We will never forget her. Jocelynne wants another child, but the doctors advise against it. She will have to listen to them.

Gabriel lowered the journal on to the grass. There was much for him to read, but for the moment his interest was only with certain matters. So he flicked the pages over.

17th February 1960

A sad conversation with Arthur. His work has been slipping and a rumour of impending dismissal has started to circulate. I visited his office to speak to him and it was clear that his work was in disarray. He has always been untidy, but his system is his own. None of us have really tried to challenge him for fear of experiencing his wounding disapprobation. Still, something had to be done, so I had left a note. Several days later, he paid me a visit at home.

He was well dressed as always, but the smile that had been such a fixture during the early stages of our friendship was now absent. This is perhaps a conscious decision as whenever he smiles the scars that criss-cross his face warp horribly. Jocelynne, as is her habit, slipped away to maintain her privacy. We talked in the kitchen. I tried subtly to raise the subject of his behaviour at work, but, as always, he made that impossible.

'I'm not concerned with what people think. My brief is my own. As long as I fulfil it, then no one has the right to complain.'

'No one's complaining about your work. You know how popular you are. You're a powerful personality. When you're up, everyone is up; when you're down, you inevitably affect the general morale.'

'So our colleagues are sheep?'

'That is unfair.'

'As are these comments. I am not responsible for the emotional oscillations of pretend adults.'

'Friends.'

'What friends?'

'You know who they are. Penny, for one.'

His laugh was bitter and derisive. 'Penny is a child.'

'Nonsense.'

'She loves like a child, she reasons like a child, she responds like a child.'

'She is loyal.'

'As child is to the sweet vendor. Whoever gratifies her or denies her gratification controls her. You have only to inveigh.'

'She cares for you.'

'She cares for herself. Her feelings for me are nothing but a way of satisfying her own miserable agenda. A way of pretending she isn't as suburban and bourgeois as her pretentious, kitsch-ridden parents, who embarrass her every time they open their affected, elocution-battered mouths.'

'Parents who were kind to you.'

'As they would be to a performing ape. "Look how well-spoken he is. Look how well his hair is combed. Check those manicured hands. My, my, what a good little ape you are. Can you leap for us? You know, we were so embarrassed when you came to the village to visit, but now that you've added a little *frisson* to our lives and the other villagers think we're terribly radical and interesting, we want you to come again. But please, don't be too forward with our daughter. We don't mind people thinking she's a bit eccentric, but don't push it too far. As you know, there are a lot of eligible bachelor farmers around here. And we always thought, you know, when we were toiling away in the old corner shop, that when we'd saved enough and Penny's private schooling paid off, she'd make the perfect wife for a pig farmer. Don't you think?" '

He grew increasingly agitated as his jeremiad reached a climax and he was unable to remain seated. 'I refuse to flatter her. And you shouldn't blur the issues at hand with these spurious assertions. Still, if you must, go ahead. Venal equivocation was never my strong point.'

'Neither', I told him, 'were arrogance and cruelty, but you seem determined to turn these into virtues.'

He was openly contemptuous. 'Why not? Others have. Why shouldn't I?'

'Now you sound like a child.'

'I've always envied children for their powers of perception.'

'You will lose your job, if you keep this up.'

He laughed at me. 'Oh DuBois, really. I have no financial constraints. I wouldn't be embarrassed for a moment if the Institute terminated my contract.'

'That isn't the point.'

'Please, tell me what is.'

'You are good at what you do. The Institute needs you.'

'Needs me.' He got up and walked around the room with his hands behind his back, apparently deep in thought. 'Needs me?'

'You heard me.' I wanted to hit him.

'The Institute doesn't need me, and, though your ego might not realize it, DuBois, the Institute could even survive without you. We are unimportant. Do you know why we're unimportant? Because we don't do anything. We don't affect anything. We have no power. This island worked perfectly well before we arrived.'

'Hardly.'

'And it will work or not work, it will abuse, corrupt and destroy as it always has. I cannot pretend that Cromwell's children want anything other than the solitary use of their playing fields.'

'So you just give up?'

'I've never given up anything in my life.'

'Then what are you up to?'

'I'm not up to anything. Why should I be up to anything? This is the problem with you people – you think that anyone who adheres to a different strategy is misguided or deluded.'

'And this strategy involves alienating all your friends and neglecting your work, which includes defending the rights of your fellow –'

He exploded. 'Defend who? Defend what? I stand up for myself. Why should I defend any man who cannot rely on his own wits and fists?'

I could hardly believe my ears, and told him so.

'Oh, DuBois, you really are priceless. You sit here in your quaint little flat, earning your so-righteous little crust, and pat yourself on the back daily for having the fortitude to turn your back on your inheritance. You clothe yourself as the common man, but retain the arrogance to think you can lead him.' His eyes rolled upwards in thought. 'What is it that quaint American kept repeating the other day? "Let freedom reign, let freedom reign." '

'Arthur, you are too foul.'

He waved his hands in the air. 'Lordy, Lordy, I'm so fucking gaudy. I ain't got time ta pick cotton, ain't got time to suck tobacco, Lord set me free! Set me fr-e-e-e-e!'

I was lost, utterly lost.

'Your father was a good man, DuBois, but you spurned him. I watched you with that Yank the other day; your sycophancy was quite appalling.'

I could only stare.

'The man is not Moses and he is certainly no Gandhi. These times don't require a new Mahatma, no matter how velvet-voiced.'

'Then what do they require?'

He held his fist out to me.

'Nonsense,' I replied. 'The world isn't a bar room.'

'Oh, I see. We must appease, because we are outnumbered. Look around you, my confused friend – we outnumber them.'

'Them? Listen to yourself. One silly girl rejects you and you want to shoot every czar in sight.'

He had the good grace to laugh, and for a moment it was as if the weeks had rolled back. But the levity was short-lived. 'I am an African, my friend. The thought of following an American who has been stripped of all culture and heritage is anathema to me. All you will get from these people is pithy emotional diatribes that may well draw tears from the liberal establishment, but will not change anything.'

'Is that supposed to relate to me?'

He sat down again and lit up a cigarette, an annoying smirk on his face. 'Where are the legislative changes, DuBois? Where are the multitudes of your fellow countrymen, banging on the doors of their local council chambers demanding registration? Where are the hoards, breaking down the various mechanisms of education?'

'I might have some respect for you, Arthur, except for the fact that you've spent every minute of every day I've known you sucking up to every white woman who ever offered to lift her skirt. One girl turns you down and you become a new David, anxious to lead his people to a blazing Zion of his own making.'

'All right,' he said, holding up his hands in mock surrender, 'enough of this. Let's go for a drink.'

We walked quite some distance, passing several pubs along the way, despite my protestations, to a place that was almost a mile away, but which Arthur insisted on. It took some time for us to be served. We were the only Negroes except for one small fellow who sat with a group of men some distance from us. I believe they were busmen or something. Their conversation sounded jovial, but was full of talk about the Labour Party and the role of the unions in empowering the working class.

Our chap was being encouraged to recruit more 'coloured' people into the union. He was bright-eyed and eager and clearly determined to do his best. Arthur had nothing but scorn for him and loudly vented his opinion that political organizations for the empowerment and education of the Negro should be run entirely by Negroes.

I confess I found him tiring and, as his voice continued to rise and rise and his insults grew more vicious, offensive. Eventually the barman came over to our table and asked us to leave. Arthur told him to go away. The barman grabbed him. Arthur whipped out a knife and held it to the man's throat.

It was horrible. Arthur swore and shouted. He drew some blood. The man wet himself. Our fellow Negro came over to try to calm things down. Arthur's anger increased, and he cut the barman across the face. He then pushed him away, screaming invective even at me. His knife flashed several times across my face before he stormed out of the pub. Shocked and frightened, I chased after him.

I was fearful as I approached, but he began to laugh and told me not to worry. 'That bit at the end was all show, old man. Just so no one could say we were in it together, you know, in case there are any follow-ups with the police.'

I walked alongside him, speechless. We made our way quickly through several backstreets. I had no idea where we were going. Eventually, I found my voice. Why did all this nonsense occur? We could have gone elsewhere. We knew plenty of other pubs that were much more friendly. Damn it, the place hadn't scorned us, after all. He was the one who had started all the trouble.

Arthur told me calmly that he had gone to that pub because he had heard that it had a reputation, that it was often visited by Teddy boys. I was furious. He had no right to take me to such a place. Was he insane? He couldn't go around attacking people.

He looked at me as if I were a dim-witted child, and laid a hand on my shoulder. He told me that I had to learn to be calm; that I must face difficult moments with resolve. 'I have learned that when you come to an impasse you must speed through it.'

We stood together, under a street light on a street full of classically English middle-class housing. I looked at my friend and studied that face, with its dreadful incisions. I realized that I was talking to someone who had truly sped through an impasse far greater than any I had ever known. This was a Paul who had been trying subtly to tell me of his trip to Damascus.

He smiled at me, conscious of my new awareness. 'Good,' he said. 'Good.'

I was unsure what to do. He was full of conviction and purpose. My own confusion weakened me considerably. But there was something I had to ask.

'Arthur?'

'Yes?' That little smile had reappeared.

'I came across something the other day – I'm sure you did too. It was about your ex-girlfriend, Sharon Goldmeir, or rather about her parents.'

The smile grew.

'There was an accident.'

'An accident?' He reached out and wiped some sweat off my forehead. 'DuBois, old man, are you suffering from flu or some such? You don't look too good.'

His humour got the better of my reticence. 'Did you have anything to do with it?'

'I had everything to do with it.'

Many minutes passed without anything being said between us. At some point he just turned and walked away. Again I followed. I do not know how, but at some point we reached his home, which was several miles from where we had started. He opened his door and stopped to talk to me.

'It isn't that terrible, DuBois, not when put in the proper context.' He spoke of injustices across the globe, of cultural and religious genocide, plunder, rape and murder. 'So all in all, this really is not something to get over-excited about, is it?'

He asked me if I wanted to come in for a drink. I said no, and made my way home.

Jocelynne was sleeping when I returned. I lay down beside her and enjoyed her peace.

Gabriel passed quickly over information that fascinated and disturbed. He could return, but for now there were other matters that concerned him. The motion of the flicking paper fanned the air, but provided little other comfort. He read again from the ninth entry in December. The year was 1962.

9

Again we argue. I cannot understand her. She talks of her needs and I of mine. We share the same fears, but not, it seems, the same concerns. The doctors advised her that it would be unwise to conceive another child, but she feels enough time has passed. I can't agree. We have grieved for our child and survived her passing. I could not bear it if something happened to Jocelynne. Our lives are moving smoothly. Her theatre company is flourishing: she has a healthy mixture of sponsorship and local-government grants. The company's existence is cause enough for celebration, its financial security a minor miracle. She leads a full life. My work provides me with enormous satisfaction. We are happy together. I see no need to endanger anything. We could adopt. There are many children who would benefit from having a secure home, with loving parents. There is no need for us to be obsessed with producing children. But she insists. She insists.

10

She has not spoken to me for over a week. I am hurt. But I must be strong. I know that no good will come of it. She is obsessed with her dreams and their messages. Why will she not listen to me?

12

I came home to find a drawing. It was of a woman with no stomach. Her stomach had been scooped out. The ground about her feet was barren. It was filled with other horrendous images. I gave up. I cannot not make love to her. She will not consent to us using protection. I cannot fight. The decision is hers.

15

We spent Christmas alone. J. was happy to do so, since she believes that it will be our last Christmas alone together. I have told Rupert that he is no longer welcome in my house and that J. can meet him at his house, workplace, anywhere that excludes me. The hypocrite promised to speak for me at his church. His wife is upset with me, but has chosen to forgive me. She is a sweet creature, simple but sweet, but to be honest I will not miss her or that intolerable brood she seems intent on raising in piety and holiness.

Our light came from candles. The food was simple, but delightful. J. had bought herself some presents. They were all for an infant.

Gabriel moved on to the next year, concerned only with one thing.

22 February

Jocelynne is pregnant. She is ecstatic. Friends and cousins, many of whom form the core of her theatre company, were invited over and much drink was downed. An impromptu song-and-dance performance broke out and everyone was entertained with folk stories, poems and improvisations. It was wonderful. The caricatures of our West Indian celebrities back home were painfully accurate, but the impressions of the English, their mannerisms and accents, reduced everyone to a state of hysterics. Jocelynne is so full of life, so exuberant, that it seems inconceivable that any harm might come to her.

March

Jocelynne is showing. The swelling has brought all my old fears to the fore. I approached Penny and she told me of a doctor she knows who would perform an abortion. I waited until our evening meal and brought the subject up with Jocelynne. She surprised me with the calm with which she listened to my suggestion.

'No, no. It not fe me.'

'I just think you should consider it.'

Her eyes rolled up for a few moments. 'Deh, it done. As me seh, it not fe me.' She touched her stomach. 'Dis chile is mine. We knoh each oddah. Me woan' betray de trust it place wid me.'

'It's nothing but gelling flesh and bone. It doesn't know the meaning of trust.'

'Doan' talk so about de chile.'

'I don't want anything to happen to you.'

'Nuttin' gwine 'appen.'

'You don't know that.'

'Yu caan' seh oddahwise.'

'I fear otherwise.'

'Den doan' fear. Me mind is clear.'

June

We lay in bed last night, the warm swelling between us. I could feel the displacement of J.'s organs as she moved two fingers down from her rib cage, counting the weeks of the baby. She had been worried for she hadn't felt any movement, but last night the child moved. J. screamed and grabbed my hand. Her face was glowing with pleasure and as we felt the child do whatever it was doing, and guessed the parts of its anatomy, my heart soared with her. The life-force of our baby was there. It was undeniable.

'It move,' she said over and over again. 'It move.'

She began to weep, the tension she had been carrying pouring out of her, leaving her weak. I held her tight, mindful of the life she carried. As I held here, my own resistance broke and I wept freely with her. I kissed her enlarged breasts, I kissed her stretched skin, soft and rubbery to my lips, and listened for the child. She stroked my hair and whispered, 'Seh hello to ya son.'

I asked her how she knew it was a boy.

She rubbed her stomach. 'De chile rest diffrant. It is a bwoy.'

She couched her opinion in terms that she felt I would respect, for I know that she regularly discusses what she believes to be visitations from the child with her friends. Whatever – a boy she said, and a boy I expect.

August

A package containing letters from my family has arrived. My father has written and invited us to visit him. He speaks once again of his sadness at our previous tragedy and wishes us well for the future. He advises me about my work and has sent me a long list of pointers, as well as a number of contacts. My mother has sent me some seeds from her garden and hints that my father's health is less than she would wish. I have been hearing this from various members of the clan for several years. I have prepared myself for his death; we have said all that needs to be said between us. William has sent me a picture of his wife and their child. Meredith has sent me a beautiful letter as well as some poetry that she has asked me to pass on to J. for criticism. How gentle and honest she is – the best of us all, by far. But I want nothing to do with them. My child will have nothing to do with them. We are part of a new beginning.

Martin pushed his wheelbarrow along the cemetery path. A broom fell off and broke Gabriel's concentration. The old man stooped and picked it up, his bald patch glinting in the sun. Gabriel moved determinedly on to the heart of the matter.

20th December

Where do I begin? With the birth of the child. The child was born on the same day as its mother. November 16th.

Gabriel's cheeks burnt. For the first time, he knew when he was born. He said it out loud, 'November the sixteenth. I was born on November the sixteenth.' He was elated, almost giddy. All his life he had told himself that birthdays were silly romantic things that were highly overrated, and his own heartfelt joy embarrassed him. Still, the smile on his lips was quite obstinate, and did not pass away for some time. He read on.

We had gone to the hospital. I was allowed to stay with J. for some time and help her. A few hours later, she was taken away. I was informed that there were complications. I wasn't surprised, for I had foreseen this event for months. The doctors and nurses merely played their part in a scenario which I had run through countless times, every minute of every day. Perhaps that explains my detachment as the nightmare played out its course.

As a series of staff walked past me with their heads bowed, I was calm. I remained calm as the doctor, solemn-faced and gently spoken, asked me to accompany him to his office.

I waited in a calm vacuum of preparedness as he spoke to me of 'serious complications' and a 'life-threatening situation'. It seemed as if he was speaking in slow motion. I could not speed him up to his inevitable conclusion. As he neared the finish, I took a breath and looked deeply into his eyes before releasing the words, 'I have no choice. Save my wife.'

I waited for him to nod in acknowledgement of my choice. But he surprised me. He changed the lines of the script and said, 'I'm sorry, you didn't understand me. Your wife has given specific instructions that the baby's life is paramount.'

I must have sat there looking like a fool, for he kept on saying things I didn't understand. In truth I couldn't even hear him, for everything was obliterated by a long unbroken ringing in my ears. I remember he came round the table and placed a hand on my shoulders. He took out a piece of paper. It was true, Jocelynne had written exactly what he had told me. I realized that the paper was in fact a death warrant.

I tore it up. I screamed and shouted. He had no right to take the word of a sick, irrational woman seriously. What did he expect her to write? I forbade such a thing. I threatened to sue him, the hospital, the county, everyone. He tried to calm me down, but I was furious. How dare he present me with such nonsense? I demanded to see my wife.

He took me to see Jocelynne. She was already in a deep coma. Her face had become swollen and rubbery. Her eyelids were puffy, her lips a strange

201

purple. I could not bear it. I remember being helped out of the room and sitting on a bench in a hallway that smelled peculiar, as people in white clothing moved past me.

Someone sat with me.

Eventually the doctor emerged again. My back hurt. It was as if a dozen knives had been planted along my spine. I had never felt more tired. I am sure that the person who sat alongside me was propping my frame up. I had no strength. Everything had left me.

The doctor told me things.

I had a child. A son.

He was born with some sort of sack, a 'transparent veil', over his face.

He told me that Jocelynne had passed away.

My darling wife joined our sweet child on November 29th. They lay together in peace.

The journal fell from Gabriel's hands as he covered his face. He was unable to face the world and the truth that lay beneath him for quite some time. When he read again it was with eyes that found it difficult to accept the brightness of the sky and the greenness of the grass that rose about him.

4

I have tried to join my loves several times.

On the first occasion, the tablets and the alcohol sickened me and caused much pain, but I recovered. The rat poison was nearly successful, but Penny and her new husband broke down my door and took me to hospital. The police and the social services have warned me that I might lose the thing if I carry on like this. The thought does not worry me. Penny speechifies: I must be strong for the child, Jocelynne would have wanted me to carry on, blah, blah, blah.

Why should I carry on? I have nothing left. Why should I raise the creature that murdered its own mother and strangled my life? I have been told constantly that it looks like its mother, but that fact brings me only pain. How can this thing succour me? How can it love me? How can it make me smile? It has no thoughts. It only sleeps, cries, urinates and defecates, and then begins the whole cycle over again.

I do not understand this. Cuffay was in my life for only a flickering instant, but brought me immeasurable joy. This thing has been in my life for even less time, but has created untold destruction. How is it possible that two children can be born from the same parents, and yet one be filled with goodness and hope, the other with evil and despair?

It is best I give this thing away, for I cannot promise that it is safe with me. I look upon it and am filled with revulsion and horror. I loathe it. Every breath it draws is an affront to my sense of justice and fairness. Every movement is a slap in my face.

Gabriel decided that he had had enough for the time being and, after collecting himself, walked away.

Evening had fallen and the intensity of the heat had faded as he walked out of the cemetery. A coach filled with policemen was parked outside, and every head turned and watched him as he passed by. He ignored them, but the intensity of their aggression made itself felt along his back. The car was still warm, so he opened the door and waited outside it for a few minutes until he was prepared to face the escaping heat. As he got in, he could see in his rear-view mirror an officer studying his car as he spoke into a shoulder mike. Gabriel pulled away very slowly, hoping to cause as much irritation as possible.

Gabriel was stopped by the police twice on his journey to and through Brixton. Each time he was warned about his driving before being allowed to carry on. As he parked outside the youth centre, Rachel, carrying a six-pack, bounced over to him. An impressive and extremely mixed gathering had formed. Several fires burnt in open metal bins. Crates had been turned over for seating. Empty beer bottles and bent bottle-tops lay on the ground. The aroma of marijuana was strong and musty. Sonia called out his name and offered him a beer. Sonia's hair was in long braids, each strung with red, blue and green beads. She was dressed in black. 'Here,' she said, holding a petition out to him, 'sign this.' The petition demanded a full investigation into her brother's death. Gabriel signed it. 'I'm glad you came, Gabriel,' she said with a note of familiarity that disturbed him. 'Rachel said you weren't very political and like to keep to yourself.'

Rachel punched her on the shoulder. 'I said no such thing.'

Sonia laughed her way into Edwin's arms.

'Isn't it sweet,' said Rachel, 'the two of them getting it together. He'll be good for her – he's got a good head and a good heart.' She paused, indicating the apparently downcast figure of Jeffrey, next to an animated Guptah. 'Be careful what you say. He's a bit upset with Rowena.'

Guptah was in full flow as they drew near. 'St Paul's is what it was all about,' he said. 'The pigs rushed into that café. They started shit and they got shit. The people retaliated and defended themselves.' He paused briefly to flash a smile at Rachel and Gabriel before carrying on. Jeffrey was clearly surprised to see Gabriel and wasn't sure whether to glare at him or not.

'You know, over twenty of those fuckers got fucked up. It was the first time we showed them that we're not like our parents – that we're not content to bow and scrape and offer another chapatti. We need more of it, I tell you.

'I remember the days when I used to shit myself if I saw a skinhead. When the Anti-Nazi League suggested we actually take over their place, I shat myself.'

Jeffrey's laughter was like a town crier's bell, splitting the night. Guptah laughed with him, his eyes filled with a bright nostalgia.

'Man, there was this pub – fucked if I can remember the name – when we walked in, you should have seen their faces. I couldn't believe it, the way they looked at us, like we were the maddest Pakis they'd ever seen. There was this white guy who was with us, Robert Maddox was his name.'

'I've heard of him – mad Robbie.'

'That's it, mad fucking Robbie.'

'Was he as mad as they say?'

'Mad? This whitey was insane. He wasn't anything. He was the skinniest bastard you've ever seen. A maths teacher or something.'

'That's right.'

'But put a Nazi insignia up before him, let him see a fascist salute and fuck me, the guy would pull out his red cape and kick arse!'

'I hear he was unstoppable.'

'Unstoppable? I've seen that guy destroy bars. One day, these fuckers – real steroid Hitler junkies with biceps coming out of their ears – took him on. He fucked them over like nothing I've ever seen. Bang went the bar. Bang went the windows. He destroyed the place. You know what? When we were all getting out of there, someone found part of his finger stuck on some broken glass.'

'No!'

'Yes, man, it had come off. He hadn't felt a thing. We needed guys like him. The police used to arrest so many of us.'

'Typical.'

'Yeah. But they were great times.'

'Great days, man.'

'Great fucking days. When those bastards stopped handing out their shit magazines, well, that was –'

'That was a day.'

'It was indeed. We stopped being Pakis that day, we stood our ground and marked out our territory.'

Rachel broke in, 'Guptah, don't you ever tire of talking about politics?'

'What else is there to talk about?'

'I don't know, what do normal boys talk about? Sport, women.'

'Women are my sport.'

'Yeah, yeah.'

Guptah kissed Rachel's hand. 'That's no way to talk to a brother.'

Rachel pushed him away.

He winked at Gabriel. 'And you, aren't we brothers?'

Rachel offered Guptah another beer. 'How many of these have you had?'

'Not enough, my sister, not enough.'

'I'm glad you've come round to all this sister shit, but next time I come with you to Brick Lane, you'd better tell it to your people.'

'Ah, fuck it, they just weren't used to seeing me with a black chick, that's all.'

'What are you two talking about?' asked Jeffrey.

'I went with Guptah a few weeks back to get a leather jacket from his uncle's shop in Brick Lane.'

'Oh, the sweat shops.'

'My uncle does not work in a sweat shop.'

'Whatever.'

'What do you mean, whatever?'

Jeffrey held up his hands. 'I've seen the pictures, my friend.'

'What pictures?'

'They had it on *Nationwide* the other night.'

'That was crap. They like to put on that sort of shit because it makes us look bad. They can't work as hard as us, so they make a mockery of how we work.'

'The camera doesn't lie. Rowena showed me −'

Guptah exploded. 'Rowena! Rowena! I don't want to hear about Rowena! All she does is cause trouble.'

'That's not true.'

'Isn't it?' snorted Guptah derisively. 'All she does is complain about this and that. I've never heard her say one good thing about her people, not one good thing. It's all wife-beaters, poor pay, enforced marriages, shitty work practices, it never stops. Sometimes, I tell you, I think she's being paid by the National Front. I'm not here to defend my people, but I can't jump up and down every time they do something wrong. If you want that, go to Golders fucking Green.'

Rachel and Jeffrey pointed their fingers at him and shouted in unison, 'Racist!'

'Oops!' screeched Guptah, covering his mouth and slapping his wrist before taking some change out of his pocket. 'Where's the sin bin?'

Jeffrey pulled open his back pocket. Guptah, chanting, 'I'm so sorry, I'm so sorry,' dropped in the money.

'Thou shall not speak a racist word,' intoned Rachel.

'I shall not speak a racist word, even though every word of it be fucking true.'

'Thou shall not,' she snapped, kicking him in the shin.

'You're right, oh goodly one, you're right. Even though they have screwed my uncle for years with the rent, even though they have tried to fuck dozens of my family over in business −'

Jeffrey began to laugh heartily.

'Even though they kept the best houses for themselves, and charged us a fortune for the others.'

Rachel opened a can. 'Really, Guptah, sometimes you can be quite disgusting.'

'I can, I can, I can!' yelled Guptah, pumping the air with his fist. 'I love it!'

'What?' sneered Rachel. 'Talking like a pig?'

'Yes,' he shouted triumphantly. 'Yes, I love talking like my arse is tattooed with fuck-you tattoos and Nazi flags.'

Jeffrey was doubling over with laughter. Guptah punched him on the shoulder. 'I love looking at you and calling you a black bastard every time you piss me off. I love it, it's', he leaped into the air, 'so fucking liberaaaaating!'

Rachel was completely dumbstruck.

Guptah started to laugh so hard he could barely speak. 'Sometimes I think if I spend another evening with Rowena and a bunch of spastics at those fucking right-on meetings of hers –'

Jeffrey shook his finger at him. 'Now, now, you know we can't say "spastics" any more.'

Guptah's hands popped on to his hips and his lips pursed. 'Oh, I'm sorry. I haven't seen the latest booklet from our department head.'

Guptah and Jeffrey shot out a quick-fire burst of Nazi salutes and chanted, 'GLC! GLC!'

Rachel's nails bit into Gabriel's hand. 'Never mind the fact that your own organization runs on GLC money. Never mind that you spend half your time putting up posters slagging off people who talk about Pakistanis the way you've –'

'Oh, for God's sake,' moaned Jeffrey with a pained expression on his face, 'lighten up, will you?'

'No, I will not. I don't find this kind of sick racist talk funny.'

Guptah gulped down some beer. 'I'm black, darlin', in case you hadn't noticed. I can't be racist.'

'Sometimes I don't know how Rowena puts up with you.'

Jeffrey and Guptah exchanged looks.

'What?' asked Rachel.

'Nothing, nothing,' said her cousin.

Rachel looked about the street. 'Anyway, where is she? I would have thought she'd be here.'

'She's doing her thing,' said Guptah, finishing off his can, 'I suppose.'

Rachel began to pull Gabriel away. 'Suddenly I find you two very, very boring.'

Jeffrey followed them. 'Gabriel, I wanted to talk to you.'

Rachel faced him off. 'About what?'

'You know about what.'

'Well, what have you got to say?'

Jeffrey held up his hands. 'Hey, hey, hold it. I'm not here for any more trouble. Whatever went on between you and Peter is between you and Peter. Between the three of us, I'm glad he got a kicking, he had it coming.'

'All right then.'

'But you know that what he wanted was the right thing. My mother would like to see you, so would my father. Everyone would like to see you. What's your problem?'

Rachel squeezed Gabriel's hand. 'Well?'

Gabriel held Jeffrey's gaze. 'I have no problem. I'll see your parents tomorrow morning.'

'OK, that's more like it.'

As they walked towards Sonia and Edwin, a woman shouted from a passing car, 'Get a job, you lazy bastards!' As one, the protesting group gave the woman abuse. Honking her car, her face screwed up with rage, she drove on. One of the protestors, a white Rastafarian wearing a fake-fur coat and Dr Martens boots, picked up a bottle and threw it down the empty street. Edwin called out to him, 'Hey, enough! None of that!'

'She deserved it.'

Edwin pulled away from Sonia, who held on, her eyes to the ground. 'I said none of that. That's not what this is about. If you can't maintain your discipline, then go.'

The boy smiled and rejoined his friends who all made black-power salutes at Edwin. Sonia welcomed him back into her arms. 'Did yu see dat? De bwoy caan' speak de lingo, but he suah knoh how to act like a black man.'

Two police officers came round the corner.

'I don't believe it,' said Edwin. 'They've been walking round here all day like flies on shit.'

The police officers walked slowly towards the group and stopped in front of the youth centre. Sonia walked over to them and held out her petition. 'This is in protest against the unlawful killing of my brother. There's another one trying to stop this place being closed down. Would you like to sign them?'

The older of the two men replied, 'No, I won't sign your one.'

Sonia's temper flashed to the surface. 'Then why are you here?'

'But I will sign the other one.'

'What?'

'I said I'll sign the other one.'

Sonia went and snatched the other petition from Edwin, before thrusting it towards him, determined to call his bluff. He took it calmly and wrote his name upon it, before offering it to his companion. The offer was turned down by the flustered junior officer. Sonia watched the two men carry on their way before returning to her friends. 'Would you believe it?'

Everyone studied the signature.

Edwin watched the officers disappear down the street. 'He's got some balls, eh?'

Sonia scored a line through his name with her biro. 'He's got nothing I want. Every one of those bastards should burn.'

Gabriel drove along Brixton High Street as Rachel glared at the various groups of police officers they passed. 'Look at them. They must have bused them in from everywhere. What the fuck do they think they're doing? I wish I had a gun – I'd shoot the lot of them.'

As they passed the local independent cinema she came alive. 'Hey, why don't we go to the pictures?'

Gabriel said something about her being too conventional and she slumped into her seat as if she had been slapped. As he turned on to Acre Lane she began to cry.

He apologized.

She dismissed him.

'No. I truly apologize, there was no call for what I said.'

'It's not you. You can't help being a shit – I expect it.'

'What has upset you, then?'

The car came to a halt outside her house. Across the road, a blues was winding down. Couples emerged and drove away, playing their own mixes in their cars. A heavy-set man wearing flowing clothes sat on the doorstep, eating curried mutton and rice off a plastic plate. He called out to Rachel, 'Come ovah an' talk to ya Uncle Winston.' She placed both hands against one side of her face and closed her eyes. Winston grinned and wished her well.

Gabriel accompanied her to the door, where she told him dryly, 'It's OK, go on home.'

'I asked you what was wrong.'

'Why?'

'Why what?'

'Why do you ask me what's wrong? Do you ask me because you care, or because you just like having answers?'

'I asked because you're upset and I'd like to know why.'

She opened the door. 'So that you can do what?'

He stared at her and then at the ground.

'I thought so,' she said, and strode into the house, closing the door with hardly a sound. Gabriel went back to the car and began to pull away. Then he stopped and reversed. He sat in the car for a few minutes, then picked up the journal, went back to her door and buzzed her flat. She didn't answer. He buzzed again. Still no answer. He buzzed again. The intercom clicked on and filled with her irritation. 'Hello, who is it?'

'It's me.'

A long pause. 'What do you want?'

He cleared his throat. 'I thought that I might –' He lost his voice.

'Speak up, I can't hear you.'

'I thought, considering that you were upset –'

'I was upset; now I'm sleepy.'

'Oh. In that case I won't keep you up.'

'Why did you come back?'

He took a deep breath. 'I thought that I would come and keep you company – that I might be of some assistance.'

The intercom broke up her cackle, but its essential mocking thrust remained. He turned and swore under his breath as the door lock buzzed open and the intercom shut off. As he made his way up the stairs, Rachel appeared with skin cream all over her face. She hugged and thanked him.

'You don't have to thank me.'

She pulled him into her apartment.

Marvin, his blue fur recently combed, lay on the hall floor.

'Look who's waited up for you.'

Gabriel picked the monkey up and stroked his ear.

'Look who's come to see you, it's your Uncle Gabriel.'

That was too much for him; she caught his discomfort and cradled the toy herself. She bounced on to her bed and asked, 'Are you staying the night?'

'If you don't mind.'

'Why would I mind?'

'I've been thinking about our journey.'

'And?'

'It occurred to me that I was less than understanding.'

She turned over and began to stretch. 'My back hurts.'

He sat down beside her and began gently to massage her back.

'That's nice. Where did you learn that?'

'My father sent me on a course.'

'A course?'

'He had a bad back. Stress.'

She smiled into the mattress. 'He sounds like quite a guy.'

'You might say that. Have you got any oil?'

'No, do you need some?'

'It helps.'

She turned over and held his hands. 'Do you always have to do everything right?'

'I, I –'

Laughing, she rose up and kissed his hands. 'That's it – at last, you haven't got an answer.'

Her arms snaked around him and she smothered his face with kisses. 'Isn't it nice?'

'Not to have an answer?'

'Yes.'

'No.'

Tears started to form in her eyes. 'I cry too easily. It's my weakness.'

He rubbed her tears away between his forefinger and thumb, unsure of what to do as she rolled over towards the wall and talked to her silhouette. 'I can't help it, things get to me. They've always got to me. That's why I was the class fool, because anyone could make me cry. I cried when other people got bullied, I cried when people failed exams or didn't make the swimming team. I've always been a fool.'

The shadows on her body moved with her breathing, and Gabriel noted the different skin tones along her arms, and the stretch marks on her lips. Her thigh muscles seemed to go on for ever, the slightest movement stirring muscle definition.

'I cried when I saw *Bambi*. I cried the first time I made love and every time I see kids starving in Africa on the telly. When Tom got killed in *Rich Man, Poor Man*, I wept buckets. I couldn't believe that Falcon Eddie was going to get away with it. When Guptah was talking like that, I could have cracked up there and then.'

A few of her dreadlocks had begun to bond. Gabriel gently pulled them apart before running his fingers through her strands.

'I hate hate, you know. Hearing it from someone like him, even jokingly, hurts. When I hear those words, they hurt my brain. Maybe if I had answers, if I could stop all the shit, I wouldn't be a running joke for everybody.'

He slipped his arms around her and held her tight, saying nothing as she wept and sniffed and cursed herself until she was done. 'God, I'm tired. It's so tiring. My eyes will look like shit tomorrow.' She slipped a leg between his. 'Do you like me?'

'Do I like you?'

'Yes. I know you want to fuck me and all that, but do you like me?'

He breathed her scent in. 'I haven't met anyone like you.'

'That's for sure, but that doesn't answer my question.'

'Yes, I like you. I think you're the most wonderful person I've ever met.'

A few minutes passed before she said, 'You're a recluse. You hardly know anyone.'

'That's not true.'

She turned over, her eyes glaring. 'It is true. How can you say what you've just said? It doesn't mean anything, it's just words. You haven't travelled, you don't go to clubs, you don't mix, so it can't mean anything, can it?'

He went to hold her hand. She whipped it away. 'I don't like to be lied to.'

As he laid his head on the pillow she said, 'Beds shouldn't be resting places for lies. I don't want anyone here who makes this a coffin for the truth.'

He took a few seconds to collect his thoughts. 'I've read a lot. I've met many people through my reading.'

'Words! There you go again with words!'

His own anger began to match hers. 'Why do you place such little faith in words?'

'Because that's all they are!'

'Nonsense!'

'I'm a dancer, I should know.'

'You're being ridiculous.'

She jabbed a finger into his chest. 'Don't talk to me in that tone. I will not allow you to speak to me like that.'

'Can I tell you something?'

She crossed her arms over her chest.

'You say I haven't travelled, that I don't know the world.'

'That's for sure.'

'But I have travelled.'

'Where? When? You live like a fucking hermit! You don't know anything about people. It's all just books, books!'

'Books that have shown me the lives and cultures of peoples from the ancient world. I know the France of Sartre and Genet, Calvino's Italy. I've never been to America, but the likes of Mark Twain, Alice Walker, Richard Wright and Chester Himes must have given me a fair road map.'

'So?'

'I've read about the lives and adventures of incredible characters like Bilbo Baggins, Paul Arrikis, Ulysses, Captain Ahab, Norrin Rad, Nancy spider –'

'Nancy spider?'

'Hobgoblins, werewolves, unicorns, elves, vampires and shape shifters. But for all that, you are by some distance the most wonderful person I've ever met. When I'm with you, I don't even think of picking up a book.'

She performed an exaggerated gulp and fluttered her eyelashes. 'My, my, my. To think I was complaining about the way you talk.' She lay down and wrapped herself about him. 'I order you never to say anything to me again, not unless you can top that.'

Her kisses were soft and easy and sleep came quickly to her. When he was sure that she wouldn't awake, Gabriel opened the journal.

29th December

Arthur has taken it for a week or so, to give me a break. He has decided that he is its godfather, though I have not encouraged him. For all I care, he can keep it.

I have packed all of Jocelynne's belongings away. I don't want anything to break. When I am ready, I will review our things.

Gabriel moved on to the first entry of 1964.

1

Jocelynne was a dreamer. She saw the best in people. How, I wonder, would she view the people of this country, whose shrillness increases the more our profile rises?

I wish that the electoral system of this country would promote the wise and the good instead of promoting careerist scum who seek to pay their mortgages by inciting fear and hatred. Conservative MPs, desperate to achieve election victory, are constantly waging battle, with little concern for the long-term effects of their short-term career gains.

The Conservative candidate for Smethwick, Peter Griffiths, has been shameless in seeking to harness the racists to his desperate tail. His favourite slogan is, 'If you want a nigger neighbour vote Labour.' Opinion poles indicate that although the general public tide is against the Conservatives, in Smethwick they will achieve victory. So, the die is cast. If you are facing defeat, if you have failed to deliver on tax and unemployment cuts, just promise to end immigration and get rid of 'the coloureds' and all will be well.

4

Some words do have consequences. I do not know what J. ever really achieved through her work. She made people smile, she made people think. Perhaps that is enough. But the world never stopped and took notice. No one ever walked to a stranger's house and became a good neighbour as a result. Hateful words seem to have power. In the aftermath of Smethwick a Jamaican has been shot dead. A black schoolboy has been almost beaten to death by a white gang. Black people across London are experiencing intimidation and violence.

What would she say?

I don't believe I see things clearly. The days bring pain and more pain. I read awful things. I go to sites and take photographs, I wrote down people's complaints and tales of woe. How many landlords abuse? How many shops overcharge? How many schools turn away? Different stories with all-too similar narratives.

7

The work continues. A Conservative MP has written to the Home Secretary asking that all immigrants who have been unemployed for more than six months should be deported. We shall see where this goes. I gather organizations such as the Smethwick Indian Workers Association are considering throwing their weight behind Labour candidates who appear to be favourable to the needs of immigrants. I have my doubts. The Labour Party is the lap dog of the unions and the unions will inevitably see immigrant labour as a threat. Where will these supporters of Labour go, when their masters start to complain about black competition?

9

An interesting meeting with the Indian Peoples Association in Coventry.

They were marking the hanging of Ujjagar Singh, who had founded the first Indian Workers Association in Coventry. Singh, noted for his kindness and hard work, had become something of a martyr in 1940 when he assassinated Sir Michael O'Dwyer, who, in 1919, as Lieutenant Governor of the Punjab, had approved the action of British General R. E. H. Dyer in massacring hundreds of Indians in Amritsar, Punjab.

I admired their sense of history and sense of their own place within their community. Many of them were vociferous about their disapproval of the caste system and their plans to opt out of it by adopting other faiths. I wondered about the battles we brought with us to this country – how we would resolve ancient questions and old wars within the religious and constitutional framework of Mother Britain.

The most population's perception of us is extremely narrow. How little they know of our concerns. How difficult true dialogue continues to be. For in truth, I know so little of those with whom I formed strategic unions, against those who saw us all as a single threat.

11

New organizations are springing up every week. The events in America seemed to have catalysed us. People want to seize the day. Even the space race inspires. If the Americans can attempt to conquer space, then surely we can capture our own little plot down here. I am tiring, though. The work excites, but I need to do something else. A holiday, perhaps.

What is the point of all of these endless meetings? I fight for a world that will take shape without my beloved. Her child lives and breathes, and prepares for a future that it robbed from its mother. There is no justice in the world.

12

Arthur brought the child round. He says it is time for me to take on the demands of parenthood. We sat and talked. The child lay on some blankets between us. It has a strong resemblance to Jocelynne, stronger even than its sister's. Arthur talked of his plans. It has been months since he quit the Institute and I have no idea of how he passes the days.

The subject of the Goldmeirs came up, I do not know how. I told him that his behaviour had disturbed me and that he had acted wrongly.

He asked me why I hadn't reported him to the police.

I told him not to be silly.

He was adamant: if he had offended my sense of morality, then it was my duty to report him.

I told him that such a thing was impossible.

He wanted to know why.

'You're my friend.'

'I'm grateful for that,' he replied, 'but is that it?'

'It's enough.'

He thanked me, but said he was curious about something. If my sense of friendship was so well developed, and went beyond any sense of civic responsibility, why was it that my sense of fatherhood was so underdeveloped? He picked the child up and told me that he had named it Gabriel.

I told him that he had no power to do such a thing.

He was dismissive. 'A father should always name his child.'

'You are not the father.'

'Oh, really? You gave him to me for a week and it's been almost two months. I have fed and washed him.'

I shouted something at him, told him he was a fool.

He hugged and kissed the child. 'So, I feel like his father. I've come to ask you for him.'

I was outraged and went to take the child from him. He resisted, told me that fatherhood wasn't something I could pick up and drop. We engaged in a rather unseemly bout of tug-of-war, but eventually I snatched the child from him and ordered him to stop his nonsense.

He told me that pride was no reason for claiming a child.

Pride, I said, had nothing to do with it.

He wanted to know what had. As far as he was concerned, the child did not know me, my touch or my smell. I was a stranger to it.

I yelled, 'I am its father!'

He laughed at me.

I was incensed. I spoke to him as I have never spoken to another human being.

When my venom was done he held up his hands and said, 'I suppose, if you feel like that, then you must be the father.'

His manoeuvring became clear to me. I allowed my revaluation to settle, and to my horror found myself beginning to weep. Thankfully, he felt the need to leave the room and was away for some time as I wept with my son.

Later on, the child asleep, we talked. The conversation turned to fatherhood. He made it clear that he had enjoyed his time with Gabriel and the experience had convinced him that even if he married and had children of his own, he would also like to adopt. He was in no doubt that the country was filled with 'incompetent' parents, and children who could do with the 'love and guidance' that he possessed in abundance. He spoke of the need to travel, to get out of England and see other places. He was even considering going home for a few months.

I asked if anyone would be accompanying him.

'No one who interests me romantically.'

We were silent for a time. Once again we had returned to that topic.

I asked him how Sharon was doing since the tragedy of her parents.

He seemed uninterested. 'She has been having problems of her own.'

'Problems?'

'Yes. It seems the poor girl has been suffering from a series of accidents.'

A hammer started knocking on my heart. 'Accidents?'

'It seems she's suffered a run of misfortune . . .'

'And?'

'And I'm not exactly unhappy about it.'

'I see. Did you have anything to do with these "accidents"?'

'In what sense?'

'Were you responsible for any of them?'

'Yes.'

There it was. Such a little word, pronounced in a tiny breath, but it brought so much.

I asked him what he had been responsible for.

His lips pursed. 'Oh, the odd thing. Letters to her bank. Leaked medical details. A wrecked car.' He smiled. It was the smile of a child dipping his fingers into a jar of honey. 'It seems the poor thing was attacked on her way home.'

I couldn't look at him.

'It was quite a vicious attack. It made the papers. Didn't you come across it?'

I shook my head.

'Of course not. How silly of me. I apologize. You've had other concerns.'

Eventually I found my voice. 'How vicious?'

'Pretty vicious.'

'How is she?'

'I haven't seen her. You understand that I am not welcome in her family, so any attempt at seeing her would have been futile, but I've kept up with the reports and asked people at the hospital in my own little way.'

'And?'

He sighed that weary sigh of his and feigned mock concern. 'Let us just say that even her sizeable inheritance may not be enough to tempt a suitor to her door any more.'

I was disgusted and told him so.

'Oh,' he said in that damnably pious way of his, 'I see. I am no longer a gentleman.'

I told him that he never had been.

'You're quite right,' he said. 'I suppose that's always been the trouble. Underneath all this wonderful refinement I'm just an animal.'

I told him not to play games with me. He would not advance his cause by conforming to an antiquated Shakespearean model of the Noble Savage, no matter how appealing he found it to be. I was sure that that was the role in which he seduced most of his conquests. They delighted in his manners and smooth ways, but loved it when he let rip with a little 'African' temperament.

He clapped his hands and laughed uproariously. 'Oh, DuBois, I do so love it when you let your claws show. But for your obvious qualities of gender and breeding, I might even call you a fine old cow.' This amused him even further and he was almost dancing with glee. 'That's it, a right cow.' He was quite incoherent with the hysterical power of his laughter. 'Oh, don't you just love them?'

He mimicked a cockney accent. 'Cow! Slag! Cunt!' The swine was slapping his thighs with laughter and to my shame and disbelief, I found myself laughing with him as he pointed a finger at me and screamed. 'Oi, you slag, come over 'ere! Wot now, me old cow? Aw now lovey, shut ya trap and pass me the bacon!' His thumbs slipped behind his belt and he bent his knees. 'Evening all!'

Laughing like an asthmatic hyena I begged him to stop.

'Oh, I say, what a marvellous drop-shot . . . Mind the gap . . . Darling, would you like to fuck before or after we take tea? And please can I do it on top this time? Mummy says I'll never sit upright on the horseys if you keep shagging my rump off.'

I implored him to stop. Eventually he did. Exhausted and on the verge of tears, I asked, 'What are we going to do?'

He told me there was nothing to do.

'You can't go on like this.'

He asked me sweetly, 'Why not?'

'Because you can't. It isn't right.'

'If I understand you correctly, you are saying I cannot go on because of some moral imperative.' He patted me gently on the knee. 'DuBois, I like you, you know that, and if the truth be known, I admire you. You are a decent man. For all that has happened to you, you carry a spark of innocence around with you.

'I haven't known innocence for a long time. I've feigned it, I've reached for it, I've tried to fuck it, but I haven't touched it for many years. I understand – because of my own lack of, let us say, moral fibre – that there is no true morality in the world. There is only the morality of power.

'When I was attacked, I tried to defend myself, but there were too many of them. At first they were swift and brutal. But eventually they slowed down and indulged themselves. It is a horrible moment, DuBois, when a man beats you and you realize that there is nothing to stop him but himself; that you are completely and utterly in his power.'

I looked at his face – the scars, the broken nose, the torn eyelid – as if for the first time.

'But there is a clarity within the horror. A man comes to understand that the jousts of courtship and intellect are empty and meaningless: any man of physical power can take it all away. It's a good lesson. One I've been playing half-heartedly during my little pub brawls and all that.'

I told him that he wasn't involved in a game.

He was insistent that it was a game like everything else. I was to think of the West Indian cricket experience. Had not the national team laboured for years against England, until, eventually, the sporting lessons were absorbed and returned with interest?

I told him to stop his nonsense. His life was real, not a twisted metaphor for flannels and wet lawns.

'If you say so,' he said. 'I only used it because I hoped it would be instructive.'

I asked about the lessons Sharon was supposed to have learnt.

He didn't seem to care. She was silly and shallow.

'Why were you dating her, then?'

'Because she appealed to me.'

'What was it in her that appealed to you?'

'Her innocence,' he said. 'I thought she was innocent. I looked in her eyes and she seemed free of everything that I saw in her kind. I couldn't understand how a white person could grow up in this country, in these times, and have eyes so completely free of hate. I believed that if such a person could love me, then everything might be possible. That I might be worthy.'

'Worthy of what?'

'Something bigger than me, bigger than everything. When she betrayed me, I fell from grace. I was humiliated, destroyed. I followed her once. She was dining with a white guy. I could see what he was. He had nothing: no sensibility, no awareness of the world. He was conservative, blue-eyed and utterly boring. It was as though I had meant nothing to her. I couldn't understand how she could fuck the living antithesis of me.

'We had talked of everything, you see – my past, where I grew up, everything. I'd talked to her of what it was like to be a black man. I had shown her what it was to be me!

'She was a sensitive person. She talked to me of what it was like to be Jewish, to be, if you like, a "white nigger".' He chuckled an empty, sand-blasted chuckle. 'She spoke of the discrimination and despair she'd experienced and how she could understand what I was going through. She once said to me that she'd had dreams since she was a child of being raped by some blue-eyed blond aristocrat. She'd felt as though she had been raised to be a nice Jewish girl who would be acceptable to her father's gentile friends. She had to be as good as their daughters. The ultimate accolade would be if some rich WASP asked for her hand.

'One day, she made a point at a lecture she attended, to which the lecturer said, he wasn't Jewish enough to make such a comment. She was crushed. She came to me and wept in my arms, like a wounded animal, promising to kill herself.'

He stopped for a moment and collected himself. 'She was extremely sensitive. I saw it when we met. I was drawn to it. There's something phenomenally attractive about brittle women, don't you find? It wasn't the first time she'd spoken of suicide. She had a thing about it.'

He had begun to cry. 'Forgive me,' he said, wiping the tears away. 'I'm rambling, I know.'

I told him to go on.

'I suppose I liked this inner fragility; it made her seem even more special. After the lecture, it seemed what I was – my vitality, my sense of right and wrong – enabled her to carry on. It came from my blackness, you see. It was this part of me that refuted this lecturer's claims and embraced her. I wrapped her in it. I warmed and protected her with it.

'The more we were together, the more she changed. She revelled in that intrinsic buoyant alienation that our people carry with them. She walked taller because of something essential and unique to me, which I had never given to anyone else, DuBois – my soul.

'When it ended I could barely understand, but I could have forgiven. Yes, I was damaged. She had taken an essential part of my being and I couldn't get it back. I tried, I tried so hard, but I couldn't. My soul would not return, even though I needed it for sustenance.

'If she had gone out with someone remotely like me, I might have understood it. So he was white, but he could have been politically aware, he might have had black friends, something! But to be so utterly devoid of any of my characteristics, any of my – The whole matter was beyond my understanding.'

His eyes widened with exasperation.

'If you could have seen him, DuBois, you would have wept for me. He was, I suspect, the whitest man ever to walk the planet. He had no sensuality in him, no dance, no song, nothing! She admitted to me once that he was no good in bed, that he might as well have masturbated when he was with her. Can you imagine?! How could she stay with a man who couldn't even pleasure her? Why did she stay?'

He looked me straight in the eye. 'Why? This question vexed and haunted me. I concentrated on it with a power that I have never had before, and doubtless will never have again. Then one day, like sun breaking through cloud, the truth came to me.'

He paused dramatically before continuing. 'I realized, DuBois, that she was a charlatan. For all her looks, inside, where it truly mattered, she was spiritually malformed. For all her bravado, she was a coward.

'I walked in this blackness because I had no choice. But she, for all her professed Jewishness, could walk amongst white people at will. If she didn't protest when they made their vile jokes about Jewish religious habits, if she kept quiet when they denied the Holocaust, she could claim this whiteness and its hierarchy for her own.

'If, eventually, she had shown some fire, some passion, I could have forgiven her. If she had looked into the eye of her seducer and said, "Arthur is worth more than you," I would have rejoiced. But she didn't. She had found her master and rejoiced in her enslavement.

'No fist, no blow has ever hurt me the way that creature hurt me. I can never forgive her betrayal. She humiliated my race and she spat in the face of every Jewish woman who ever looked the enemy in the eye and said "Fuck you".

'Did her mother escape extermination, just so she could fuck someone who will never let her celebrate one day that is of any significance to her true people? I would have observed every ritual, everything, just to wake up to her each morning. But I was shit to her. And whatever I do, I will never get her smell off me, or recover the piece of me that she took. My spirit will always wander the earth, incomplete and crippled.'

I was sorry for him.

He had no interest in my pity. Things were exactly the way they were meant to be.

I had no idea he was so fatalistic.

He looked at me in that particular way of his that signalled the delivery of a spectacularly pithy statement. 'I understand fate, DeBois,' he said. 'When a man accepts the overwhelming power of destiny, he is becalmed. This knowledge has helped me enormously. Perhaps it will help you.'

I asked him about Sharon.

'What about her?'

'Does she share this same opaque determinism?'

He thought about this for a time before replying, 'I imagine, with a face like hers, the answer must be yes.'

He left shortly after that.

I sat in the darkening apartment. Arthur had been my only source of stability and radiance. Now I was alone. Chaos clamoured outside my window. I had only to open it and inhale the thickening halitosis of the world, to decide I wanted no part of it.

A police siren wailed outside the room.

Gabriel, glad of the distraction, left the journal.

Two police cars had pulled up outside. Winston threw down his plate in disgust and walked into his house, slamming the door behind him. The police rang his bell repeatedly. Finally the door opened and Winston came storming out, swinging a pickaxe. The police scattered as the axe smashed into their cars. Winston didn't stop until he was surrounded by destruction. Sweating with anger, panting with hate, he charged back into his home. The stunned officers tried to collect themselves. Screams filled the street as the remaining party-goers came rushing out. Winston hurled abuse from the window, threatening to kill anyone who entered his home uninvited, then disappeared inside. The police called for reinforcements. More police cars arrived. Two of the officers had guns.

It was the first time Gabriel had ever seen firearms.

A wait-and-see strategy developed, as the police installed themselves outside the house. Gabriel returned to the journal.

February 1964

A most interesting day.

Weary of looking at the clothes we had bought for Cuffay, I decided to put them to immediate use. The boy looked quite fetching in them. Since my helpers, Gladwin, Penny and Mrs Grimestone were not around to kick up a fuss, I took him for a ride in his pram.

Women, strangers all of them, stopped me and told me how beautiful my baby was. It was quite startling. My mind runs over and over the moment I first answered 'What is her name?' with, 'Cuffay, her name is Cuffay.' Most of them seemed to think Cuffay was an unusual, but lovely name. How my heart beat when I was told how sweet she was, what lovely eyes she had. It was quite thrilling.

I walked with pride today.

I took her into supermarkets, clothing shops, toy shops, and on and on. I drew tremendous satisfaction from picking out a baby dress for her from Marks and Spencer. I returned grinning as I rarely have before. How great was my fall when I undressed her and found his penis between his legs. It shattered everything. I left him there. His screams meant nothing to me. I will not rush to him every time he wails.

The boy is like a puppy and all puppies can be trained. I will not be his servant. He has controlled my life enough; I will reclaim it. He can cry all he likes. In truth, the thought that he is unhappy is almost satisfying. It is good that he experiences pain. I see no reason why he should be spared that which has destroyed me.

3

Today the dam broke and the waves of despair that always lurk, like hungry crows, at the back of my mind washed over me. I was unable to do anything but sit in the shadows.

Gladwin came to see me and would not go away. Eventually I allowed her in.

She is studying English literature at college in the evenings, but her interest is in Afro-Caribbean/American writing. A passion that she is kind enough to thank my dear wife for. She was sympathetic to my mood, but urged me to get on with my life and my work. I was not to allow my mind to dwell on its unique torture, I must shut out everything and work, work, work. I tired of her entreaties, but she went on, sat me down and began to read from some of her books of poetry.

She was moved by the poems. 'I love the words. You know that I've always been ignorant and slow.'

I told her this was nonsense.

'It's true. If I had been cleverer, then Rupert and I might have made it.'

I felt sorry for her. She still carried a torch for Dimmer-than-a-dung-beetle-high-on-shit-fumes. I suppose her loss connected to my own and I was able to relate to it. Still, I had to be blunt.

I told her that Rupert was a fool and that his wife, for all her sturdy character, was a simple thing, barely above peasantry; her only recommendation was her willingness to convert Rupert's sperm into screeching brats.

'I was capable of that,' she said forlornly. On a litmus test of emotions, she was a shade above Thoroughly Pathetic.

I told her that his new wife was just a nice girl from home.

'I am a nice girl and my home is his real home. More, I come from a much better family. My parents would have been horrified if I had married beneath myself and taken on Rupert, but I would have done so.'

Still she went on, so I cut to the heart of the matter. 'You are too kind to Rupert. It is clear to everyone but you why he picked her.'

Her eyes flashed angrily, but the answer to her rejection, her personal Holy Grail, was within sight, so she virtually ordered me to tell her.

I barely paused for breath. 'It is quite straightforward. His wife may be simple, but she is fair skinned.'

Her mouth dropped.

'Rupert, like most Jamaican men, is obsessed with pigment. He considers himself enormously lucky to have a woman of her skin tone as his wife. He has guaranteed that his children will be fairer, thereby ensuring, in his eyes, greater social mobility and eventual access to a superior gene pool.'

The poor thing hardly knew where to look. But since she had come to help me move on, it was only fair that I returned the good deed.

'In all the time I lived with him, you were the only woman I ever saw Rupert with who was darker than himself. He could spot a "red-skinned bitch" – yes, I think that's how he put it – from the other end of the street. The truth is, when he saw my interest in his sister, he happily confided in me that we shared the same tastes. I have no doubt that Jocelynne was his favourite because of the lightness of her skin. I often imagined his glee as he paraded his youthful, well-toned sister about, fending off the boys who weren't good enough for her company.'

'Why', she asked, 'did he go out with me?'

Reluctantly, I carried on. 'He told me that you were the only woman he knew who would suck his cock before marrying him.'

She left.

I dropped her books out of the window on to the street for her.

She had been a good friend but she must not trespass.

9

Cecil Banks has just finished a survey of white and black attitudes. We have all found the results interesting and a local radio station is planning a debate around his findings. It seems that:

1. The mass immigration of West Indians to England had more to do with restrictive immigration laws in the United States than any deep-rooted love of the mother country.

2. The average age of the West Indian settler is twenty-three. Most of them are skilled workers. Of the men, 13 per cent are without skills; the same can be said of only 5 per cent of the women. Twenty-five per cent of the men and 50 per cent of the women are non-manual workers. Over 60 per cent of the employed males in GB work in jobs that they are over-qualified for.

3. The West Indian immigrant force-fed a diet of British history and culture before his arrival in the mother country regarded himself as a 'kind of Englishman'. They have experienced great shock and disappointment at the racism they have encountered.

4. As for the English: 50 per cent of Britain's white population have experienced no contact with a person of colour; two-thirds hold clearly racist

views. They see blacks as heathens who practise head hunting, cannibalism, infanticide, polygamy and witchcraft. Commonly held views are that blacks are inferior to Europeans, ignorant, illiterate, sexually promiscuous and have brought unpleasant diseases into the country.

Thirty-five per cent of the English consider themselves only mildly racist. Thirty-five per cent consider themselves extremely racist. This group objected to mixed marriages, miscegenation, having blacks as lodgers or guests in their homes and blacks working.

They all agreed that blacks should be kicked out of Britain.

My, my, what a picture. Elizabeth sits on the throne and holds out her sceptre over her animal kingdom. I wonder if Her Majesty's thoughts reflect her people's? I wonder how many blacks she has dined with, laughed with, shared intimate thoughts with? What effect would it have if a black was to hold a senior post in the royal household?

Perhaps she has a black lover somewhere? An African, maybe? Perhaps he visits her, as her husband pops off to see his own mistress, a Swede or French woman, no doubt.

My son, despite the views of his countrymen, is *English*. His passport carries the same legitimacy as the monarch's. The Englishmen who foreshadowed him placed the heads of their enemies on pikes for public display, and merrily slaughtered the children of their Catholic rivals. The druids and holy women of this isle were branded as witches and massacred. The Vikings brought their own particular diseases, as did soldiers returning from the Crimea who were overfond of their horses. Illiteracy was an accepted condition throughout the Elizabethan era. Alcoholism reached epidemic proportions during the Victorian period. Throughout these times, not a single Englishman was stripped of his birthright for any of these crimes. So why should we or our children, who have not committed any unlawful act, forfeit our lawful rights? Who are these sinning bigots to tell my son he does not belong?

But what a shabby little thing it is he holds out his hand to. The long shadow of empire has faded into the cosy warmth of nostalgia and antiquity, whilst the creeping darkness of post-war futility and geo-political irrelevance descends. Somehow I doubt that my son will be gleefully raising his hand when his geography teacher asks him to point out the island of his birth on a world map.

June

3

Arthur has been arrested. He is to be charged with attempted murder.

4

I have been unable to visit my friend, but I have spoken to his lawyer. It seems that Arthur, while attempting to defend himself from a beating (another brawl in a pub), stabbed his attacker almost to death. His lawyer fully expects him to be sent to prison.

5

I have spoken to Arthur's father and was surprised by his reticence. He seemed unconcerned by his son's predicament. His view was that Arthur had been a source of constant trouble and embarrassment to him, and that it had only been a matter of time before something dreadful occurred to him or he brought harm to somebody else.

I learnt much about Arthur, his childhood and his rebelliousness. I gather that Arthur bears a strong resemblance to his father.

It is almost comical. We have led truly parallel lives. We have both made similar journeys to escape the long shadows of the men who sired us. Look where they have led.

6

The Institute is not going to involve itself either officially or unofficially. None of its members want to become involved. Penny is adamant that she cannot and will not participate in the affair. She is married, she has a child, she has made a name for herself, blah, blah, blah. She has read the police reports and is in no doubt that Arthur is guilty as charged. She is of the opinion that he has been unstable for some time, and believes him to be a danger to himself and to others. It is an opinion shared by too many. Even the director beseeched me not to throw away my reputation on Arthur. I have no one to consult. If J. was here I could ask her advice, but she is gone.

10

I managed to see Arthur today. He was in good spirits. We laughed and joked. He passed me a newspaper. The MP of the man Arthur assaulted has given an interview to his local paper:

This incident shows the difficulties of placing people of different races and cultures together in a situation that begs for violence and anger to flourish. Those who come to this country must come with respect and a healthy fear for the full powers of the law, should they cross the line.

Arthur was amused by this. I told him that his lawyer had better be a good one. He told me I had no reason to worry. He seems to expect that his cause and charm will carry the day.

17

I sleep badly, but alcohol helps. I wish that I liked the taste of spirits better. Toxic they may be, but they are a welcome anaesthetic.

18

I attended the first day of Arthur's trial. It was a battle to be there, for my diary is increasingly full. Arthur, always the showman, got his barrister to deliver a shock by pleading guilty. More. His barrister informed the court that:
– Mr Kembo had been involved in a long series of fights against Caucasians since his arrival in the country.
– Mr Kembo wished it to be known that he considered his life to be more valuable than any Caucasian's.
– Mr Kembo wanted the court to be aware of a series of attacks that he had carried out against a Sharon Goldmeir and her family.
There was uproar in the court.

Arthur smiled at me. I didn't know what to do or think. But for the sure grin on his face which told me that he was indeed the Arthur of old, I would have been sure that his mind had turned.

Still, he looked immaculate in his blue silk suit and people were commenting on how handsome he looked as they left the building.

19

The English are indeed amazing. Arthur has become a cult figure. One of the tabloids, in the light of his pugilistic abilities, is referring to him as the 'Brown Bomber'; another, rather mockingly, as 'Arthur X'. Some teenagers have been demonstrating outside the court-house in support of him; it seems they find him a 'brave' and 'cool' figure. One must never forget that this country has a greater capacity for surprise than any other. It is a nation of eccentrics and individuals who hate their own class more than anything else on this planet.

22

The case against Arthur proceeds quickly.

The highlights?

Arthur's pub victim. A middle-aged man who drew much sympathy, even though he was well built and obviously used to brawling. He was slow of speech and seemed confused by proceedings.

As for Sharon Goldmeir, her appearance was devastating. Penny (who despite her previous determination to have nothing more to do with Arthur has turned up to see the proceedings on several occasions) was shocked by the damage to her face and had to leave the public gallery. Sharon had clearly been destroyed by the attack. She trembled throughout her appearance and the prosecutor made constant reference to her need for medication. She spoke eloquently about her relationship with Arthur and his conduct after she had rejected him. She seemed pleasant – even, dare I say it, good.

Worse was to come. Arthur's colleagues from the Institute had been approached by his barrister to be character witnesses. No one had come forward. Imagine my shock when Rupert took the stand as a hostile witness. The egomaniac actually brought his wife and eldest child along.

Rupert spoke as someone who had known Arthur for years and had enjoyed a close relationship with him. He had volunteered his services to the court as a 'concerned citizen'. He spoke of the distrust that he'd always felt towards Mr Kembo and provided numerous examples of Arthur's sexual conduct, his belligerent attitude towards white women and his 'offensive politics'.

The pig hardly knows Arthur, but he left the court with warm words from the judge, who praised him as a 'model citizen and a sterling example to all newcomers to our shores'.

Arthur greeted this statement with high laughter and was threatened with removal by the judge.

23

I visited Rupert in a state of near fury. How could he have done such a thing to a friend – to his benefactor?

He would have none of it. I should be grateful that he had come forward and 'saved the good name' of us all. He had shown that West Indians – Arthur was a Nigerian, after all – were hard-working and law abiding. His church and his life were proof of that. He was not going to allow his church, through his association with Arthur, to be destroyed. I had disgraced his sister's memory. He had redeemed it. My organization was out of touch with the needs of the common people. It was his responsibility to articulate the wishes of his flock and speak for them with honesty and without fear. He had received a number of phone calls from concerned citizens who wanted to donate money to his ministry. He'd even been booked on to a radio show.

The man made me sick. I told him so.

He told me what he thought of me.

We vowed never to speak to each other again.

He is scum. He will always be scum.

24

The final day of Arthur's trial was quite stressful. He had refused to see me, but had asked that I come along and witness the handing down of the verdict.

The public gallery was filled. It seemed all the regulars from the Milford Arms were either in the gallery or waiting outside the court building. Penny was clearly distressed and held my hand throughout. Callaghan flashed the odd smile, but had little stomach for the proceedings.

The court seemed harsh and exclusive, full of regalia, symbols and tradition, and peopled by strange citizens who seemed to breathe a rarefied air unfit for consumption by normal mortals. There was no one of power in that court who might be called a contemporary or peer. But they judged him. He was found guilty. Before sentencing, the judge asked him if he had anything to say. With a slight clearing of the throat, he stood. He was utterly composed and chillingly succinct.

'I have pleaded guilty, but I have no guilt. I would do as I did again and again and again, without question or remorse. When a white man attacks me, I know the cause of his action, as well as what my response should be. I do not regret defending myself, or pleasuring myself as I made a victim of my attacker.'

He ran his hands over his face. 'My skin is inviolate. It is my bond, my word, my faith. I know who I am. I know what I know. My skin is my badge. I am a black man. No person of another race will ever violate my body.'

The judge, I am sure, wanted to interrupt him, but found himself fascinated.

'I would rather see every white person in this room perish than see one black child suffer the indignities of the hate and spite assembled here. I loathe each and every one of you. Do what you will. You are irrelevant.'

And with that he sat down.

Someone yelled bravo.

Someone shouted obscenities.

Many booed.

More hurled insults.

Penny buried her face in my shoulder.

Callaghan whispered, 'The man is mad, but he's got balls.'

I was lost.

I was lost as the judge passed sentence and he was taken away.

I was lost as we left. Nothing made sense to me.

Not the journey home.

Not the price of the whisky from the off-licence.

Nor the walls of my bedroom, or the comfort of my pillow.

I lay awake all night and still nothing came to me. Everything, except for the dullness of the alcohol, was without purpose or sense.

25

I awoke with an awful headache and with Arthur's words still spinning around in my mind. I was appalled by him.

His words shocked me.

I was moved. I was impressed.

I was disgusted. His ego and self-satisfaction were shocking. He had no sense of reality.

He was in control. He was enormously dignified.

I envy him nothing. He was foolish. Full of hot air. The judge found him ridiculous. The jury thought him mad. His friends choked on their shame.

I envied his courage.

His courage?

Yes, his courage in the face of the enemy.

There was no enemy. He
succumbed to the enemy. His hate
shouldn't be elevated to anything
beyond its vile nature.

He was alone. He wasn't afraid. He
didn't feel the need to defend
himself from the so-called great and
the good. He was magnificent.

I think of her face. I think of his
brutality. She must have been quite
pretty. No man has the right to do
that.

Stop thinking like a man. Remember
what she was. You owe her nothing
and him everything. His skin was
his badge. He was a black man.
That is all that counts.

She was a woman. A human being.
They joined as one. He stamped his
foot like a child when she ended it.
Arthur the pseudo-English gent who
couldn't handle being treated like a
spear carrier. A spoilt and vicious
child.

He acted as a man.

I can understand, I will never
understand his actions.

Arthur.
You were my only friend.
And now I've lost you.

WHY DO PEOPLE LEAVE ME?!

WHY?

26

Today was without a doubt the worst Monday of my life. Work was a chore, a bore. Mercifully, the director gave us the day off.

29

A letter from Arthur's father. He thanked me for befriending Arthur and standing by him, but advised me to forget him. He no longer considers Arthur to be his son. My, what a world it is when sons have to grow up in the shadow of such fathers.

32

I have taken a leave of absence.

33

A spent the evening at the Milford Arms. Newspaper clippings of Arthur's trial adorned the wall. Callaghan spent a great deal of his time talking to customers about his relationship with Arthur. He was witty and descriptive. He exaggerated certain incidents and underplayed others, portraying Arthur as a larger than life figure whose madness, once understood, was comical and quite endearing.

2nd September

A letter arrived this morning. It is from Arthur and contains a visitor's pass to his prison on the Isle of Wight. How can I say no?

19th September

Yesterday I went to see Arthur. It rained relentlessly all day. I could listen to weather from all around the world and identify English rain.

To reach the prison, I had to board a special coach near the Elephant & Castle underground station. The coach was packed with working-class women, with grim faces and dead eyes. Many of them were accompanied by children. There was just a handful of tough-looking men, several with scarred faces. There was little laughter throughout the journey. I was struck by how unhealthy many of them looked. Their skins were pallid, their clothes cheap, their hair dull. The children were restless and without focus. Every person on the coach smoked and we drove through the wet streets in an unmoving cloud of tobacco. When I opened a window, a small, bullish woman immediately closed it again.

Though the group dispersed on the ferry, we were watched by many. It seemed that our reputation had preceded us. The staff in the tuck shop were cool and offhand, often glancing at us with contempt, even disgust.

The prison waiting room was a strain. Most people studiously avoided any contact with each other. One woman stared resolutely at the floor with unfailing concentration. Nothing existed for her but the man she was about to visit.

The women who had finished their visits came out with their heads high. It seemed a point of honour not to show emotion to the prison guards. One woman, emerging with her crying daughter, gently insisted that she 'Calm down,' but when the girl persisted gave her a sharp smack on the head, ordering the child to behave herself. Family honour had been besmirched.

When it was my turn to enter the visiting area, I went with a painfully beating heart. I offered the contents of my pockets to the guards, who were strangely courteous and quite free with their smiles and reassurances. I had imagined they would be hard and brutal, but they were incredibly normal. Resigned to their fate, it seemed they just wanted everything to go smoothly, without any hiccups or melodramas.

I entered a hall adorned with impressive paintings and filled with small tables observed closely by grim-looking men in uniforms. Red-faced women kissed and hugged their men passionately, as if they were alone, then sat, hands touching with a trembling desperation. Children, unable to concentrate for long periods, cried and played amongst themselves. Stony-faced guards said nothing as smuggled cigarettes changed hands, opting instead for conversation with colleagues.

Arthur caught my eye from the middle of the hall and I joined him. He had shaved off all his hair and looked quite fit. An envelope rested on the table in front of him. He rose to meet me and we embraced with heartfelt emotion. It was quite wonderful, and as I sat down I realized just how much I had missed him.

'DuBois, old man,' he began with the familiar smile on his face, 'it is good to see you.'

'And you, Arthur, and you.'

We fell silent for a time, until we found ourselves breaking into broad grins and laughing merrily. It was a good feeling.

He told me I was looking well.

I returned the compliment.

We spoke of his surroundings. The works of art on the walls had been produced by inmates, and had already been exhibited on the island. Arthur, too, has begun to paint and believes he is developing into a competent artist. He was pleased that I had brought him a packet of cigarettes and insisted, despite my reservations, that I pass them to him. He was right to be unconcerned, as no action was taken.

He asked about Gabriel.

I told him that the boy was well.

He misses my son.

I joked that I would happily send the boy to join him.

He wasn't amused.

We talked of the Institute and former friends.

He informed me that a series of letters had come to the prison from his so-called 'friends', carrying messages of regret but making it quite clear that they had no intention of visiting him. I was surprised – he wasn't, and said he didn't care anyway. He was dealing with the truth and had no time for soft lies or misleading manners.

The conversation turned to politics. His knowledge of current affairs was as informed as ever. Eventually he drew my attention to the envelope that lay between us.

'I want you to pay attention,' he began, laying out several documents on the table between us. 'My lawyer has worked on these for several weeks and he will be carrying out my instructions to the full.'

I was asked to study the deeds to his house and several small portfolios. The house had been signed over to my son. The investments were also for him and were to be held in trust until he was eighteen. I couldn't understand why he had done these things and told him so. The strangest look was in his eyes as he laid his hand on mine.

'I've done these things because I believe there is a need for them. I have watched you with my godson and, to be frank, I have my concerns.'

I said nothing.

'You were always a bit too self-absorbed for my liking.' He waved away my interruptions. 'It is true that Jocelynne forced you to relate to aspects of the world, but now she is gone and –' he performed that eloquent shrug of his shoulders that I had always envied, 'and you have become as you were.'

'And?'

'And as Gabriel's godfather, I have made certain provisions to counter your undeserved and spiteful apathy.'

My ears rang.

'Your place is too small. I suggest you consider moving to my house as quickly as possible. Perhaps with more space you might find yourself being a bit more agreeable. I know that you have a penchant for the antiseptic, but please try not to remove every vestige of character from the building.'

And with what he repacked the envelope.

I took it. I considered throwing it in his face.

He saw my expression and wagged his finger at me. 'Don't be silly, old man, take it. It's all I have to give you. When I'm in my cell, the knowledge that you will be enjoying the property will be of no small comfort.' He patted my hand. 'There really is no reason for you to disappoint me, is there?'

I asked him about his fascination with my son.

'I was fascinated with his mother,' he said. 'It's the least I can do. A way of marking her journey, if you like.'

I'm afraid that my eyes began to water.

He gripped my hand tightly. 'You're my friend. If the truth be known, you're the only true friend I've ever had. I wish that was some sort of compliment, but –' That shrug again. 'Take what I have to offer you, please.'

I accepted.

'One more thing.'

'Yes?'

'I would appreciate it if you didn't visit me any more.'

I was shocked and wanted to know why.

'Because', he said firmly, 'that is my wish. I have a long haul ahead of me here. Please don't make it any harder. I will survive this on my own.'

He was being ridiculous and I told him so. He told me that he wouldn't be sending out any more visitor's passes, 'So you don't really have a choice.'

There was nothing I could do. My silence confirmed it.

He stood up and held out his arms. 'Come.'

I hugged him and he held me with that enormous, hidden strength of his.

'Come, old man,' he said as I began to weep, 'don't do that. You'll ruin what little reputation I have left.'

I made my goodbyes and walked away without looking back. My time with him had been short and I had to wait for my fellow travellers to complete their visits.

The journey home was most strange. I think I was in shock. It had been a thoroughly horrible day. I couldn't remove Arthur from my mind's eye. He stood there, smiling a smile of ridiculous charm and warmth that caused me to smile as I cried. It seemed impossible that this image would be the last one I would have of him, before the years took their course and we would meet again.

November

The system grinds on and brushes the troublesome under the carpet. Arthur has been sent to Broadmoor – an institution that caters for criminals who have been declared insane or pose a threat to themselves or their fellow inmates. I have written a letter of protest, but expect little satisfaction.

12th December

My son and I moved into our new home today. I brought J. with me, she will be happy here. It is as spacious as promised and has a lovely garden. The street is quiet and free from continuous traffic. The neighbours are mostly elderly, so we will have peace at least. I have not notified any of my wife's bloodhounds of my move or new address. They will not interfere with my life any more. As for the boy, he has his own room and the garden to play in. We will, I hope, be able to coexist without much friction or dissension. I will carry on.

Gabriel encircled the sentence 'I brought J. with me, she will be happy here' with a red pen, before jotting down a few thoughts.

My father was a specific man. This entry is precise. It reflects his intentions, which he carried out, and his hopes, which were dashed. His reference to my mother and its rich metaphysical cadence is glaringly dissimilar to the rest of the piece. I believe he believed she was with him, that she was a part of him. I was always aware of her absence.

He paused.

No, that isn't true. I told him once that I had dreamt of her and he was furious. He beat me because I was not worthy of her. I never mentioned the dreams and her words again. I told myself I was stupid, that the dreams were a pleasing cartoon and no more.

He read on. There were no more entries until March 1965.

Arthur is dead. He started a fire in his cell, then chained himself to his door. I cannot bear to think of how he must have suffered. I have been informed that he has left a letter for me. I hope to receive it soon. Death, Death and more Death. Jocelynne, Arthur, what was the point?

There are so many files at the Institute of blacks who have come to this country and died here. I imagine these people starting their journeys in the West Indies, their optimism and excitement, and then their end. Murdered by a Teddy boy. Beaten by an extortionist. Run over by a drunk. Gassed by a faulty leak. Prescribed the wrong medicine by a doctor. Heart attacks. Cancer. Tumours. Lung disease. Sickle cell anaemia. Slippery bathroom floors. On and on and on, stories with abrupt endings.

I know Arthur's tale.

His name will mean nothing to anyone else.

All that potential, all that charisma.

A mental institution.

A fire.

Suicide.

For what?

For what?

For what?

Can anyone tell me?

Gabriel moved on until he came to a page with a letter pasted on to it.

20th June

Finally, I have been allowed Arthur's letter.

Gabriel read the letter. It had been written on several sheets of toilet paper.

Dearest DuBois,

After all this time, I feel I should break my silence. I have decided to end my incarceration. I will not allow these people to control my life any longer. Enough is enough. I cannot bear the boredom any more. Their games bore me. The rules are simple but trite, and I haven't the patience to upset them any longer.

I didn't want to surprise you. I know that you are easily hurt and wanted you to know that this happened on my terms. Unlike your dear wife, I chose this. I controlled it. I was happy with it.

Take care,

Your friend.

Matthew had written underneath the letter:

I cannot go on. But I am too weak to do what I should, so I do go on, shaming myself with my inability to do what is right. I should never have come here. This place has brought me nothing but agony.

The next entry was for April 1968.

Martin Luther King has been murdered.

Shot by a creature named James Earl Ray.

He was only thirty-nine years old!

Riots have erupted across America. The land of hope and glory burns to the tune of hate and despair. Blacks across America, and for that matter across the world, have lost a beacon of light. They have shown us that they will give us nothing, that they are prepared to exterminate the best and the brightest of us. We will swing from the trees, we will lie unburied on dirt roads, we will hang in police cells, we will be shot on balconies. Whatever it takes, they will do it.

They are ruthless, while we are weak. They are unforgiving, while we attempt to forget. They are ruthless, while we offer the other cheek.

King is dead.

Imagine what that piece of metal did to his flesh.

How long did it take for his spirit to move on?

What were his last thoughts? Were they of his own futility or an overriding hope?

All those marches, all those speeches, all those triumphs, all those awards, all those tears, all those handshakes, all those smiles, all those pleas, to end like that. Bleeding to death in a hotel, alone without his family.

How little was the man who fired the weapon? How great was his sense of triumph? A soldier fighting for his cause, a martyr to the flag and its white states? How many slaps on the back will he receive from those who arrested him? How many winks and nudges from those who turn the key to his prison cell? How many congratulations and good wishes from those who pass him in the exercise yard? No doubt there are many who consider the murderer, not the slain, to be the true American hero.

At night when he sleeps, how many times does he see King's last gesture? How tiny the motion, how white the finger that commanded the bullet that drew the red blood from his brown body, so that the black and white of the news reels could shock us over and over and over again.

The newspapers say that such an act could never happen here, that racism in England is of a different order. They say that the people of Great Britain are linked by the threads of empire, culture and history, which are stronger than the weak glue that binds American citizens together. They say that America is a violent country which resolves its problems violently. Whatever. If one thing is certain, it is certain that King loved his country.

I have played the recordings of his great speeches over and over, and they are mighty.

And if America is to be a great nation this must become true. So let freedom ring from the prodigious hilltops of Hampshire. Let freedom ring from the mighty mountains of New York. Let freedom ring from the heightening Allehenies of Pennsylvania! Let freedom ring from the snowcapped Rockies of Colorado! Let freedom ring from the curvaceous peaks of California! But not only that; let freedom ring from the Stone Mountain of Georgia! Let freedom ring from the Lookout Mountain of Tennessee! Let freedom ring from every hill and molehill of Mississippi. From every mountainside, let freedom ring.

When we let freedom ring, when we let it ring from every village and every hamlet, from every state and every city, we will be able to speed up that day when all God's children, black men and white men, Jews and Gentiles, Protestants and Catholics, will be able to join hands and sing in the words of the old Negro spiritual, 'Free at last! Free at last! Thank God Almighty, we are free at last!'

Where is the hate?

This is a man who loved every aspect of his country: its air, its environment, its architecture, its culture, its music and theatre. Even though it rejected him, he opened up his arms and sought to embrace it. He never once called for an act of sedition or terrorism or murder.

How is it possible for such a man to be laid low by so petty an individual? Is that what they teach us? That such a great man can be taken away by the worst, the most inconsequential, the most ignorant. They have told us, 'You dream because we allow it. Our towns are not for you. Our religions are not for you. Your preachers speak in our tongue and we can close their mouths when we choose to.'

A white woman stopped me today and said she was sorry for what had happened. She wanted me to know that she didn't think like 'that', that she supported King's aims. I didn't know what to say to her. If he was her champion, it was because she allowed him to be. I despised her. My life, my aspirations are beyond the whims of her fashionable politics. I am more than an opportunity for discord between this woman and her parents. My life has substance. I live.

We all live.

King is dead and we go on.

It is only a few days since his death, but the dream doesn't seem so bright. I went to a memorial in King's Cross and the black speakers were visibly chastened. They lacked confidence. It was as if the loss of their champion had weakened them before their audience. The spectre of James Earl Ray hangs over them all. How many people will change their minds and not call their sons James this year? How many more will do so?

I wonder whether, in this heaven that King so fervently believed in, there is a hall where the assassinated and the martyred meet and discuss their deeds. If so, I wonder if they are happy about the future that has been ushered in by their blood. Do they laugh at the rope marks about their necks? Do they chuckle at the tar and the feathers that have bonded to their skins? Do they speak with fondness of the fires that consumed them, and the guns and the endless cowardly bullets?

Do they think of Colorado and Tennessee and Mississippi with affection? Do they look down on Hull, Leeds, Bradford, Sutton, York and Glasgow and wish us well? Or have they found out something else, something they desperately want to tell us?

When I walk along the streets of London I am never overcome by an overwhelming need to embrace my Hasidic brother, nor do I feel compelled to rush over and break bread in the houses of my Catholic neighbours. I cannot even begin to visualize a day when I might join hands and sing, 'Free at last! Free at last!'

Then again, I am not a godly man. I am not a man of love or vision. I cannot transcend the limitations of my heart, or reject the truth of my eyes when they fill with the image of my enemy. That is why I will not be missed, why I will never inspire people to tears or song. Still, when giants have walked the earth, it is not possible for pygmies to eradicate their footprints.

The romance of King's voice will always overcome the doom-laden messages of the apocalyptic Cassandras with their messages of race hate and easy violence. For all my cynicism, as King's voice reaches that wonderful peak and he chants 'free at last' over and over, for a second – a wonderful, joyous second – I rise with him and I believe.

This flight transcends the motion of a bullet and the imprint of blood-stained concrete on cooling cheek. I do not know what land I flew over – its rolling fields and immense valleys were clear to me in the heat of my imagination but it is beyond my ability to evoke them when I am calm and easy – but I know that King, momentarily at least, helped myself and millions of others to find it. In fact, he strode across that mythical mountain range with us. I can never thank him enough for that.

Gabriel moved on to March 1973.

9

The child has been relatively good of late and I have not had to discipline him. It seems the detention cupboard was an inspired decision. He seems to have got the message. Still, you can never be quite sure with a sly child. They often are at their worst when they seem at their best. Still, I am older and far wiser. Whatever nonsense he tries, I have seen it and tried it myself. He will learn. I would swap him in a second to have Arthur back.

11

I will have to take Gabriel out of his present school.

This will be his fourth move.

He was in a fight with a boy who, it seemed, kept approaching him. The boy liked him and couldn't understand why he was so quiet. For his pains, Gabriel attacked him.

The teachers want him removed.

The head teacher, an amateur psychiatrist it seems, has suggested that Gabriel is a disturbed youngster who requires professional attention.

I am unimpressed with this view.

The boy's only redeeming feature is his individuality. I will not repress it. I hope he goes his own way.

In truth, I would rather he learnt to defend himself than be a victim for every pale bully who fancies abusing him. Every black parent owes their child that. I will see to it that he enrols in some defence classes – boxing, whatever.

12

The boy asked questions about J. I beat him rather severely. He is not to mention her. He will not mention her.

April

4

A remarkable day.

I had walked with the boy to the park near the cemetery. I have always found cemeteries fascinating and took a stroll through it. Gabriel dawdled so I walked on. I forgot about him until I was ready to leave. I found him sleeping by a headstone near where I had left him. He was in a deep sleep and refused to wake, despite my proddings and raised voice. Uneasy, I picked him up and headed towards the cemetery gates. He awoke and began to speak in a voice that was not his own. He seemed confused, scared, unsure of who I was or where he was.

I was angry. I could not understand why he should play such a game. I ordered him to stop his nonsense, but still he spoke with a ludicrous accent and addressed me as if I was his junior.

I smacked him and pushed him in front of me. The further we walked from the grave the more agitated he became, and by the time we reached the gates he was quite hysterical. He screamed at me, abusing me in whatever tongue he was pretending to speak, and hung on to the gate of the cemetery so hard that it took all my strength to pull him away. Eventually he collapsed in a dead faint.

I carried him back to the car and drove home. I was, of course, by now quite disturbed. This went beyond play-acting. Yes, he was a bright child and capable of bizarre behaviour, but this was more than schoolboy jinks.

I took him to bed. He was running a high temperature and failed to respond to my efforts to cool him down.

Again, though apparently unconscious, he began to speak in a foreign tongue. When he finally came to, he sat before me as an adult, a confused adult, but an adult all the same. He tried to communicate with me and mimed what he needed.

I gave him a pencil and paper and he drew a sailor. Happy that I understood him, he then drew a map. It was of Iceland. Next he wrote down a name, and other things that were indecipherable to me. Though this was frustrating for him, he seemed happy that we had made progress. Satisfied, he lay down and fell asleep.

I watched him carefully for many hours. I was in no doubt that something extraordinary had occurred, but what? There was only one person who I could turn to.

Although I had not seen her in years, I hoped that Gladwin was still at the same address and drove down the Embankment to Clapham Junction. Fortunately Gladwin had not moved. She was shocked to see me, of course, and paid me the compliment of appearing to be quite moved. I told her that time was of the essence, that Gabriel was unwell and that I needed her help. To her eternal credit she left immediately with me. Yes, she began to express her anger towards me in the car, but she came, that was the main thing.

She sat with Gabriel for some time before talking.

Quite calmly, she said that he was possessed. He was, in her opinion, a 'white child' – a boy with special powers. His talent was for communicating with people in the spirit world. He was, in other words, someone whose role was to act as a voice, a speaker for the dead.

I did not laugh. I did not doubt that what she said was true. I knew, of course, of the African traditions of magic that continued throughout Jamaica and the other islands, but had never really taken them seriously. Jocelynne's sensitivity to people and the world had encouraged me to be more open-minded. This experience with the boy was extremely challenging.

Gladwin said that Gabriel must be taught how to use his gifts, so that he would understand how to pass on the advice of the spirits. She was willing to be his teacher and would introduce me to people she knew who could help him. Apparently there are many African healers in England who practise their traditional arts discreetly in privacy, who would be only too willing to educate Gabriel.

I found the concept of Africans walking the streets of England in double-breasted suits and ties, then returning home and throwing the bones fascinating, but unhelpful.

She was not pleased by my scorn and commented that I was 'just as stupid and arrogant as ever'.

I moved the conversation on and asked her to try and do something practical, if she was able. Her response was to stomp out of the room. She did not leave, however, but went into the garden and returned with a long stick, before ushering me out of the room and slamming the door.

About an hour later she emerged with the stick and claimed that the spirit which had taken advantage of Gabriel's inexperience was now in the stick. I had only to take her back to the cemetery and all would be well. So I did.

She lectured me all the way, about my ignorance, my colonialized mind, my disrespect for my own 'true' history and so on, *ad nauseam*. The cemetery was locked up, so rather foolishly, like two mad teenagers, we climbed the walls.

I took her to where Gabriel had fallen asleep and she planted the stick in the ground and ordered/pleaded/charmed the spirit back to its resting place. When she was done she turned on her heels and climbed the wall. I have never felt more foolish in my life, but as we drove back I found myself looking at this strange creature in her synthetic fabrics and cosmetics, and noticing for the first time just how truly foreign she was to the take-aways, petrol stations and Georgian mansions that littered our journey. I realized that although she could talk and think like me, it was by choice. We were not, despite appearances, the same.

I drove her home.

She warned me not to be led by my ego and told me to visit her again.

As I drove home, a plan began to form. It is a little daring, perhaps even foolhardy, but it makes perfect sense.

Perhaps after all there is some justice in the world.

5

Several days have passed since the incident. I have fed him well and made sure that he is fit. He has no memory of what happened. Perhaps it is for the best. I do not know whether I am being foolish. Perhaps I need a little excitement? Whatever, the game is afoot. Let us see where it will lead.

6

Today I took Gabriel to where Jocelynne and Cuffay are buried. I wonder how that pompous brother-in-shame-only of mine would react if he knew that I moved their bodies shortly after J.'s burial, and that he has spent years visiting, speaking and wailing to nothing more than grass and dirt. I have only to think of that imbecile at her 'grave' performing his absurd routine of appalling, self-serving hysterics and I am overcome by laughter.

Gabriel was stunned by this entry. It was some time before he was able to read on.

He was unaware that he was standing before the burial place of his mother and sister, but that was as it should be. He murdered one and brought ill luck to the other. I chatted idly with him of things of little consequence, controlling my resentment, subtly preventing him from moving on. We stayed there for hours. Nothing happened. Eventually we had to leave. I could barely speak to him. He has failed me, but that is his bent. No matter, we shall try again. I put him to bed early, so that he will be in a good frame of mind tomorrow.

7

Again no success. He questioned me and kept on doing so, even after I had told him to desist. He was nervous. He sensed something was up and seemed a touch threatened. I went to a nearby shop and bought him a drawing pad and pencil, so that he would remain calm. This did the trick. He is reasonably proficient with a pencil and produced some rather fetching drawings. I am unkind, the boy has talent, but what good ever came from being handy with a pencil? Tomorrow.

8

A complete waste of time. The boy tries my patience and seeks to hinder any success that might come my way. I know that I am owed something. This could not have happened without a chance of the scales being readjusted. I am owed something. He owes me more than he can ever repay. I will never cancel his debt, never.

9

I will wait, I will see this out. I am stronger. My will will triumph. Gabriel will learn that there are stronger powers at work in the universe than himself. Every child must learn this.

10

I am afraid that I lost my patience last night.

I tried to stop myself, but eventually in the early hours of the morning, I got out of bed and slapped him.

I was careful not to bruise him – I don't want any interference from his teachers. I have become quite skilful at it.

There are times when it takes everything I have to stop.

This rage that fills me is quite irresistible.

Sometimes, often, I am shamed by what I have done. I tell myself that I must send him away before the inevitable happens. I catch a glimpse of myself in the mirror and cannot recognize the ugliness that is reflected.

There are days, weeks when I avoid him, and times when I try to be kind and good. We have moments when I am truly joyful, when something he says or does stirs a feeling akin to pride in my heart and it seems we are as we might have been.

But then the shadow falls again and I am aware that she is gone, that we can never be normal and that he is solely responsible.

We must talk, his mother and I.

She must tell me why she did what she did.

Why did she choose this thing over me?

Why did our love have to prostrate itself before this greater passion?

So many questions.

So many imagined debates.

We have screamed and hollered and shrieked and nothing has ever been resolved.

I need to talk to her.

I need her.

It has been so long since we touched.

I cannot understand what it was all about, what we were about.

Why did we meet and begin for such an ending?

If I had known at the outset how our tale would unfold, then I would never have ushered in once upon a time. One does not discover the love of one's life in a photograph and chase her across the globe, only to have her snatched away and told, Sorry that's it. Time's up. You have no more. Others can go on, but you will stop right here. That's it. You have no choice, you have no choice, you have no choice.

11

Success.

This morning I took the boy to Jocelynne's grave again. We spent hours there. Eventually he fell asleep. At some point he stirred, making silly noises as he awoke. At first I was annoyed, but then I realized that the sound was not his. The tone was of someone else. I could hardly contain myself. It was as if someone had just proved that the likes of Newton and Brown were extraordinary con men, and the physical universe they propounded nothing but illusion.

I watched him as he looked about the cemetery. He was lost and confused and I could see terror building up in his eyes. I held him and, with my heart in my mouth, dared to call her name. It seemed to work, for he calmed down a touch and looked at me. He looked at me with eyes that belonged to another and tried to speak. I waited and waited, but no words came. I shook him and urged him to speak. He grew limp and fell unconscious. But it was fine, for as he fell I heard my name called. The caller was my wife.

Gabriel, shaking, stood up and walked around for a time. Rachel stirred in her sleep, but did not wake. He sat by her and touched her lips, before rubbing his fingers over the canine teeth at the edge of her mouth. Her eyes flickered open and she mumbled something, before sinking back into a deep sleep. He kissed her and ran his hands over her body, feeling the swell of her stomach and the hard edge of her belly button. As always, he was drawn back to the journal.

12
The boy has been ill since our experience, and is having a few days off school. I have received a letter from Penny, urging me to return to my post at the Institute. I burned it.

13
I took the boy back to Jocelynne's grave. He was reluctant to come. I am sure that this attitude contributed to our lack of success. I will have to adopt a more conciliatory approach.

14
We went to see a Disney movie, *Dumbo*. The artwork was quite shoddy in places. I understand that the Disney animators went on strike during the making of the film, so much of the animation was completed by scabs. It showed. What peculiar characters inhabit the Disney world. The puerile anthropomorphism of the characters works along specific racial and social lines that are breathtakingly offensive. The boy pleased me by being aware of the crude stereotypes, but still enjoyed the movie. He sped down the road with his arms out, copying the flying motions of the elephant. I trust this evening will help his mood.

15

Nothing. An entire day at the cemetery and nothing.

16

The director of the Institute asked me to a meeting, to discuss what my duties would be after my leave of absence. He found me to be aloof and apathetic. He was right, so I quit. He asked me to think again. There was no need to. I left the building without speaking to any of my colleagues. As I walked along High Street Kensington, it seemed that a tremendous weight had been hoisted from my shoulders. I passed the bench where I used to talk regularly with my friend. It is time to move on.

17

My frustration builds. I decided to talk to the boy.

I explained my purpose to him.

I explained his ability.

I spoke of his mother's death and his complicity.

In my opinion it was a marvellous opportunity for him to make reparation and rehabilitate himself in my own eyes. Perhaps if there is a higher power waiting to sit in judgement of his final tally, then this course of action might have helped to balance his undoubted shortfall.

The boy replied that:

a) I was behaving irrationally.

b) He had accepted his part in his mother's death.

c) He did not believe in a 'higher power'.

d) If what I said was true, then I had no right to expose him to something neither of us fully understood.

I considered his response, then sent him to the detention cupboard. I will not tolerate this behaviour from a child.

18

Three days have passed since he entered the cupboard. My own lessons of strength and resilience have rebounded on me. He is refusing to give in. This is interesting.

19

Five days have now passed since he began his detention. I have given him a minimum of food and a bucket for his waste. Despite myself, I am impressed by his fight. He will do well in this world. He understands it. In that area, at least, I have not failed him.

20

I have let him out a day after he pleaded to be released. We both understand who is master. I bathed him, for his condition was repellent. We spoke in the bathroom of his experience and his fears. His report was calm and lucid, in truth, quite chilling. I know that I would not have emerged from a similar ordeal with half as much dignity or composure.

I watched as he executed the cleaning routine that I taught him and thought of the first time I saw him. Even then, as a babe, he possessed the same quality of stillness. At the time I thought that the trauma of his birth had drained him.

He towelled himself down. His legs trembled a touch. I felt the urge to hold him and warm him. I imagined myself touching his face and pleading for forgiveness, us holding each other and promising never to fight again. In the real world, he put his pyjamas on without a word passing from my lips. He asked for my permission to go to bed. I gave it and he went. I was alone with myself. The company was hard to bear.

22

I went to the grave. I spoke to the block of stone that carries the names of my lost loves and told them that their son/brother would not be returning. I owed him that. If they were to come to me, then it would have to be by other means. I apologized for my cowardice and left.

The boy returned from school. We ate together. We were, as ever, cordial. I looked at him, unaware of any patrilineal urge to bond. His formal education will enable him to understand much of the world as I see it, but our flawed approximation of a father–son relationship will always prevent us from forming an affinitive, homogeneous view of the world.

I have come to a decision.

As soon as the boy is old enough to look after himself, we will part ways.

Gabriel passed over a number of pages, to 1976.

May

The boy continues to excel at mathematics and is equal to all the demands his private tutors place upon him. He has managed the portfolio I began for him extremely well. His advice on my stock has proved to be extremely lucrative. I am proud of him.

Gabriel flicked through more pages, until an entry for 1978 caught his eye.

2nd August
A memorable day. A turning-point, no less.

Gabriel angered me. He was sloppy in the kitchen and failed to prepare the meal I had requested on time. I struck him. He raised his hand as if to retaliate. We were both shocked. I slapped him, but he did not strike me back. That moment will surely come. It is only a matter of time. I await it. I hunger for it.

Gabriel wiped away tears as he recalled the incident, and looked for something that he knew only too well.

1979
5th July
Finally, it has come. The boy struck me.

We were watching cricket. The West Indian batting star Viv Richards was scoring freely for Somerset and the boy was enthusing about his play. I said I found Richards to be arrogant. The boy went on about him being a great symbol of black pride and confidence. I brought up Muhammad Ali. He felt that was an unfair comparison, for Ali dwarfed everyone.

Me: 'That is my point.'

Him: 'Richards represents his island and an entire country every time he bats. He is a new West Indian without the servility of those who went before. Everything about him – his batting, his physique, even the manner in which he walks to the crease – reflects a new confidence and assurance.'

Me: 'Sobers served his country even better and he did it without this man's ridiculous strutting and gum chewing.'

Him: 'Sobers the man was no threat. Richards carries his masculinity before him. He challenges all the old colonial sexual myths every time he plays.'

I began to laugh and couldn't stop.

Him: 'Well, if you don't want to learn anything then you might as well laugh.'

That did it. I went out into the hallway and picked up his cat. I held it out to him.

Me: 'This cat takes its name from Sobers, you remember that! Remember that when you wet your pants over a man who couldn't hold a candle to Everton Weekes, let alone compare with the greatest left-hander to grace the game!'

And with that I threw the cat against the wall.

It screamed as it bounced off the wall. The boy rushed over to it and tried to comfort it. As I sat down he screamed, 'You hurt it!' and charged me.

I was taken by surprise, but worse, I was actually hurt. He was vicious, clawing at my eyes, kicking at my groin. It took all my strength to hold him off. I pushed him away but he kept coming back. His eyes were truly manic and I had no doubt that he would have seriously hurt me if he could. I managed to sit on him and remained there until he calmed down.

I then told him that I would take the cat to the vet, and left the house with Sobers.

I returned after an hour or so.

He asked me where Sobers was.

I told him that the vet had put the cat down because of his injuries.

He screamed that he hated me. He hated me more than anything in the whole world. As he stormed out of the room, I knew it to be true.

I sat down.

I began to cry.

It was over. I had freed myself. This terrible obligation was over.

I stayed in that chair for hours before visiting him. He was asleep. I closed his door and packed my bags. After leaving a letter on my breakfast table – it contained the address of my lawyer and advice for the coming years – I left.

I am content.

I have been a hard taskmaster, but then again the world is a cruel place. He is familiar with its harsh eccentricities.

He understands the capricious nature of love and of deceit.

He has grasped the power of hatred.

No one will betray him. That prerogative was mine and mine alone.

He is ready, which is far more than I could claim when I arrived in this

254

country. Lacking my arrogance, he is less likely to repeat my folly. The architecture of necessity dictates all.

As for me, it is time to regroup.

The third act of my life begins.

I cannot prevent its onset, but whatever it brings, I will survive it.

Gabriel closed the journal and went to bed.

Three

Rachel worked out as Gabriel sat by the window. She had spent the morning comforting Winston's friends, who'd been upset by the manner of his arrest. After promising to accompany them to the police station, she had gone there herself and made a series of complaints to the desk sergeant. Furious and suffering from a tension headache, she'd returned home, stripped down and begun to work out. Winston was one of the few true Rastas she knew. He followed Jah, read his Bible, took the weed for spiritual purposes and lived for peace. If he'd lost his cool it was because of extraordinary circumstances.

Gabriel left his chair and picked up the journal off the bed.

'Could you pay attention to me for a second,' said Rachel. 'I'd appreciate it if you could deal with the real world for a few minutes. A friend of mine has just been arrested and you can't even put that thing down and try to help me.'

He left.

She refused to watch him drive away.

An ambulance crew carried the body of an old man out of Gladwin's block of flats on a stretcher. One of the team was handing out advice to the caretaker. 'Check on your elderly tenants from time to time. This is the third pensioner we've picked up this week. In weather like this, buildings like yours become treacherous, so use your head.' The death had attracted quite a crowd and the lifts were in constant use with tenants coming down to see what all the fuss was about.

Gladwin's door was open.

After Gabriel called out her name, she appeared in a red kikoi with new hair extensions. She was accompanied by a flustered student, who was ushered through the door with, 'Think about what I said. You've got two days to choose. Either stay and get down to studying my

reading list or leave and buy all the Falconhurst books you like. I leave
it up to you.'

Over iced coffee she asked him his opinion of the new look.

'You look quite glamorous.'

She tossed beaded strands of hair back over her shoulder. 'I feel
extremely glamorous.' The ivory about her wrists clicked and her heavy
rings cast reflections to all parts of the room. 'I feel wonderful. And
you, what brings you here?'

He handed her the journal.

'Ah.'

As she flitted through the book she released a series of light sighs
and gentle exclamations, before murmuring, 'Your father was certainly
a character, of that there is no doubt.' Her examination continued,
punctuated with, 'I didn't know that . . . Yes, yes, that is true . . . Oh
dear, what a pig. What an absolute pig.'

Tracing her fingers over the cover as if she were leaving patterns in
dry sand, she handed the journal back. 'Those were interesting days
for all of us. Are you OK with this?'

'It's been interesting.'

'I'm sure. And your mother, how did you find her?'

He thought that through.

'I mean, did you find her interesting? Did you feel you got to know
her a bit? Did you like what you saw?'

'I'm not sure how to answer that.'

'Why?'

'You said to me the other day that you looked upon the world with
different lenses –'

'True.'

'Well, I found my mother in this book, but the lens through which I
saw her was my father's. The image was shaped entirely from his
perspective. I wonder how accurate his impression was.'

'What makes you think that?'

'More than anyone, I appreciate just how jaundiced my father's view
of the world could be. He fitted people into very tight categories and
rarely attached new labels.' Gabriel placed the journal on the carpet.
'The Jocelynne who inhabits these pages is bright, but her intellect is
essentially untapped. She's ambitious, but her aspirations don't clash

with her husband's or preclude her from fulfilling her – how should I put it – wifely duties.'

Gladwin's laughter filled the room. She poured out more coffee. 'You're hard. Harder than your father, I think. It must have been pleasant reading about her arrival, her poetry. She was a wonderful poet, you know.'

'I haven't read any of her work.'

'I had some, but your father borrowed the poems she'd given me and never returned them. I was quite upset.'

'He seems to have destroyed everything.'

'That's terrible. He had no right to do that to her, to your inheritance.'

'I would like to believe that my mother was as wonderful as he made her out to be. It would be good to know that she was who Rupert believed her to be.'

She took his hand again. 'Believe what I say. I was her friend, her true friend. She was wonderful. She wasn't a saint by any means, but she was wonderful, and how many people can have that said of them?

'I remember her as a woman who could get whatever she wanted. She twisted us all around her little finger. Her brother worshipped her. She couldn't do any wrong in his eyes and she knew it. Do you know how that made me feel? I always felt that I was under her thumb in that way, that if I annoyed her or disappointed her, that would be it.' She snapped her fingers. 'No woman who failed to meet with his sister's approval or live up to her was ever going to be good enough.

'She could have had any man she wanted. Why do you think she picked your father? She wasn't stupid. She knew, no matter how much he proclaimed to despise money, he'd always have it. That she'd have it. For all her reading and writing she was a small-town girl. Matthew was the sort of man she'd dreamed about. How do you think her family reacted when they found out that one of the DuBois clan was interested, seriously interested in her? Come on!

'Rupert will tell you that the family thought hard about it. Believe me, they took all of two seconds. I was with Rupert before Josie came over. All he ever did was talk about how famous Matthew's family was. It used to drive your father mad. They couldn't meet company without Rupert bringing up his background. It was terrible.

'I tell you, Rupert thought Josie was going to be his meal ticket, make no mistake. He couldn't believe it when your father shut him out. It sent him mad. He was always carrying on about how much money Matthew had. Do you know that he wrote to Matthew's parents behind his back? They didn't give him the time of day, my friend – not a minute, not a second, nothing.

'That's all he ever talked about, how they'd treated him like dirt. Money, money, money, that's all he ever thought of. Have you any idea how much money Josie used to send back home?'

Gabriel shook his head.

'Loads! And it was her money, not her husband's. Look at Rupert now. I know for a fact that his mother lived on nothing till the day she died.'

'And Matthew's parents?'

'To my knowledge both your grandparents are still alive.'

'Oh.'

'Yes, "oh".'

She let him digest her news for a while before continuing. 'And let me tell you, your mother never asked them for anything. She sent them the odd letter so that they'd know how things were, but that was it. She had pride. She wasn't over the top about everything the way Matthew was, but she fought her corner. She wouldn't hop out of the way when these white people walked into her. She wouldn't turn a blind eye when they short-changed her, but she dealt with it with style.

'So you see, when you add everything up, I had every reason to hate her – her looks, her brother, her manner. But I didn't. No one did. She was a good person and people loved her. It was as simple as that. If you knew her, you came to love her. I loved her and sometimes I did hate her for it. I hated the way she made quality friends so easily and I envied the loyalty she inspired. Can you imagine what it was like being the best friend of someone like that?'

Her cannon-like laughter cracked off the walls. 'She was a monster. A damn monster. I remember once we were in a corner shop and I was being served by this horrible white woman. She hated me, the world, herself, her husband, her dog, the fleas on her dog, everything. She counted out my money as if I was a thief and I remember wanting to punch her face in. And you know what, when that mother of yours came over and paid for her things, the cow smiled at her like a long-lost friend and asked us to come back! Can you believe it?'

'It takes some imagining.'

Gladwin pulled Gabriel towards her, patting the floor by her chair. 'No it doesn't. Your mother had something that wasn't hard to see. Your father saw it in the picture that brought him over here. You think he was cold, but you should have seen him before. His nose was way up in the air, nothing affected him. He was like ice. He was dead inside and he damn well knew it. When he saw your mother, that wasn't love he was reaching for, it was light.'

Gladwin lifted up his hand and kissed it. 'Now, let me ask you this. So your father may have flattered her, your uncle idolized her, but where's the harm? There was another side to her and I could tell you what I know of it. If you think you would profit from it, I could tell you. Shall I?'

'Another time, perhaps.'

They left it at that.

Gabriel drove to Rupert's home.

There were no cars parked outside, but he rang all the same.

Marianne's voice came through the door. 'Hu is it?'

'Gabriel.'

She opened the door, clothed in a blue cotton gown, barefoot and sleepy eyed. 'Come in.'

He joined her in the hallway.

Arms folded across her chest, she looked him up and down. 'Yu woan' fin' me husban' heah, but eif yu wan' ihm, he busy wid de choir.'

He smelled alcohol on her breath. 'I'll go there, then.'

'An' me? Tell me someting. Wa' me do to yu, to mek yu so angry?'

'We have no quarrel.'

'Den why yu start so much trouble 'pon me son?'

He didn't say anything.

She climbed to the top of the stairs, paused, then called him on up.

A pair of thick curtains were drawn, keeping the bedroom in cool darkness. It was richly decorated in purples and blues. There was a king-size bed, but the focal point of the room was the television set, adorned with a host of framed photographs of the family.

Marianne sat down on the bed and invited Gabriel to sit beside her. *The Big Boss* was playing loudly on the VCR. An impressive range of kung fu videos were neatly stacked on top of the cupboards. A picture of Bruce Lee was pinned up between several photographic collages of her children. A pile of newspapers lay by a reading lamp.

After fiddling with her finger-nails for a few minutes, Marianne picked up a newspaper from the bed. She showed Gabriel an article about a young black man who, after being mistaken by the police for a dangerous criminal, had been shot several times in his car. He had survived and was recovering in hospital.

'It seem', she said, 'like yu caan' step outside ya house widdout someting bad gettin' up and bitin' yu. Tings nevah use' to be like dis, nevah. A wooman could walk de street widdout bein' mugged oah get attack'. Now, yu caan' even drive home widdout de pohlice shootin' yu up, jus' 'cause yu got de wrong face.'

She played with the hem of her gown. 'Me wrong to come to dis country. Me haf a good life back in Jamaica. But me start chasin' diamond an' pearl an' evary silly ting in between, wen dose kinda tings were nevah fe de likes a' me, anyway.'

Soon after, she made her excuses and kissed him goodbye.

The staff at the Albert Hall were quite accommodating and led Gabriel to Rupert. His uncle sat with Clarence at a long table on the main stage. They asked Gabriel to wait while they concluded their business. He waited at the side of the stage and watched various members of the choir run through sound and lighting checks. The choir leader was firm but good humoured and everything seemed well in hand.

Peter, deep in conversation with a suited city type whom Gabriel recognized as a government minister, came on to the stage. Rupert and Clarence shook hands with the man. The choir members fell silent and stood formally, as if they were readying themselves for inspection.

The minister shook hands with the choir leader and wished them all the best over the coming days of competition. 'You're a credit to your community,' he said. 'I hope that you inspire others by your example.'

The choir performed a brief song for the minister, who clapped along enthusiastically, even though he was frequently off the beat. When they had finished, he encouraged Rupert to keep up the good work and congratulated him on his idea for setting up a local independent black conservative party. 'We don't want to encourage separatism, but anything that helps to tap into our support at local level is welcome.'

Rupert oozed false modesty and humility. Finally, the small talk exhausted, the minister left. A general feeling of triumph and excitement was in the air as Peter approached Gabriel.

'Do yourself a favour,' he snarled. 'Leave before I make you leave.'

Rupert held up a warning finger, and shouted from across the stage, 'No trouble, yu heah?'

Peter lowered his voice. 'How long are you going to hide behind my father?'

'Now mek up, like me tell yu to,' came his father's distant order.

Peter held out his hand. 'This doesn't mean fuck all, you know that.'

They shook hands.

Rupert and Clarence joined them. 'Good, good. Me like wat me see,' said Rupert, slapping his son on the shoulder. 'Truly, de Christian spirit can ovahcome evary likkle dispute, eif yu give it a chance.'

Peter muttered something about being needed elsewhere and left the hall.

Rupert turned to his nephew. 'Gabriel, once yu an' Peter get to knoh one anoddah, yu —'

Gabriel cut him off. 'We shall never be friends.'

'So, yu look into de future now, eh? All de bookies mus' be shakin' in deh boots.'

'Unlike you, I've kept company with the truth for most of my life. So believe me when I say that we shall never be friends.'

'There's no need to speak like that,' said Clarence.

'That's a habit of yours, isn't it, Reverend? Not airing the truth.'

The eyes of both men fell on the journal. Gabriel held it towards them. 'Why did you show me this?'

'So yu can see tings right.'

'What things?'

Rupert puffed out his cheeks and threw up his hands. 'It jus' like two an' two — eif yu doan' undahstahn', yu nevah reahlly knoh how to mek four, or how to get to de trut'.'

'Whose truth?'

'Yu got it. Yu tell me how many trut's a book can hold.'

Gabriel turned and walked away.

Rupert followed his nephew. 'Gabriel?'

Gabriel wouldn't look at him.

'Gabriel, please.'

'You gave it to me, not because it would solve anything, but because it might exonerate you.'

'Exonna wat?'

'Don't play games with me.'

'Nevah.'

'How did you come by my father's journal?'

'Sorry?'

'I've read it. He would never have given this to you.'

'Believe it or not, deh was a time wen we was truly close.'

'Oh, please.'

A fit of coughing suddenly overtook Rupert. Gabriel strained to catch the words that were sandwiched between the explosions. 'What did you say?'

Rupert cleared his throat. 'Me tek it.'

'You took it?'

'Ya fadah lef' me no choice. Me wan' some a' Josie's tings back. He refuse to han' dem ovah, so me tek de book to force his han'.

'You're unbelievable.'

'At de time, it seem like de right ting to do. Anyway, me nevah look at it, not reahlly.'

Gabriel, lost for words, could only shake his head in wonder.

Rupert beckoned to Clarence, who moved over to join them.

'Rupert was right to show you the book. I stand by what we did.'

'This book has nothing to do with the disappearances,' Gabriel said to Rupert. 'There is no mention of the eggs. It was an act of ego to let me read this, nothing more.'

'Nonsense.'

'It hasn't solved anything.

'Den yu nevah read it right.'

'We have to go to the police.'

It was as if someone had slapped Rupert in the face. 'No way. We mus' deal wid dis.'

' "We" cannot solve this.'

'No!' shouted Rupert, silencing the choir on the stage. They were quickly ordered to continue with their business. 'Look about yu. Wat yu wan', fe it all to go bye-bye? Do yu?'

'The dead girl on my door –'

'Let me tell yu someting right now. Me na come all dis way to end in shame an' failure. Evaryting I got, I got thru hard work an' sweat. Eif me fadah slip a silver spoon in me mout' de day me born, me nevah see or taste it! Can yu see it? Can yu? No one, no one, gwine see dis bwoy fall.'

'And Mary?'

'De trut'?'

'The truth!'

'No doubt about it. It wud be a seriaas, seriaas wrong eif a man in my position could not carry de same unjus' burden dat afflict his flock. De Lord will lead us thru all dis. Trus' me.'

At that moment, Peter's voice reverberated through the building. 'Father! Father!' As Rupert looked for him, he burst through the main doors into the auditorium. 'She's here, Father! She's here!'

Mary followed him into the auditorium. Everything about her was immaculate. Smiling nervously she stuttered. 'Daddy –'

Rupert's scream, wild and utterly joyous, started an outcry on the stage as everyone rushed towards the girl. Rupert picked her up and held her with all his strength, ignoring her squeals of pain and planting kisses all over her face as she burst into tears. Peter, crying freely, embraced the two of them as the choir and Clarence milled about them.

Rupert, beside himself, ran his hands over Mary as if to ascertain that she was real. 'Me caan' believe it!'

'I'm fine, Daddy, I'm fine.'

Her father exploded, pumping his fist at the roof. 'Tank yu Lord! Tank yu!' He thrust his finger, ramrod straight, at his nephew. 'See! Me tell yu! Me tell yu! Yu seh yu doan' believe. Well, believe now. Yu seh yu doubt. Well, doubt no moah!' His frame shook with emotion as his passion transformed him. 'Doubt no moah, sinner! De Lord will forgive wen yu ansah his call an' believe in de irresistible force of his powah! Believe an' he will forgive all a' ya sins!'

Amens and salutations swelled from the choir as he swept down the aisle towards his nephew. The outstretched finger curled back into his fist, the bones of which cracked as he shook it, and tears streamed down his cheeks. 'Believe. Believe, befoh de world gobble yu up. Accept his word an' knoh de trut', dat de whole world knoh to be true.'

Silent, he returned to his daughter and held her once more.

Gabriel looked on as Rupert quietened everyone down, sat next to Mary and asked the questions everyone wanted to ask. She tried to answer calmly, but quickly became agitated and signalled for a smartly dressed man who had been quietly watching the proceedings from the doorway to come over and join her. Ill at ease, eyes to the floor, he took hold of her outstretched hand.

'Dad, I'd like you to meet Errol.'

Rupert looked at Errol as a prize breeder surveying a misconceived crossbreed. 'Errol?'

'Mr Wills.'

They shook hands.

Peter covered his face and let out a muffled, 'Oh, God!'

'Dad, I have something to tell you.'

'Damn right. Yu up an' go widdout a word an' mek us all sick wid worry. Now yu just walk in like – like –' He looked Errol over. 'An' hu de hell is dis?' His temper began to rise. 'Was it yu hu tek me girl?'

Mary slid in between them. 'No, Father, he didn't take. We're married.'

Peter looked away.

The choir gaped.

Rupert's lips began to purse. He looked to his right, to his left, and eventually produced the longest sucking of teeth that anybody had never heard. Mary started to say something. He silenced her with a slight motion of his hand.

'Wat? Marry? Marry wen?'

Her voice was barely audible. 'Just after I left.'

'Jus' aftah yu lef'?' His fingers drummed on his leg as he studied the watching faces with their popping eyes and slack jaws. 'Young lady, me got news fe yu. Yu didn' jus' up an' go to Marks an' bloody Spencer! Yu go! Yu go!'

Errol ventured, 'Mr Wills?', but got no further.

'Shut up, fool!'

No one moved.

'An' weh yu go? Wat yu do? Wa' de hell gowan aroun' heah?'

'I'm pregnant. I didn't want to tell you before I – before we got married.' And with that the tears came. 'I knew how you'd react. I was afraid to tell you. I knew that if we weren't married, then you'd never forgive me.'

Rupert was unable to speak for a few seconds. 'Forgive? Forgive wat?! Forgive a daughtah hu caan' control de smallest itch wen it rise up between her legs, an' hu scratch it like a dog. Yu caan' act like a decent, Christian wooman! Yu got no control. Yu jus' go an' betray, yes betray evary principle me teach yu, an' mek a fool outta me!' He turned to Errol. 'Anyway, how me knoh dis fool be de real fadah, an' not som idiot yu drag off de street?!'

'Daddy –'

'No! None a' dat Daddy shit! Out! Get outta me sight!'

Rupert rose and pointed to the door. 'Out!'

Mary ran out.

Errol followed.

Rupert collapsed on to a chair.

Peter tried to comfort him. 'It's all right, Dad –'

Rupert pushed his arm away. 'All right? All right?'

'I –'

His father clipped him on the head. 'Doan' jus' stan' deh, go an' get ya sistah. Go!'

Peter went after Mary and Errol.

Family and friends gathered rapidly at Rupert's house to celebrate. Mother and daughter were inseparable. Brother and sister swapped jokes. Cousins passed drinks around. Friends handed out continual congratulations. Rupert, having had chance to cool down, welcomed Errol into the family. The press were called and handed a brief statement. The police arrived and expressed their anger at having so much of their valuable time wasted. Much apologizing was done.

When the moment was right, Rupert took Gabriel and Clarence to one side. His mood was upbeat and optimistic. 'Well, Gabriel,' he began. 'Ya uncle tell yu. Yu doan' listen, but he still tell yu.'

Clarence shook his hand. 'You were right again. All we had to do was keep faith. I can hardly believe she's back.'

'Well, now me baby back, we can put dis awful episode behind us.'

Gabriel seemed unconvinced. 'You honestly believe that?'

Rupert placed a hand on his shoulder. 'Yes, yes, certainly. Tek a look aroun' an' tell me wat yu see. Me tell yu. Family. It is all deh fe yu, evary bit. De pas' is de pas'. Yu is me sistah's son. Me caan' forget dat.'

Gabriel said goodbye and left.

Gabriel woke up the next morning having come to a decision. He went into the garden, dug up the earth just under the tree-infant and uncovered an envelope wrapped in a plastic covering. He refilled the hole, then returned to the house, collected the eggs and set out on his journey.

The envelope contained a single sheet of letterhead. A few years ago, it had been sent to Gabriel's lawyer with instructions regarding the sale of some shares. After acquiring it, Gabriel had noted on the back of the letter the exact route that would take him to the address it had been sent from. With the paper now beside him, he sped along the motorway to his destination.

It took him just over two hours to reach Cambridge. Once in the city, he wasted time negotiating the one-way system and asking directions from people who had no idea where the village he was searching for was located. Eventually, he went into a travel agency and, after waiting for a couple of students to complete their business, was given a very specific set of instructions by a cheerful travel adviser.

After several wrong turns he found the village of Willingham. An elderly man trimming his front hedge directed him to the correct house. It turned out to be a Tudor cottage, which lay at the back of a long driveway that contained a Mercedes and an MG. Children's bicycles lay on the expansive front lawn, along with T-shirts, water pistols and Action Man dolls. As Gabriel walked up the drive a swarm of young boys rushed round from the back of the house, wrestling and kicking at each other. The eldest, a freckled, skinny thing with straw-blond hair, stopped in his tracks and gawped at Gabriel.

'I'm looking for a Penny Windsor,' said Gabriel.

'No one called that lives here,' said the boy.

Gabriel hesitated.

'There's only my mum, Penny Addcock.'

'Perhaps that's her. Could I see her?'

The boy screamed, 'Mum!' and, chased by his gang, ran into the house and out of Gabriel's sight. A woman's voice shouting at the boys to be quiet reached Gabriel where he stood waiting on the lawn. 'Someone's here to see you!' yelled back the boy. 'That's still no excuse!' was the reply. More youthful screaming, then the sound of doors slamming and then quiet.

Through the door, her throat red from bellowing, came a plump woman with shoulder-length hair. She wore flip-flops, shorts and a thin cotton shirt. 'Hello,' she said. 'What can I do for you?'

'My name's Gabriel DuBois. I've come to see my father.'

Her face flushed a deep pink as she covered her mouth and took a few steps back. 'I don't believe it!' she gasped. 'You're Gabriel – I don't believe it!' Grinning from ear to ear, she rushed forward and embraced him. 'I'm Penny. I'm an old friend of Matthew's.

He shook her hand. 'He talked often of you.'

She shook her head. 'I can't believe it. This is amazing, absolutely amazing! Come in.' Calling out, 'Tom! Tom! Come quickly!' she led him into the house.

A door opened and an enormous bear of a man emerged, bending down to avoid banging his head on the low door-frame. 'What on earth is the matter?'

She caught hold of his arm. 'Nothing's the matter. This is Gabriel – Matthew's son.'

'Well, well, well. This is a surprise.'

Tom and Gabriel shook hands.

'Your father isn't here just at the moment,' said Penny. 'He's popped to the shops to buy a newspaper.'

'Would you like something to drink while you wait?' asked Tom.

Gabriel declined and Penny offered to show him round. The back garden was enormous, and was ablaze with colour. Penny informed him that it had featured in several magazines. But Penny's pride and joy was the orchard, which was stocked with a huge variety of fruit trees. 'It's a real pleasure, planting things, waiting for them to grow,' she said. 'There's nothing I love more than selling my produce at the market. Nothing comes close.'

A swarm of wasps buzzed over a compost heap. 'Don't mind them,' Penny said. 'You just let them get on with it and they're no harm to anyone. You should have seen this place when we took it over. It was an absolute mess. But we've made something decent out of it. Your father's been very good at giving design hints. Useless at the actual work itself, but marvellous when it comes to thinking it all out.'

She pointed to a barn down at the end of the garden. 'That's Matthew's place. We handed it over to him and he's quite happy there. It's perfect for a bookworm. He's been very productive in the last few years, writing all hours of the day. He can be quite brilliant.'

From where they stood they could glimpse part of the road where it curved round the side of the house. Along this stretch a tall man came into view, wearing a blue shirt and black jogging pants, a rolled-up newspaper under his arm. Gabriel watched him, surprised by the signs of age that had appeared on his father's face and body. His gait was slower. He stooped slightly.

Penny called out to Matthew as he came round the side of the house, but he didn't respond. She tried again, but he carried on and went inside the barn.

'He gets like this sometimes. Hang on while I tell him you're here.'

She followed Matthew down the garden, knocked on the barn door and went inside. Gabriel waited and waited until Penny, flustered and embarrassed, emerged. 'Look, I'm sorry, but he told me to tell you that he doesn't want to see you.'

'Would you tell him that I won't leave until I see him?'

She went back inside. Raised voices filtered through the door. She came back with the same message. 'This is an awful position for me to be in. I really don't know what to do, but you must understand, right or wrong, he is my friend.'

'I understand,' said Gabriel, before moving past her and kicking open the door.

Matthew stood in the middle of the barn, chewing his nails. He glowered at Gabriel. 'How dare you come into my home like this?'

They were the first words that Gabriel had heard from his father in years. He'd often imagined this moment of reunion and the dialogue that might pass between them, but he hadn't even come close.

Penny said quietly, 'I'll leave you two to it,' and walked briskly back to her house.

Gabriel closed the door behind him and stepped inside his father's home. The room was fully carpeted, with central heating and everything a recluse might need – television, cooker, microwave, juice extractor, weights, hi-fi and books. Books were everywhere – on shelves, in boxes, piled up on the floor, stacked on cupboards, under the bed, everywhere.

Matthew lit up a pipe and turned the hi-fi on. Etta James began to sing 'I'd Rather Go Blind' before the tape was fast-forwarded to a more restrained Ella Fitzgerald number. 'You surprise me, Gabriel.'

'How?'

'I hadn't expected to see you so soon. I thought it would be at least three more years before you turned up.' Matthew turned and sank on to his bed.

Gabriel sat down on the floor. He studied Matthew – his soft belly, slim arms and almost delicate fingers, the lack of hard muscle, his physical smallness.

Matthew blew out a stream of smoke. 'Would you turn the kettle on? I've picked up the habit of enjoying tea, in weather like this.'

And Gabriel did. Just like that, he found himself standing at the stove lighting up the gas ring, and filling the kettle. As he sat down again, Matthew asked, 'You filled the kettle with enough water for two. Why?'

As his cheeks burned, Gabriel took a deep breath. 'Is there a water shortage?'

'That quip might impress children in a school yard, but I'm afraid it leaves me cold.'

'Since I didn't spend that much time socializing in school yards, I can't comment.'

'True. Still, you didn't miss much. Or is that the purpose of this visit? Have you come to complain?'

'No.'

Matthew studied his watch. 'Then what?'

Gabriel removed the journal from beneath the back of his shirt and passed it to Matthew.

'I haven't seen this for some time. How did you come by it?'

'Rupert.'

'Ah. It did occur to me that he might have taken it, but –' He fell silent and, with a shrug, placed the journal under the bed.

'How is Rupert?'

'His church is well established. His children are well. He has respect from many quarters.'

A few lethargic puffs, then, 'He's worked hard. He's never claimed a Welfare cheque. All of his children have received a decent education. I would imagine that he considers himself a "success".'

A whistle from the stove.

Matthew made himself a cup of tea. 'I think this is best, don't you? Then there is no pretence of this being anything more than . . .' Another shrug, and then silence.

'More than what, exactly?'

Matthew's shoulders rose and fell laboriously, as if the effort of breathing was a great trial. 'More than what we both know it to be.

When it's over, which I trust will be soon, you will go on your way and I will carry on with my life. In my home, with my friends and the garden and my reading. Everything will be . . . fine.'

'You've been writing.'

'Dabbling. Commentary, reviews, nothing of consequence.' He looked about the room. 'I have a magazine here, somewhere. *House and Garden*, something like that. Some of your work is featured. You're highly regarded in certain circles.'

'I enjoy my work. Like Rupert, I sustain myself through my own efforts.'

'Indeed.' A smile appeared.

'Considering that you've never known the fear of being without money, you have a curious lack of respect for people who seek to enjoy a similar comfort.'

'Perhaps.' Another glance at the watch. 'Is that it?'

'No.'

'Oh dear.' Matthew lay down on the bed.

'I want –'

'You want?'

'I would like –'

This seemed to disturb Matthew. 'What you would like is of no importance to me. Surely you know that by now. I mean, surely that is understood. You can't have come all this way expecting to break the ground rules.' He moved quickly to a shelf and removed a book. 'Really, I expected better. We spent enough time in each other's company to . . . we had an understanding.'

'You lied to me about my mother.'

'I will not discuss her with you, or with anyone else for that matter.'

'You lied about where she was buried.'

'I did what I had to do.'

'Where is she?'

Matthew shook his head.

'Where is my sister?'

'No. No. That is not for you.' He made for the door. 'Now you will leave. Go, please. I wish you well for the future, but that is all.'

Gabriel, struggling to think clearly in his father's presence, found to his horror that he was beginning to hyperventilate.

Matthew mumbled contemptuously, 'Nothing changes, does it?'

Gabriel, straining to control himself, didn't reply.

Matthew looked over to the main house. Penny and Tom were talking in the kitchen. He closed the door quietly so that they could not see into the barn. 'You shouldn't have come here. Why risk stirring up old memories and bad feelings? You'll only hurt yourself.'

Gabriel forced himself to look Matthew in the eye and said, 'That will never happen again. It was the last time.'

'I hope so. I really do.'

Gabriel stood and offered his hand.

'Is that what you want? Will it comfort you?'

They shook hands.

Gabriel went to leave, but stopped by an antique desk and took a quick look through some of his father's personal effects.

'Do you mind?' said Matthew.

The desk was clean and neat, with an Olivetti typewriter and several completed articles. Gabriel picked up a piece titled 'Figures of Fun' which examined the humour and reception of black comedians such as Charlie Cook and Lenny Henry.

'What are you doing?'

Gabriel took a lighter from his pocket and set fire to the essay.

Matthew took a deep breath and sat back down on his bed.

'Where is my mother?'

'No. I won't give you that.'

Gabriel set fire to another essay.

'Those don't mean anything to me. You can burn all you like.'

They watched the flame eat through paper.

'Go on, do what you like. You can't bully me. Is that all you learned? How to be vicious? You can't hurt me. You're not important enough. Those things aren't important enough.'

Gabriel flicked the flint as he looked out of the window at the main house. 'It's a dry day. That Tudor roof will go up in minutes.'

'What?'

'I swear to you, if you don't tell me where my mother is, I'll set fire to your friend's home. If they try to stop me, I'll do whatever I have to do.'

Matthew looked him up and down.

They stared at each other.

Matthew raised his hands and clapped slowly.

Gabriel handed him a pen and a sheet of paper. 'I don't want your applause, just information.'

'I'm not sure whether to be ashamed or proud,' said Matthew as he scribbled on the paper.

'I don't care.'

Matthew waved the pen at him. 'Don't ruin it. You were doing well. You were original, your own self. Don't go repeating me. Learn from me, but don't mimic.' He handed the paper back.

Gabriel glanced at it. 'Where is this place?'

'There's a cemetery down the road. I've bought a private plot. I'll take you there.'

'I'll find it by myself.'

'No. I won't allow you to go by yourself.'

They left the barn.

As they passed through the village a number of people waved to Matthew and greeted him as he went by. He stopped to chat to an elderly woman, who reminded him that the bridge club would be having their annual general meeting soon and that he must attend. He assured her he would. Gabriel was introduced. This caused her much shock for she had no idea that Matthew had a son. Matthew was sure that he must have mentioned Gabriel before. Not at all, not once. With excuses given and promises made, they carried on.

The cemetery was tiny. No local person had been buried there for over twenty years. Since the expansion and upgrading of a cemetery in a nearby village, it functioned mainly as a short-cut from the nearby men's club to the corner shop. Matthew led him to the back of the cemetery. In a neighbouring field, two children were having a riding lesson. The instructor barked out instructions while their parents looked on.

'Here,' said Matthew.

They came to a fenced-off area about ten foot square. In the centre of the smoothly mown grass was a brass vase bearing the inscription, 'Jocelynne and Cuffay, my eternal loves'.

Matthew joined them. 'I kept their ashes with me for a time. When I moved, Penny suggested I lay them here.'

Gabriel stepped on to the grass.

'Well,' said his father kicking away some twigs, 'here we are. I'm sure it's a bit of an anti-climax, isn't it? It's been pleasant having them to myself.

'One thing about living out here, you get a feel for nature. I have been known on the odd occasion to hold a lengthy conversation with sunflowers. I don't doubt that they are receptive. They're unquestioning. They either get sunlight or they don't. You smile at them or you don't. It's all quite orderly, really.'

Gabriel knelt by the urn and absently poked the ground with a long twig that he'd found.

'I want you to know', said Matthew, 'that I have no regrets.' He stepped back as Gabriel plucked the stick out and stood up. 'Is that it? I'd like to go home now.'

Neither DuBois spoke as the car wound its way through the village back to Penny's home. As soon as the car pulled up Matthew opened the door and got out.

He paused for a moment.

They looked each other over.

Then Gabriel drove on.

Gabriel knocked on the door loudly.

After a few moments, Rachel appeared in the doorway, dressed in an oversized jumper.

'Hi,' she said, and hugged him hard.

They sat in the kitchen.

Steam rose from microwaved salt-fish-and-dumpling soup. Gabriel's food remained untouched.

Rachel picked bones from her teeth. 'You look tired.'

'I could do with some sleep.'

She reached out to stroke his face.

Muffled voices reached them from the bedroom.

Rachel said quietly, 'Guptah and Jeffrey are here.'

'In your bedroom?'

'In my bed.'

He let out a long, weary sigh and rubbed his eyes. 'I suppose you will say it's none of my business?'

'What, if Guptah and Jeffrey are in my bed?'

'What else?'

'Where else would they sleep together?'

'I don't understand.'

'You can be very dense when you want to be. Jeffrey can't take anyone home. Guptah certainly can't. So I offered them my bed.'

'Jeffrey and Guptah?'

'Don't look so shocked. Why do you think Jeffrey was so interested in the campaign? The poor thing keeps so much to himself, when Guptah came on to him he thought he'd died and gone to heaven. They'll be good for each other.'

'If you say so.'

She jabbed his nose lightly with her finger. 'Don't look like that. I can't stand it when people look like that.'

'Like what?'

'Oh, please.'

'I didn't come to talk about Guptah and Jeffrey.'

'Well, you'd better get used to them. This is the only safe house they've got.'

'Then we'll have to spend more time at my place.'

Rachel went to the fridge and pulled out some beers. 'Is that your way of inviting me over?'

Gabriel took an envelope out of his pocket. 'There's something in here I'd like you to read.'

She sat down. 'What is this? Some contract? Rules about the bathroom? Dos and don'ts on weekend stays?'

He sat beside her. 'Before you read it I have something to say to you.'

'What?'

'I want to be with you.'

She crossed her arms. 'You want to be with me?'

'Yes.'

She slid a beer over to him and picked up the envelope. 'OK, go for it.'

He looked her in the eye. 'I will never lie to you. I will never betray your confidence. It would not upset me if I were to go through my life without knowing any other woman. You're obviously more experienced than me, so it would be stupid of me to imagine that I could satisfy all your needs, but I hope that we could come to love each other equally in every way.

'If you are willing to attempt to build something –' his eyes rolled upwards as he searched for the right word, 'something glorious with me, then open my gift. If what I say frightens you, hand it back and we'll go our separate ways.'

Rachel studied his stillness and sense of purpose. 'Black man, I'm not a coward,' she said, 'otherwise we wouldn't be here. An' believe me, me do a lot moah lookin' den yu.' She paused before opening the envelope. 'Just don't let me open this and be disappointed. I'm tired of being disappointed.'

She studied the page momentarily, then, her cheeks flushing, read out:

Rachel, before I left the womb your face was the last image I saw, and as I turned away from the bright light of this new world, it was your name that I called for comfort.

She stopped momentarily, before carrying on:

From that first day, in countless places – a torn picture, a moving image, the cusp of a melody – I have searched for you. I watched you disappear in sliding shadow, heard your fading echo in cooling water and came so close, so terribly close to giving up. Now that you have come to me and the waiting is over, I lie beside your love and find it warmer than that of my mother's birthing cradle. The hand I grasp is firm and sure and the light – ah, the light.

Off the chair she came, wrapping her arms about him, kissing his face and neck, wetting his skin with tears. 'I didn't think you'd go for it. I thought that you'd end up settling for some Sunday-school girl.' The chains round her ankles clinked against each other as she made herself comfortable on the floor. 'Thank you,' she said, smoothing out the paper on the tiles. 'You're very brave. I've always wanted someone who was brave. That's all.' She hugged him with a strength that brought pain and cast whispers in his ear. When her words for him had finished, she said, 'Jeffrey's scared you'll say something.'

'It's none of my business.'

She led him by the hand to her bedroom door and knocked gently.

Someone mumbled, 'Come in.'

They found Jeffrey and Guptah sitting fully dressed on the bed. Guptah looked warily at them through a cloud of cigarette smoke. Jeffrey seemed to be studying something outside the window. 'Guys,' she said, 'I'm going home with Gabriel. I'll see you tomorrow.'

'Sure,' said Guptah.

As they headed down the hallway, Jeffrey caught up with them.

'What time will you be picking me up?'

'What time is best for you?'

'Any time.'

'OK. Me see yu wen me see yu. Jus' be ready, right?'

'Right.' For the first time, he looked Gabriel in the eye. 'Gabriel?'

'Yes?'

Jeffrey hugged him. 'Go well,' he said.

The journey home was slow and untroubled.

He rested while she drove.

She asked why he was so tired.

He made some excuses.

She said, 'You were quite sweet with Jeffrey.'

He told her he didn't want to speak about Jeffrey.

So they didn't.

The house was extremely quiet.

Gabriel stood in the living room for a few minutes, considering the number of people who knew where he lived and who visited without welcome or permission.

He called an estate agent.

The agent arranged a time for a visit and Gabriel hinted that he would be willing to take a drop in the true value of the house if it meant a speedy sale.

Afterwards, he went into the garden. The tree-infant looked well, but he wasn't up to conversation and merely pushed the twig he had brought back from Willingham into the ground alongside his friend.

Rachel joined him, and he told her about Sobers and how long he'd lain under the tree.

'I make friends easily,' she said. 'I'll show you how to do it. Once you know how, it's easy.'

She held him tightly, then, arm in arm, they returned to the house and went upstairs.

Rachel sat down on the bed and unzipped a pocket in her jacket. 'I have something for you.'

She held out an embroidered jewellery box.

It contained a ring.

'I went and had it expanded for your finger . . . Just in case.'

Gabriel joined her on the bed.

'It belonged to my grandfather. It will look nice on you. I think you'll know how to respect it.'

He tried the ring on. It fitted well enough.

'My mother always knocked me for carrying it around, but I think it kept us in touch. I miss him . . . And I have felt him around, you know, sometimes.' She held his hand. 'Do you think it's stupid, letting death get you down? Worrying if it ends everything?'

He kissed her hand. 'I've never been afraid of death. I just want to exist well between its appearances. I know that the soul is linked to the movements of the universe. If particles of the same soul meet, then I think it's because a greater, more majestical motion has brought them together. Energy doesn't dissipate because of absence or death.'

She ran her fingers over the ring. 'That would be good. I'd like to think that was true.'

Gabriel held her face and kissed her gently on the lips. Her tears wet his fingers and salted his mouth. He lowered her head to the quilt, helped her remove her clothing and fed upon her vagina long after his belly was full.

Gabriel didn't sleep, but lay next to Rachel, studying her face in the gathering dusk.

The doorbell rang.

Taking care not to wake her, he went downstairs.

A dark-skinned boy, wearing a pristine white shirt, black trousers and spotless shoes, stood on the doorstep holding out an envelope. 'Mr DuBois,' he said, 'this is for you.' Gabriel recognized him as the boy who had recently dropped off the egg.

The envelope was without a return address or postage stamps. As

Gabriel turned it over, the youngster stepped forward. 'I have to wait until you've seen what's inside and given me an answer.'

Gabriel closed the door on the boy and stepped back into the hallway. The envelope contained a number of photographs, newspaper clippings and a message. The photographs were of Roberta Brown and James Watson, still easily recognizable although years had obviously passed between the children's disappearances and the taking of these snaps. Brown was smiling into the camera; sitting on a chair studying a book; building a brick wall. Watson was reading a book; standing in a field; sitting on a bench with a group of other children. The clippings recounted Watson's disappearance and interviews with his parents. The message, printed by hand on a blank card, read, 'If you're interested, follow Marcus's directions.'

Gabriel opened the door.

Marcus had not moved.

'Come inside, while I bath.'

Gabriel spent a leisurely bath studying the photographs and newspaper cuttings until he was ready. He found Marcus in the kitchen, reading out to Rachel a poem by Josephine Bennett. The boy quickly placed the book down on the table and put his arms behind his back.

'Why did you look so guilty?'

'It's not my book. I should have asked your permission.'

'You don't have to ask anyone's permission to read, especially not when someone's spent so much time writing it for you.'

'For me? The writer didn't do that book for me.'

'How many people do you read a book with?'

'No one. I read books by myself.'

'So it's an exclusive relationship.'

'Not when you then examine it with other students.'

'But at the time of reading.'

'Then', the boy concentrated fiercely, 'the experience is an act of mutual creation between the writer and the reader.'

'A unique experience?'

'If you suppose that everybody creates different images from the same words.'

'Hears different voices?'

'Has different feelings.'

'So?'

'If you think of it in that way, maybe the author did write the book for one person.'

'For you, perhaps?'

Marcus shook his head and smiled.

Rachel complimented Marcus on his reading of the poem before scolding Gabriel. 'Why must you spend so much time in your head? Why not just enjoy the way he said it?'

Gabriel took another book down from his shelf. 'Marcus, I'd like you to have this.'

The boy took the book. 'Have you an answer?'

'You have directions for me?'

'Yes.'

'Shall we go, then?'

'Yes.'

Rachel followed them to the door, before grabbing his hand. 'Go where?'

He found his set of spare keys and handed them to her. 'I've got to take him home. I might be gone for a day.'

'And what the fuck am I supposed to do?'

'Whatever you like.'

She watched him lead Marcus to the car, took a bet with herself on how long he'd take to look at her and began to count. His glance came earlier than expected.

Marcus guided him through the evening traffic, past the Embankment, through Battersea to Clapham Junction. They parked the car and went into the station. Without explanation the boy walked to a ticket booth, bought two tickets and carried on to platform five. When Gabriel joined him at the top of the stairs, Marcus advised Gabriel to continue along the platform and waited by a bench.

As Gabriel moved on, a crackling tannoy informed passengers of the impending arrival and destination of the next train. A station attendant waited for him to pass before slopping water over closed-off stairs. Sweet papers, cigarette butts and can rings littered the concrete. A fluttering movement grew in his stomach as he passed stained posters for new movie releases.

Out past the last waiting room with its single-bar fire, beyond the illumination of the station lights, under a signpost declaring the name of the station, Gabriel found a man waiting.

His face was gaunt with striking cheek-bones. The dreadlocks on his receding hair-line were a pure white. Despite the warm air he wore a light overcoat over his slim frame. He offered his hand. 'Hello.' His palm was cool to touch, the finger-nails elongated and brown. 'I wasn't sure you'd come.'

'I couldn't really say no.'

He squeezed Gabriel's hand. 'You can always say no. My name is Arthur. I'm not sure if it's much of a recommendation, but I was a good friend of your father.'

'What do you want?'

'What makes you think I want anything?'

'Mr Kembo –'

'My name is Arthur. Having chosen your name, I think it's only fair that you enjoy mine.'

Gabriel took the envelope from his jacket and produced a picture of Roberta.

Arthur examined it. 'She was quite lovely, exquisite really.'

'And James Watson?'

'Oh dear,' said Arthur, responding to the bite in Gabriel's voice. 'I hope you're not going to be as precious as your father, it really is too late in the evening for that.' He shivered as he pocketed the photograph. He signalled for Marcus to join them.

The boy trotted down the platform. 'Yes, Sir?'

'Hand me another cough sweet, please.'

The boy reached into his pocket.

Arthur tapped the top of the book Marcus was clutching. 'What's this?'

'Mr DuBois gave it to me.'

Arthur lifted Walter Hammond's autobiography from Marcus's grasp. On the inside cover was the inscription, 'To my dearest friend, Matthew. May this bring you much joy and no little enlightenment. Your friend, Arthur.'

'A good choice.' He slipped the book back.

'Your sweet, Sir.'

'You've done well, Marcus. I'm proud of you.'

'Thank you, Sir.'

A train pulled in. Passengers disembarked and pushed their way on, until the station attendant blew his whistle and the train slid away.

Arthur turned to Marcus. 'Are you watching?'

'Yes, Sir.'

'What do you see?'

The boy straightened up and licked his lips nervously. 'The system.'

'In what regard?'

'The way it works. Who the train serves. Who serves the train and the people on it.'

'More detail.'

The boy pointed to the signal box. 'A black man works in the box, but it's a recorded white voice that announces the destination.' His finger moved on. 'A black man is cleaning the platform. A white man is supervising an Indian man do a job that doesn't need supervision.'

'A simple conclusion.'

Marcus's eyes were filled with an intense anger. 'They exploit us, as they've always exploited us. If I was out here, that's all they'd expect of me.'

'And what do you expect from them?'

'Nothing. I want nothing from them.'

'I didn't ask you what you wanted. I asked what you expect.'

'I expect the same.'

About thirty yards down the platform, by a framed timetable, a ginger-haired woman caught Marcus's gaze. His undisguised aggression took her by surprise and she blushed a bright red. Confused, she tried to outstare him.

He cussed her and began to walk forward. Arthur called out his name. The boy came to a halt.

'Come back.'

With clenched fists and tight lips, Marcus returned.

'Calm yourself.'

'I hate them,' spat Marcus, barely able to contain himself.

Arthur smiled wanly at Gabriel. 'We'll wait for the lad to calm down.'

Another train pulled in. The woman boarded it. As it left the station, she took one last look at Marcus through the window.

'Look at her,' said Arthur. 'She's been scared out of her wits. What do you imagine she'll say to her husband? I'm sure that she won't just talk about Marcus. She'll remember that there were three of us. And

Marcus, he'll be bigger, much bigger and older. You and I? We'll have egged him on and laughed at her.'

He watched Gabriel watching him. 'Shall we go?'

'Where?'

'To my home. We can't talk here.'

Arthur and Marcus went back along the platform and out of the station.

Gabriel came after.

Arthur told Gabriel to drive over Chelsea Bridge. They headed over the water towards a barrage of flashing neon that caused Marcus to gawp.

'Forgive him,' said Arthur. 'He's not used to the glamour of the city, certainly not at night anyway.'

Gabriel studied Marcus in the rear-view mirror. Every passing cab and car seemed to intrigue him. Leather pants, studded jackets, brightly dyed hair, flesh-piercing jewellery, garish rings, all drew steady proclamations of disbelief.

'Over there,' said Arthur as they passed over the bridge and parked along the Embankment. 'Will it be safe to leave your car here?'

'No, and I won't.'

Arthur unbuckled. 'In that case you'll have to get used to following my speed. I drive much more slowly than you, I'm afraid.'

Marcus accompanied him to a run-down Land Rover parked by the road. Its engine took some time to turn over, but eventually he moved off, with Gabriel following behind. Arthur was indeed a slow, almost pedantic motorist and when he pulled into a garage for petrol he apologized.

Gabriel made light of it.

Arthur advised him to fill up his tank.

'Where are we going?'

Arthur pulled a pout. 'Come now, Gabriel, show some patience. I know it's something the young lack nowadays, but try to indulge me a little ... The London skyline is quite beautiful at night, isn't it? I always like to catch the sunset. The Thames takes on a certain magic at night, don't you think? Many years ago, back there where we parked, a youngster was very badly beaten.'

He had Gabriel's full attention again.

'A few days after Powell's first colourful speech, a boy walking home was attacked by a man from a passing car. When he was done, the driver sped off. He was never caught. The boy, thankfully, recovered in hospital. I remember coming along here and finding traces of blood at least ten feet from the scene of the attack. I wondered how it was that a boy could be beaten in broad daylight in the rush hour and no one stop it.'

He paid for his fuel and they drove away.

They averaged 50 m.p.h. along the motorway. Despite the earlier heat of the afternoon, the evening was almost chilly. It was impossible to pick up any independent black stations on the radio, so he settled for Radio Luxembourg. When they had been driving for just under three hours, they turned off the motorway and continued along several side roads.

On they went, over bridges and around sharp bends that appeared out of nowhere, passing the dim outlines in the darkness of cattle and idle harvesting machines in vast fields. The Land Rover came to a halt and Arthur got out to open a gate. Beyond, a road so narrow as to be practically invisible rose up an extremely steep hill. Arthur called out to Gabriel, 'Close the gate after you,' and drove on.

At the top of the hill they entered a small forest that was entirely unsuitable for the Volvo. Gabriel parked, and joined Arthur in the Land Rover. Marcus was sleeping.

'Not far to go now,' said the older man.

Gabriel sat back and looked around. The darkness was complete, and it was impossible to see anything beyond the rays of the headlights. All that could be heard was the sound of the engine and the animal night-life beyond.

They continued through the forest, until they reached some flat land on the far side. From what Gabriel could make out, it looked bleak, inhospitable and unfriendly. But in the distance was a small farm. As they drew near, Gabriel could see that the main house had seen better days and the few barns were in need of fixing. Much of the surrounding land was fenced off. Placards warned trespassers that they would be prosecuted and electric fencing emphasized the message. There were no footpaths for the public within sight, and it seemed highly unlikely that anyone would choose to come to such a desolate spot.

They approached another gate with 'PRIVATE PROPERTY' emblazoned across it. The gate was padlocked. Arthur handed Gabriel a key and asked him to open it. As he turned the key in the lock, the air filled with the sound of barking and two huge shapes lunged at him out of the darkness. Arthur ordered the dogs away, but they continued to sniff and bounce against the newcomer.

The dogs accompanied Gabriel as he approached the main house. As he drew level with the vehicle, Arthur asked him to carry Marcus inside. The boy was deep asleep and he barely stirred as Gabriel lifted him out.

Every window in the house was covered with padlocked shutters and it took Arthur some time to open the heavily reinforced front door. A light was turned on to reveal a sparsely furnished kitchen which, with its coal stove, cast-iron pots and row upon row of preserved jams, might have been the model for an all-too predictable painting of rustic life. A large wooden table took up much of the space. It had been set for breakfast with five places. Marcus lifted his head and looked around blearily. Arthur crossed the stone floor to another door, which he unlocked to reveal a flight of stairs. He then gently guided the disorientated boy upstairs.

'Alone at last,' he said on his return. 'It's been a long day.'

The keys were dropped on to the table and a glass of water eagerly gulped down.

A high-pitched squeal echoed through the night. Arthur locked the stair door and took Gabriel's hand. 'Pigs. At first the noise drives you mad, but after a while it can seem quite musical. Would you like to take a walk around?'

They walked in the blue-grey light of the crescent moon past an old Mini, some rusting washing machines and broken computers to a small barn that held an impressive collection of stores. Food, tools and stationery all had their place. A range of fabrics, feathers contained in plastic bags, coat-hangers, pegs and cleaning materials were stacked alphabetically in one section; pens, paper, ink, typing ribbons and rulers in another. The entire building was well insulated and free of damp or rot.

'It pays to be self-sufficient. You save countless trips and much money.'

Arthur took him to the next barn. It was set up as a classroom with several rows of desks. The windows were double glazed. On the blackboard had been chalked the question, FREUD: VISIONARY OR

FAKE? Below this was written: 'Formulated before the discovery of Mendel's Laws: a) the chromosomal theory of inheritance; b) the recognition of inborn metabolic errors; c) the existence of hormones; d) the mechanism of the nervous impulse.' Various other comments spotted the board, such as 'no scientific basis', 'rooted in Western literary traditions', 'Talmudic influences' and 'Rabbinical Messianic ideologue'. A number of words had been written in large letters: CRUELTY, WILL, RETRIBUTION, VENGEANCE and APOCALYPTIC.

Arthur surveyed the room with satisfaction. 'It's not spectacular, but it serves my needs.'

'What needs are those?'

Arthur wagged a finger at him. 'Gabriel, there is no need to be so sly. If you have any questions, ask them honestly, and I will answer with equal merit.'

Gabriel stepped out of the classroom. 'Shall we go on?'

They approached another outbuilding. Arthur opened the door to reveal several pigs sleeping on some straw. 'I like them,' he said. 'They're honest and easily satisfied. Apart from all the blood and guts when we kill them, they're most agreeable.'

'When will you kill these?'

'Oh, not for some time yet.'

The scents of the farm lay undisturbed in the cool air as they made their way to a nearby field. Arthur, lighting their way with a torch, slipped his free hand through Gabriel's arm and smiled warmly. 'I was quite excited today. The thought of seeing you again was most . . .' His voice tailed off as they concentrated on avoiding the mud and discarded rubbish. They came to a large, fenced-off area, in the middle of which appeared to be a number of low huts.

'What are they?' Gabriel asked.

'Pigsties.'

'Do you sell your pigs.'

Arthur flicked some hair out of his eyes. 'No, no. I tried it many years ago, but it means you have to deal with other people. One of the reasons I bought this place was because of its "splendid isolation". Fortunately, I don't have to rely on others for my income.' He tapped Gabriel's hand. 'And you – I gather you've become part of the Thatcher revolution. A self-employed entrepreneur, no less.'

'I hadn't thought of it like that.'

'I had no idea when I named you that you'd become one of the many thousands beavering away to power this failing nation back up the league tables.'

'Why Gabriel?'

Arthur pulled him on. In the silent darkness it seemed as though they were the only people on earth. 'Why Gabriel? You were beautiful as a baby. That is one thing you can be grateful that you inherited from your mother. I suppose I was taken with you – your innocence. It seemed appropriate. Mind you, it is not your real name.'

'No?'

'No. I gave you another name.'

'Which is?'

'No, no. That is for me to know. Like all secret names, it has power. Knowing it might free you from me.'

'I've never felt any other way.'

'No?' Arthur walked away, prodding the earth with his toe. 'You identify yourself by that which I gave to you. You have spent virtually all of your life in the home I gave you. Your father was my closest friend. So tell me, how have you been free of my influence?'

Gabriel took a few seconds to reply. 'I've never considered myself under your influence.'

'You're lying.'

'How would you know?'

Arthur paused. 'A long time ago,' he said, crossing his arms as he looked up to the sky, 'I thought that my life had been blighted by several things – my colour, my romanticism, my need to trust others. But then, after much reflection, I realized that it was in fact how others engaged these aspects of myself through manipulation and deceit that was the problem. So I set out to correct this. I taught myself a system of truth-telling. After much refinement it became foolproof. I know immediately when someone is lying to me. Would you like to learn the system?'

The concentration that Arthur brought to bear on Gabriel was intense, almost as tangible as the air on the younger man's cheeks. 'There are several things I can give you during your stay. This is one of them. Keep in mind that once you have a process of understanding man, everything he says to you becomes questionable.'

'I'll have to say no to your gift.'

'If only I'd been as wise at your age. I spent my life searching for its meaning. Now that I've found it, I'd give anything to be an ignorant fool again. One day, when a truth presents itself to you, you'll realize why it was best hidden from you.' He rubbed his eyes. 'I'm tired. Let's go to bed.'

They went back to the house. Arthur prepared a mattress for Gabriel in the lounge that was awash with books, papers and gramophone records, wished him goodnight and went upstairs.

Gabriel awoke to find Marcus and one of the dogs standing over him. Marcus told him not to worry – Herod looked fierce, but was quite nice actually. Would he like to wash before breakfast? Gabriel got up and followed Marcus through the kitchen. Arthur was busy cooking and barely acknowledged his greeting. The farm looked entirely different in the bright morning sunlight, not nearly as harsh or inhospitable as it had seemed the night before. As they headed for a barn, another boy approached, carrying a towel and a wash bag. He stopped and stared at Gabriel, his manner hesitant, even fearful.

'This is Mr DuBois, Malcolm,' said Marcus. 'Mr Kembo's friend.'

Malcolm bowed his head slightly.

'He'll be staying with us for a few days.'

Malcolm dipped his head even further and carried on.

Soapy water poured out of a pipe that ran down the side of the barn. An older boy was washing himself under a makeshift shower. He looked at Gabriel with a bright curiosity and something that might have been resentment.

'Martin, this is Mr Kembo's friend, Mr DuBois.'

His greeting was polite, but cool. Since there was no more space, Marcus and Gabriel waited for him to finish. After Martin had left, Marcus handed Gabriel a towel and some soap. 'I'll leave you to it. You can join us when you're ready.' The sharp shock of the unheated water removed any last vestige of sleep from Gabriel.

Breakfast was served.

Arthur and his companions stood to greet Gabriel, only relaxing once he had sat down in the free chair at the end of the table. The meal consisted of vegetable dishes and fruit, and was entirely free of dairy products.

'The boys are curious about you,' said Arthur. 'They've heard much about my exploits with your father.'

Through their munching and chewing, each boy fixed his glance on their guest.

'I've told them not to ruin your stay with non-stop pestering.'

Gabriel ate an apple and prepared himself for the day ahead.

The meal over, the boys went outside and began a series of stretching and isometric exercises, gently competing without malice or mockery. Arthur fed the dogs as the boys worked up a sweat. He agreed to Malcolm's request for a run, and when the boys called out for the dogs he sent them on their way. As the group sped about the field their laughter grew more ebullient, until the boys gave up their sprint and began to wrestle with the dogs.

Arthur stretched out his arms and took a deep breath, releasing the air with a sigh. 'It's a beautiful morning. The kind of morning I once imagined woke this country up every day.'

One of the dogs was a bit too rough for Marcus's liking, so he kicked it, continuing his assault until it backed away and kept its distance.

Arthur whistled. The boys began to jog back.

Arthur wiped down the blackboard. The boys lifted up their desk tops and pulled out pens and writing pads as Gabriel sat behind them.

Arthur stood before a table stacked with books. 'A few weeks ago, we began a conversation on Freud and took a rather serious detour. A former student raised certain matters that caused much rancour amongst us. Two of you have approached me to voice your concerns. I suggested some reading and you've spent the past week with this material.' He wrote CRUELTY on the board. 'Marcus?'

'Yes, Sir?'

'When did Liverpool's first slave ship set sail for Africa?'

'In 1700. It was called the *Liverpool Merchant*.'

'Correct. You will recall that by 1771, one-third of all ships were slave traders, and that by 1772 Liverpool controlled 42 per cent of the total European slave trade. By the 1780s, the city accounted for three out of four of the slaves transported to Jamaica; of the nineteen British firms that transported slaves to Jamaica after 1781, all but three were located in Liverpool.'

'I will try to remember, Sir.' Marcus glanced at his note pad. 'I found an amusing quote, Sir.'

'It is?'

'It's an advertisement from the *London Advertiser*, printed in 1756. It reads, "Matthew Dyer intimates to the public that he makes silver padlocks for Blacks or Dogs; collars etc." '

Malcolm burst out laughing. 'Maybe we should give him a call?'

'Could I ask you a question, Sir?' said Marcus with a glint in his eye.

'Of course.'

'Have you heard of the phrase "St Giles Blackbirds"?'

'Well done, Marcus. Yes, I have. It refers to a group of slaves who were freed in London around 1772, the period you've been researching. The former slaves were unable to find work and became destitute. They lived in slums in the St Giles area of London, so earning the nickname 'St Giles Blackbirds'. A quaint name – are we to assume that the former slaves were met with humour and goodwill?'

Marcus replied, 'Most definitely not, Sir. In 1720 a naval surgeon, watching slavers at work, compared the scene to a cattle market. The Africans offered for sale were, quote, "examined by us in like manner, as our Brother Trade do Beasts in Smithfield; the Countenance, and Stature, a good set of Teeth, Pliancy in their Limbs and Joints, and being free of Venereal Taint, are the things inspected, and govern our choice in buying".'

Marcus shuffled through his notes. 'This is an instruction from the firm of Isaac Hobhouse & Co. to the commander of one of their ships: "Let your endeavour be to buy none but what is healthy and strong and of a convenient age – None to exceed twenty-five years if possible, among which so many men and stout men-boys as can be had, seeing such as most Valuable at the Plantations . . . So soon as you begin to slave, let your netting be fix'd breast-high fore and aft and so keep 'em shackled and hand-bolted, fearing their rising or leaping Overboard." '

Arthur looked at Gabriel. 'And were these ships happy places?'

'Not at all, Sir, not even for the whites who sailed on them.'

'The whites?'

'Yes, Sir. Many of the white sailors were mistreated as well. The trade seems to have attracted sadists and psychopaths by the hundred.'

'Yes, yes. But can you concentrate on those people whose suffering concerns us?'

Marcus, embarrassed, mumbled, 'Of course. In 1771 a ship named *The Brothers* returned to Bristol, with over thirty-two members of its own crew having died as a result of the captain's ill-treatment. A free black seaman called John Dean –'

Arthur wrote JOHN DEAN on the blackboard.

' – had been mutilated. The captain had tied him face-down on the deck, poured hot pitch over him and cut his back open with a hot knife.'

Malcolm joined in. 'I found that one of the methods of forcing open the mouths of slaves who refused to eat was to shove hot coals against their lips, or pour molten lead on them.'

'So,' said Arthur, tapping the blackboard, 'cruelty is an apt word.'

'Most definitely,' said Malcolm, his eyes bright with a fierce anger. 'I found this document. It contains the testimony of an Isaac Parks, who in 1764 was a sailor on the *Black Jake*. Parks gave evidence that the captain of the *Black Jake* flogged to death a baby who wasn't even a year old for refusing food. He then forced the mother of the baby to throw the child overboard.'

'And we know', said Arthur, underlining CRUELTY, 'that in the early part of the eighteenth century the children of slaves were branded at the age of three.'

Malcolm held up his hand. 'In 1865, Governor Eyre of Jamaica put down a rebellion of pig farmers at Morant Bay. During a thirty-day rampage his troops killed 439 black people, flogged over 300 others, bashed out children's brains, ripped open the bellies of pregnant women and burnt down the homes of over 1,000 suspected rebels.'

Martin's hands were trembling. 'How many of us have they killed? Eight million, ten, fourteen? We're shit to them – you don't count shit. You can wipe out anyone you like if you think they are shit.'

'Evil, they're evil,' snapped Malcolm. 'They destroy everything they touch. If they can't kill us with their drugs, they kill us in their wars.'

'Should we be surprised by their cruelty?' asked Arthur.

'Like you said, Sir, they're animals,' said Martin. 'You can't expect anything else from animals.'

Arthur picked up some papers. 'I showed you that truth, but when I asked you to try and imagine how such a creature came into the world, you all came up with some rather arresting ideas. Martin, would you like to read your piece?'

Martin left his chair and took a sheet of paper from Arthur's outstretched hand. 'I thought long and hard about this,' he said to the other boys. 'I tried to think why such a creature should have been created. Why introduce something that would cause so much harm? I could not come up with an answer, but then I had a dream and it helped me.'

He read from the paper:

In my dream I travelled to a great city in the ancient world, that may well have been the Utopia that the cities of Atlantis and Shangri-La became echoes of.

I travelled through the city and I came to a tall building. It was made of the purest glass. In one of its great halls I found a spherical room.

Inside the room, a great man, a scientist, was working on a grand experiment. He had collected material which he believed contained all that was evil, base and animal in man. He had stored it in a safe place away from sight, but its smell could be detected from many miles away.

There was an explosion. When the dust from the explosion cleared, the scientist found at the door to the safe place, sitting on his haunches like an ape, a white beast.

Over the following centuries that white beast learned by imitation to walk like man and to speak in his tongues. Eventually, by trickery and subversion, for that was his nature, he overcame man and began his reign of terror and abuse.

In my dream, the white beast enslaved man so it could study him and learn how to walk and talk. But man refused to bow down and began to fight back and retake his world. The beast was hunted down and eventually wiped out. The world rejoiced and rediscovered the splendour it had once known. For with the beast's death, all evil ended.

He lowered the paper. 'Was it like that for you, Sir?'

Arthur waited for him to sit down before replying. 'Perhaps. I think all of us have dreamed of that immaculate city, that perfect age. The dream, the vision appears at many times, in many places: in a burning house with crosses outside; on a ship surrounded by vomit and blood; perhaps, even, when a man is on the ground being beaten senseless by cowards. Who knows? Let us just be glad that it comes.'

He examined the boys carefully. 'I suspect that there have been times when each of you has thought me the cruellest of men.'

The boys denied this. They seemed genuinely hurt by the accusation. He quietened them. 'Don't deny it, please. I know the truth. Malcolm?'

'Yes, Sir?'

'I recall our journey here. Oh, how you screamed and wailed – I had never heard such sounds.'

The boy smiled. 'I didn't know any better.'

'What were you to know? Your world had been turned upside down.'

'I thank you for that, Sir.'

'Thank me?'

'Yes.' Malcolm looked to the other boys. 'I would like to thank you, Sir, we all would.'

'I don't understand.'

Malcolm stood up, and took a deep breath to steady himself. 'I knew nothing of the real world before you, Mr Kembo. I lived in lies. Lies that my parents had not prepared me for. They were weak. The whites had corrupted their brains. They were slaves. You have given me knowledge and strength. When I think back to how I was, I'm ashamed. Everything I have, I owe to you.'

He sat down.

Marcus and Martin stared at Arthur with something beyond adoration.

Clearly affected, Arthur turned away from them for a few moments. 'Was the world as you knew it so bad? Can you separate it from the one I've shown you?'

'I can,' said Martin. 'I remember it as a world that I didn't understand properly. I remember going to school and being afraid that I'd be called small and worthless. I was afraid in the cellroom that the brainwasher would talk about things I didn't know about and didn't care about. I'd sit there, learning their liestory, constantly looking at images of human beings in chains being sold by whites, being beaten by whites, serving whites, cleaning up after whites, even praising whites. Then my white brainwasher would talk about these things taking place in Britain's so called greatest period.

'I'd be criticized in other cells because of the way I spoke. When I said that was how my parents talked, I was told they spoke bastardized English that wouldn't get me anywhere.

'What were the terms of success, Sir? My parents brought me up like a disguised wog. They raised me to be perfect for the whites, when we all knew I only stood a chance if I was more than perfect.

'So do I feel sorry that I was taken away from a Caucasian world I was being groomed to fail in? No. My mind was polluted by their filth. If you had to be cruel to clean it out, then I praise your cruelty. There are millions of black people in this world whose minds have been whited out. They carry their pale mask with pride. We shall never be able to help them. They'll go down with the white beast and they won't be missed.

'I think of the serfs who brought me into the world and I'm shamed by their weakness. I think of the bondsboy I was and I'm ashamed of his fear. You've made me strong. I'm a warrior now.'

'No regrets?'

'None, Sir.'

'And you, Malcolm?'

'None, Sir.'

'And you, Marcus?'

'None, Sir.'

'None?'

'None.'

Arthur passed him a piece of paper. 'Would you read your contribution out?'

Marcus rubbed out a crease along the side of the paper before speaking. 'I don't know where the white came from, or why we have been locked in this unending war. I know that man defines himself not only by his capacity for war, but his capacity for peace. I feel sorry for the beast, for he's as much a child of the Creator as myself. We all act according to God's will, so the beast must be playing out its role. You don't hate a dog for fouling or a pig for grunting. I hate the beast for its actions, but it has no choice. We have no choice before God either. I understand my duty.'

Martin and Malcolm raised their hands.

Arthur denied them the opportunity to speak. 'Marcus, I find much kindness in your words, some might say it is a –'

'Weakness,' interrupted Martin.

'I don't suppose this means you've been hiding MLK posters under your bed,' said Malcolm.

Arthur held up his hand to silence him. 'Perhaps the word we are looking for is compassion? Who knows. But Marcus, your empathy makes me think you might have some insight into why my former student was so obsessed with our "cruelty".'

The boys fell silent.

Arthur drew a chalk ring round CRUELTY on the board. 'Isn't that what she accused us of?'

Marcus's eyes remained firmly fixed on his desk.

'No insights, boys? No opinions?'

The silence continued.

'Well, perhaps, that is some form of answer. Class is over.'

The boys thanked him and left the room.

Arthur wiped the blackboard clean.

Gabriel watched Malcolm, Martin and Marcus through the window as they chased after the dogs.

'They have no regrets,' said Arthur. He put his hand on his godson's shoulder. 'Come.'

'I had a vision once,' he said as he packed away the study notes. 'It was of heaven. It had a remarkable resemblance to Lord's. I sat down and watched Jack Hobbs and Victor Trumper opening the batting against a new ball attack from Dennis Lillee and Wes Hall.'

'Lillee and Hall aren't dead yet.'

'Oh, yes they are. The good Lord just sent down replacements to keep us happy.'

'You're terrible.'

'If you think I'm terrible, just imagine the two of us sitting in the members' stand, sipping some fruit wine, perhaps, as Trumper's wicket fell and the Don came out to bat. Can you imagine the Master and the Don together, fending off a bowling quartet of Lillee, Hall, O'Reilly and Lindwall?'

Gabriel's eyes rolled appreciatively. 'Who would bat at four?'

'Well, first of all you must understand that time works differently in heaven, so the fact that Jack and Donald batted together for what we'd understand as a time-span of four days didn't really affect the game. After Jack goes down, as chairman of the selectors I really feel we must have a leftie in, so the almost irresistible claims of Hammond, Richards and Ranji must be put to one side. A man renowned for his effortless power and uncanny ability to split the field comes in. A certain G. Pollock.'

'A South African?'

Arthur held out his imperious finger. 'My boy, we're talking cricket, and great cricketers must be placed beyond trifling things such as racial harmony.' His laughter boomed about the room. 'At number five, I discount May, Richards and Weekes and bring in the matchless George Headley. A player of verve, improvisation, exuberance and terrifying power, who I am sure in this exalted company will rise to even greater heights.'

'Number six?'

'My boy, we need not even mention his name.'

'At seven?'

'At seven, I plump for Clyde Walcott. His average scoring rate and the manner in which he makes his runs is enough for me. Since I love batting, I'll take a great batsman wicket-keeper over a great wicket-keeper batsman. I have no interest in watching dreary accumulators and obsessive technicians. The bowlers have already been picked. As for the opposition, would a team of the discards,' he chuckled at the word, 'such as Weekes, Hammond and Hutton, be capable of defeating my favourites?'

'It would be quite a game.'

'Oh, can you imagine? And just think, the likes of Miandad, Rowe, Miller and Archie Johnson would be constantly at my door demanding selection. The old-timers like Grace and Spofforth would be in the nets howling with rage. Oh, my, my, my.'

Time passed as they conjured up strikes and runs until Arthur rubbed his godson's knee. 'But that is in heaven. My concerns are with more daily matters. Come.'

They left the classroom.

Arthur led Gabriel up a smallish hill, indicating the boundaries of his property as they reached the top. Wheezing a touch, he stretched out his arms and said to Gabriel, 'Take a deep breath. You won't find this quality of air in the city.'

'There's much here that's absent from the city.'

Arthur chuckled. 'You're quite intense, Gabriel. You really should relax.'

'Rupert has shown me the eggs.'

'Yes?'

'I've read my father's journal.'

'And?'

'And I've come here for some answers.'

'Ah, answers.' Arthur took out a packet of cigarettes as he sat down on the dry grass. 'Would you like one?'

'No.'

'Do you copy your father in everything?'

The look on Gabriel's face caused Arthur to raise his hands defensively. 'All right, I take that back. A few years ago, I would have happily taken issue with you, but I'm an old man now, so let peace ring out.' He pointed to the distant hills. 'Let peace ring out from the snow-capped rockies of Sellafield. Let peace ring out across our swamped cities. Let it ring!' He struggled with his lighter. 'But most of all let this damnable gadget work.'

Gabriel took the lighter and clicked out a flame. Arthur lit up and sucked deeply. Holding up the packet of Benson & Hedges he sighed, 'These are the only things I can rely on.' A few more puffs, then, 'Questions, Gabriel. You're fairly alight with questions.'

'My father's journal?'

'Indeed. I suppose you have questions about your parents?' Arthur's brow furrowed as he spent a few moments in mock contemplation. 'Let me see. Your father? There was a time when he would come to work and I would think, "This man has come to do good." ' He paused. 'Yes, that will do for him. As for your mother, she was exactly what she claimed to be – a woman who performed poetry.' And with that he fell silent.

'Is that all you have to say?'

'What do you want me to say?'

'I want answers.'

'And what then?' He cut Gabriel off. 'You must get beyond answers. An errant knight has a guest. It might be a search for the Holy Grail or for the most beautiful woman in the world, or for a magic ring, perhaps? He faces incredible dangers, he escapes from impossible situations. While he's on the quest, he's innovative, imaginative and completely focused. Then one day he finds the object of his quest and says, "I've found what I've been looking for. It's over." Just like that he stops, and all the creativity and energy that went into the undertaking disappears. So? What do you think will end when I hand out one of all the possible answers I could invent for you?'

'I want the truth.'

'The truth? I've spent years living in truth. Before I began the search for truth I spent months in my little cell, conditioning myself for what was to come. I knew that it would be ugly, that it would break a weak man, so I dispensed with weakness. I knew that it would demand a fearful effort of will, so I released my mind. I stand here stronger than any other man, because I breathe and exhale truth. You are not ready to deal with my truths.'

'Tell me a truth.'

Arthur held out two fists. 'I've two for you. Pick one.'

Gabriel tapped the right fist.

It opened. Arthur examined his palm. 'The woman who bore you lived her poetry. She thought and acted as poet. She joined your father because it was a flight of fantasy. As for the drama of your birth, she played out her role. Like all creators she understood that her story had to have a beginning, a middle and an end.'

Gabriel tapped the other fist.

'Ah, although this truth has been covered for many years by fantasy and romantic delusion, it still shimmers. Let us examine it. Your mother was not some rural chocolate virgin. She had at least two back-street abortions before she came to England. That is why her first child was so weak, and why she was unable to survive your birth.'

'How do you know these things?'

'I asked her. She was honest, I'll give her that.'

'Did my father know?'

'Of course not. The conversation was between two friends swapping intimacies, growing closer.'

'And the egg with my mother's name on it?'

Arthur lit up another cigarette. 'That was an act of symbolism. A marking of lost promise. Nothing more.'

'And Rupert?'

'Rupert crossed me.'

'He crossed you?'

'I had given him money and he crossed me.'

'You took these children because of −' Gabriel was lost for words. 'I don't understand.'

Arthur held up his fists. 'Pick. See which one holds the Grail.'

'You're being ridiculous.'

'And you're all too predictable. Nothing I've said is true. We aren't characters in a Republic serial adventure. I offer you answers and you believe everything, when others would refute every word.'

He began to walk down the hill, stumbled and lost his balance.

Gabriel helped him to his feet.

'Look at you,' said Arthur. 'You're magnificent. Whatever I say, you just deflect it and allow it to pass on. I can't hurt you.' He stroked Gabriel's face. 'What should I say to you? Should I speak of the moment I came to my truth? Is that truth strong enough to obliterate all the truths you carry within you? Shall I tell you the moment when I broke? Will it prove much more terrible than your moments of defeat? So I came back. How much will that triumph differ from your triumphs? And if I tell you these things, what then? Will you embark on the journey of my life and tell yourself you understand?'

Arthur turned and walked back to the farm, pausing to call out, 'But you will never understand. For I have found a truth greater than all others. Without that knowledge, without that strength, you can never walk along the same path.'

With his head held high, he returned to the main house.

Gabriel spent the afternoon sitting by himself in some of the more uncultivated acres of the farm. Arthur's students carried out some repair work on the Land Rover, took swill to the pigsties, exercised the dogs, then returned to the classroom for more discussion. Several pigs emerged from a barn and wandered freely.

Gabriel remained in the field until the evening came and Marcus fetched him for supper.

Everyone ate thick pork chops, potatoes and a selection of home-grown vegetables, with home-made ginger beer. Arthur was proud of his cooking, but lamented the unavailability of spices, which prevented him from creating the food of his childhood. 'These boys have African minds and English stomachs, a volatile combination if ever there was one,' he observed.

The conversation turned to Marcus's trip to London and much laughter filled the kitchen as he described the fashion that he had seen.

'So,' said his teacher, 'you found the fabled halls of Babylon quite attractive?'

'It was certainly different.'

'And you're anxious to return?'

'In time, Sir, when I'm ready.'

'Martin, you enjoyed your trips there?'

'Not really.'

Arthur served Gabriel another chop. 'Martin and I went to London several months ago. We visited his parents' home.'

Martin grew angry. 'My parents, Sir? I only call you father.'

'It was all I could do to stop him breaking down the door and bringing his sisters back with us.'

'We shouldn't have left them there.'

'Why not?'

'It was wrong to leave them in that mockery of a life. They have the right to be here and to live in truth.'

Arthur swallowed a mouthful of potato. 'I'm sure if Martin had his way we'd be out every weekend raiding nurseries.'

Marcus and Malcolm burst out laughing.

Martin returned to his food.

Everyone ate in silence.

Gabriel excused himself and left the table.

Dust stung Gabriel's eyes as he stretched out in the darkness, smelling the aromas that rose from the ground. The barn that housed the pigs sounded like a room full of angry children. Gabriel went and looked in on the grey shapes as they moved about their enclosure, but within minutes their noise became unbearable and he left.

One of the dogs lay on its belly, looking out over the pigsties in the nearby field, its manner watchful and disciplined. Hands in pockets, Gabriel approached the animal. It looked up at him but was unconcerned. The farm, open spaces, motionless trees and darkening sky seemed to offer a hint of infinity. Everything was different from the city landscape that he knew so well.

The dog rolled over and Gabriel tickled its belly, the creature taking pleasure from the scratching until something caught its attention. In an instant it was on its feet, growling menacingly. Gabriel waited for a predator to appear, but nothing came. Eventually, the dog relaxed again.

Gabriel continued to stare across the field, its silence in marked contrast to the noise from the barn. On an impulse, he climbed over the fence. The dog slipped through the gate and accompanied him.

They crossed the field until Gabriel came to a sty. In reality it was more like a little hut, with four walls, a sloping roof and a latched door marked '1'. He went down a slight incline and found himself recoiling from the pungent smell that hit him. The remains of the food that the boys had brought earlier in the day lay to his left; to his right, a collection of stools brushed over with earth and dirt. He tried to look into the building, but this proved impossible, so he began to slide back the lock that held the door.

The dog growled, but after receiving a tap on the nose it backed away into the field. The door, unevenly framed, dragged over the ground as Gabriel pulled it open. There, on the ground, lay a boy, asleep under a blanket. His red hair was cut to the scalp. Freckles covered his cheeks, and the clotted green of slumber spotted his sandy eyelashes. One arm, pale as unflavoured yoghurt, lay above the blanket, which reeked of stale urine. Held tightly in his fist, which sleep had failed to unclench, was a Mars bar wrapper.

Gabriel stepped forwards, sat down and stared at the ground. The dog came over and licked his face. The saliva grew cold on his cheeks, Gabriel's breathing slowed, his eyes lost their focus and he went somewhere else.

Arthur waited for over an hour before deciding to fetch his godson. After instructing the boys to prepare for bed he went outside and headed directly for the pigsties.

He found Gabriel sitting in sty one, watched over by the dog. At first he thought the youngster was being petulant, but it quickly became clear that something was amiss. He shook Gabriel gently before passing a hand in front of his eyes. Nothing. His pulse was fine, however, and he didn't seem to be in pain.

Arthur examined the face before him and recalled the moment of their meeting at the train station, when it had seemed that Jocelynne was walking towards him. But her eyes hadn't been as hard as his, nor her cheek-bones so prominent. Her lips had been as full, her fingers equally long, but Jocelynne's hair had been relatively short, even thin, not nearly as abundant as this mane.

He released his godson's real name into the air and held him for a time, away from judging eyes, before closing the door to the sty and returning to the house.

*

The boys had changed into their night clothes and were listening to one of his old jazz records, a live recording of Thelonius Monk, in the lounge.

'Lads.'

They turned to face him.

'Shall I make some of my special hot chocolate?'

The offer had never been refused and tonight proved no exception. Marcus came into the kitchen to help him. 'That's a lot of milk, Sir.'

Arthur rubbed his head. 'I'm going to make some for the others.'

'The others?' Marcus did a double take. 'You don't mean the Jinn?'

Arthur lit the stove. 'The Jinn? Is that your name for them this month? It's not as colourful as the last one.'

'The Nagas? That was OK, but we like this better.' Marcus dipped a finger into the milk, ignoring Arthur's exaggerated scowl. 'Isn't it bad to disturb their routine, Sir?'

'Perhaps, but there's nothing routine about tonight. Tonight is the first time I make my world-famous hot chocolate for my godson.'

Marcus walked over to the table and fiddled with one of the chairs.

'Is something wrong, Marcus?'

'Not really, Sir.'

'What is it?'

'Your godson, is he staying?'

'At this moment, I honestly couldn't say. Why?'

'He seems very nice, but will you be spending more of your time with him, Sir?'

Arthur went and took Marcus's hand. 'Listen to me. Gabriel is very special to me. During the time I spent with him, I came to understand many of the responsibilities that I've fulfilled with you. You are my children, the truest of the true. I chose you. I claimed you as my own. I've shown you the dangers of this world and I've done my best to improve your chances of survival. I'm proud of you.'

Marcus began to cry.

Arthur took him in his arms.

Marcus held on tight, before walking into the lounge and summoning his friends.

Before downing their drinks, they all clasped hands and Arthur spoke. 'We sit here in strength, unafraid and unbowed. Our skin is sacred, our minds are pure, our hearts beat with pride. The spirit that moves us speaks with the lost voices of those who have gone before. Our voices have been heard, we have made ourselves known.'

Everyone enjoyed the chocolate. Arthur joked about the pressure he had been under to ensure that the concoction was as wonderful as the last time. Martin was sure that he had figured out the recipe. Arthur challenged him to prove his boast. Martin assured him that he would do so tomorrow. A wager was struck and Arthur announced it was bedtime.

One by one the boys came to him and hugged him. He wished them a good night's sleep, then left the house with a blanket and two mugs of chocolate.

Arthur ordered the dog to move away as he placed the blanket around Gabriel's shoulders. To pass the time, he focused on a star and imagined himself looking up at it from his parents' backyard.

When Gabriel finally began to stir, Arthur leant forward and asked him if he was all right. Gabriel shrank away from him and began to take deep breaths. For a moment, he seemed unaware of where he was, but it all came back to him as he registered his surroundings.

Arthur offered him a mug. 'It's colder than it should be, but better than nothing.'

Gabriel's hand trembled as he took the mug, spilling some of its contents. Arthur drank with him. 'Gabriel,' he said between sips, 'you have to see this through the eyes of someone who needed to know.'

Gabriel squeezed his palms against the remaining warmth of the mug, stood up and went to the door. The field was as he remembered it. The other sties were as quiet as this one. He looked inquiringly at Arthur, who nodded. 'Yes, there are other Jinn.'

Gabriel put his mug down, bent down and gently picked the sleeping boy up.

'Be careful,' said Arthur.

The child stirred, then, finding himself in Gabriel's arms, began to panic. 'I didn't do anything! I didn't do anything!'

'It's all right,' said Gabriel, 'calm down.'

The boy saw Arthur and began to scream. Arthur held out a reassuring hand. 'You've done nothing wrong. Mr DuBois will put you back and you can sleep.'

The boy wet himself.

'You're scaring him, Gabriel. Put him back.'

'No.'

The boy began to struggle. 'Put me down, please.' He peed again, the warm liquid seeping through the blanket on to Gabriel. Gabriel lowered the boy to the ground. 'I won't hurt you,' he said gently.

Utterly lost, the boy stared at Gabriel before turning to Arthur, who said, 'Everything's all right. Just be quiet.'

The boy stopped struggling and avoided looking either man in the eye. Gabriel removed the stained blanket. The boy's pale skin was suffused with bright red marks, and scars littered his body.

'The boys can be quiet vicious sometimes,' said Arthur.

'Your students did this?'

Arthur let out a spirit-weary sigh. 'Oh, Gabriel, if only you could see your face. It really is too – too . . .' He hadn't the energy to finish.

Gabriel wrapped the blanket around the boy again. The child held it tight against his body, looked up to Gabriel and grunted. When Gabriel didn't respond, he grunted again, the sound a perfect reproduction of the pigs in the barn.

'He's trying to please you.'

Gabriel tried to sit the boy down. Once more the screams came, only stopping when Arthur took a Mars bar out of his pocket and handed it over. The boy ripped open the wrapper and chewed the sweet with an intense sensuality.

'They don't get treats that often.' Arthur lit up a cigarette. 'It helps to maintain discipline.' He saw tears on Gabriel's cheeks. 'So, not everything passes you by.'

'What's his name?'

'Montreal.'

'Montreal?'

'I took him five years ago from a maternity hospital in Montreal Street, Birmingham. All of them are named after the places where they were found.'

Under Gabriel's gaze, Montreal began to grunt.

'It can become rather tedious, but –'

'Tedious?' Gabriel left the sty and headed for another.

'Gabriel! Gabriel, this is silly. They are not worth it.'

Gabriel ignored him.

Arthur snapped at Montreal, 'Go help him with Wood Green.'

Montreal scampered after Gabriel.

Gabriel waited for Montreal to join him before opening the door. A girl, perhaps about eight, slept in a blanket. Montreal tried to wake her. 'Wood Green, wake up, wake up.' She was too sleepy to move, and drowsiness prevented her from screaming as Gabriel picked her up and carried her over to sty three. Confused, she went to crawl down into it, and within seconds she was fast asleep.

Gabriel found a plump boy of nine or ten, with a mop of straw-like hair falling over his eyes, in the third sty. Having woken as soon as the bolt over his door was removed, he was sitting up by the time Gabriel's face appeared. Gabriel held out his hand. Despite the cool, sweat appeared on the boy's forehead.

'Trafalgar,' said Montreal, 'you've got to go with the mister.'

Trafalgar refused to budge, and started to jabber. A film of sweat spread over his face.

Gabriel looked at the other children, then back into the foul-smelling sty. He sat inside the doorway and began to undress. Trafalgar covered his eyes. Naked, Gabriel waited.

After a few minutes, Trafalgar sneaked a look through his fingers. Gabriel turned and allowed the boy to see his body. Eventually, Trafalgar edged forward. Gabriel lifted him up and headed for sty four.

'That's enough,' said Arthur. 'You have them all.'

Gabriel went on to the remaining sty. The door was open and it was clearly empty. Beyond the sties at the far end of the field were four earth mounds. Gabriel took a step forward, but Trafalgar pulled at his hand and shook his head.

Arthur joined them. 'It's cold, Gabriel. At least put them under cover.'

'I'm not putting them back.'

'They aren't allowed in the house. The field is their home. You must –'
He saw the scars on Gabriel's body. 'Who did this to you?'

'Who do you think?'

Arthur's voice faltered. 'Matthew?'

Gabriel walked past him to sty one. Arthur took his time before joining him. 'I suggest you get dressed.'

'And them, they're virtually naked.'

'When will you stop? Really! If I had known you were given to performing these rather bad imitations of Sidney Poitier, I would never have brought you.'

'What are those mounds?'

'An irrelevance.'

'Answer me.'

Arthur shrugged dispassionately. 'Research. Exploration. Whatever.'

Gabriel picked up Wood Green and began to settle down in the sty.

Arthur sighed deeply. 'All right, you can bring them in, but only after you've washed them.'

Wood Green began to squeal.

'Do you see?' Arthur grabbed Gabriel's arm.

Gabriel pulled away. 'Stop it.'

Montreal desperately beat his clutched fists against the floor, but was unable to stop himself urinating. The other children scampered away from him.

'Animal! You can't even control your fear! You were born into filth and filth is all you can create.'

'Stop it! They're children.'

'Whose children? What is their inheritance?'

'What are you talking about?'

Arthur moved over to a pile of papers, pulled out a folder and opened it. 'I'm talking about this, the writings of an Edward Long, whose descendants squat before us.' He began to read: ' "For my own part, I think there are extremely potent reasons for believing that the White and Negroe are two distinct species." ' Arthur held Gabriel's gaze. ' "When we reflect on . . . their dissimilarity to the rest of mankind, must we not conclude that they are a different species of the same genus? . . . Nor do orangutans seem at all inferior in the intellectual faculties of many of the Negroe race; with some of whom, it is credible that they have the most intimate connexion and consanguinity. The amorous intercourse between them may be frequent . . . and it is certain that both races agree perfectly well in lasciviousness or disposition." '

He thrust the sheet of paper at Gabriel. 'I ask you again, whose children? Did men such as this write for the fairies? No, they sought to ensure the continued superiority of their children, of their descendants. Well, here they are before you.' He clapped his hands twice. The children began to howl and scratch their bodies as if they were monkeys. Three more claps and they stopped instantly.

Another piece of paper was held up. 'Listen to the voice of one of their predecessors, a James Hunt, head of the Anthropological Society of London in the 1800s. ''The Negro is inferior to the European. The Negro becomes more humanized when in his natural subordination to the European than under any other circumstances.'' '

This paper was also flung at Gabriel. 'Well, here are those superior Europeans. I am an African, and having investigated the nature of subordination, I find this to be a most enjoyable circumstance.'

Arthur pushed another sheet into his hand. 'Read this.'

Gabriel read: 'The intelligence of the average Negro is about equal to that of a European child of ten years old. A few, a very few, go beyond this, but these are exceptions, just as Shakespeare was an exception to the ordinary intellect of an Englishman. Left alone to their own devices they regress into a state little above their native savagery.'

'Here', said Arthur, standing over the children, 'are some average European children and we have seen how they behave when left to their own devices. Here are the children of empire and genocide!' He prepared to clap his hands.

'Don't,' said Gabriel, 'please.'

'Don't confuse your pain with theirs. I have my scars too. Shall we strip and trade them off? How many of us have been scarred by their people? How many have been tortured and killed? Yet you have the gall to stand here and ask me to stop!'

'There is no need for this.'

Arthur's mouth dropped in disbelief. 'No need? No need?!' He walked about the room gathering his thoughts. 'Who are you to say that to me? Have you shared my life, my pain?'

'I've read about –'

'You have read! You have studied words! You have formed images from those words, but you have not experienced, therefore you are without understanding!'

'I –'

'No!' Arthur's voice filled the room. 'It's beyond your pain. Unless a man experiences the pain that produced an idea, he'll never understand the origin of that thought. You don't know my pain.'

'I know pain.'

'Your own pain, not mine.' He tapped his temple repeatedly. 'I've trained myself to look into the eyes and heart of every human being who comes my way. I've lived through what's in their heads. I know their pain.' He waved another sheet of paper. 'I can live this. It's a record of Klan violence. Read it out.'

Gabriel took the page and began. 'Sam Davis, hung by mob in Harrodsburg, 28th May 1868.'

'I was there.'

'W. M. Pierce, hung by mob in Christian, 1868. Geo Roger, hung by mob in Bradsforville Martin county, 1868. Silas Woodford, age sixty, badly beaten by disguised mob. Cabe Fields, shot and killed by disguised men. James Parker, killed by Klan –'

'I saw his death. I saw his murderers.'

'Noah Blakenship, whipped by mob, Pulaski county. William and John Gibson, hung by mob in Washington county.'

Arthur began to call out each name out with him. 'F. H. Montford, hung by mob in Jessamine county. Albert Bradford, killed by men in disguise, Scott county. Terry Laws and James Ryan, hung by mob at Nicholasville, 1868.'

Arthur took Gabriel's hand and placed it against his forehead. 'I've lived through every hanging, every murder. When I close my eyes, the screams of the dying haunt me. I lie in bed and build a face that fits the scream. They have made themselves known to me.' He held out his arm. 'Smell me.'

Gabriel sniffed him.

'What do you smell?' He sniffed his own armpit. 'I smell shit, vomit, the salt of the sea, the blood of my fellow travellers. I can wake in the night and walk with the motion of the sea. Three weeks ago, I lost the power of speech, for a muzzle had bound my jaw. This morning I could hardly move, for in the night my ankles had been broken.'

He picked up a bundle of papers. 'These are stories that have been given me. A Perrie Bote, castrated for looking at a white woman in France. A Martin Whyte, kidnapped and boiled alive for walking down the wrong side of the street. In this one pile I have over ninety such tales. They aren't from press clippings. These people have come to me so that I might record their tales. To me, Gabriel. I have been handed a great responsibility and I cannot, will not shirk it.'

He walked over to the children. 'Do you think those voices call out for peace? Do you think they ask me to forgive those who have abused them?' Arthur moved quickly over to a shelf, picked out a book and thrust it into Gabriel's hands. 'Turn to page sixty-two.' As Gabriel flicked through the yellowing pages, Arthur paced the floor, his head in his hands. 'Move to the second paragraph down. Now read it out to me.'

Gabriel began to read: ' "The ship", said Dr Alexander Falconbridge of the slaver *Tartar*, "was fitted up with a view to preventing slaves jumping overboard. But an opening was left in the netting set above the rail in order that refuse might be dumped overboard, and through this, many a Negro leaped to his death. Others managed to secrete rope-yarn or strong twine, by which a noose was made and secured to a cleat overhead and so the slave strangled himself to death. One tore his throat open with his fingernails. Many others, to kill themselves, refused to eat." '

Gabriel found his voice being drowned out by Arthur's. 'They were flogged to compel them to eat, but this failed so often that it was the custom for all slavers to carry a tube-like instrument designed for use by surgeons to force food into the mouths of patients suffering from lockjaw. This was driven into the mouths of obstinate Negroes, smashing lips and teeth, until food could be forced down the throat. Instances were described where the lips were burned with coals and hot irons to compel the Negroes to open their mouths and swallow food.'

Arthur snatched the book away from Gabriel and shook it at him. 'Don't you understand? These words, these stories aren't just dashes of ink on a page – they're a call to arms. This place didn't come from nowhere, it came from experience, from books such as this, with tales, reminiscences, memories such as the ones you've just read out. It came about because I decided to live in the truth that had been beaten into my skin. I offer this room to you. Read at your leisure and understand. Come to know the world as it has presented itself to me. Any honest reading will inform you of the moral authority that empowers my actions.'

The sound of Montreal's anxious breathing came to him. 'I can't stand this,' he snapped. 'Put them in the corner, while I give them something to drink.'

Gabriel guided the children to a corner and helped them with their blankets. As he lit the fire, Arthur returned with a tray of drinks and passed them to the children, saying, 'Drink up. Just get it down quietly.'

Flopping down on his favourite chair to a chorus of slurping, he mumbled, 'Let's just pray that one of the lads doesn't come down or there will be hell to pay.'

Gabriel sat by the fire.

They looked each other over.

Arthur smiled. 'More questions?'

'Roberta Andrews?'

'I told you, she was exquisite.' He sank into his thoughts. In time, he began to cry. 'Oh dear, this really isn't –' His finger slowly rose and directed Gabriel to a shelf. 'There. To your left . . . up, up . . . there.'

Gabriel pulled down a blue folder with the name 'Roberta' printed on it in black ink.

'It contains much of her writings since she joined us. She was a fine thinker.'

On the first page was a drawing of four figures, captioned 'Martin, Marcus, Malcolm and Me!' A little poem read,

> *I love my family,*
> *I love it more than anything,*
> *It is a greater thing than*
> *Anyone or anything else.*

Gabriel passed over several sheets of paper until he found the following:

It is a horrible world that I have been born into. I wish I could change it. Father Kembo is here to protect me, but I can't help being scared. I worry for my brothers. I worry that one day the world will smash them. They are brave, but I don't know if that's enough. I will never let anyone harm them.

Then:

I am a warrior. My strength is my own. I give it freely. I will not be denied. I can make the world whole again.

'Move on to the end,' said Arthur. 'The rest is irrelevant.'

Gabriel came to writings that had been smudged and crumpled with re-reading.

Tottenham hurt himself today. He had been carrying tools from the workroom and fell badly. I was not angry for there was nothing to be angry about, but Martin, upset by his carelessness, beat him. I asked him to stop. Nothing is gained by viciousness. We argued. Even if Tottenham and his like are the foulest of the foul, we only hurt ourselves by acting like beasts.

The great spirit in us must be dirtied by such acts. If Tottenham fell from grace, it is surely because his people embraced brutality. We human beings must remember why it is that we walk so tall. We do not keep a tally of the brutal.

I visited the graves of the beasts whom Father Kembo had taken many years ago. He explained that his patience was not what it might have been and that accidents had occurred. The ghettos of Washington and the townships of South Africa teach us that accidents do not just happen. Every action has its source in deliberation. Therefore these dead ones were always, from the moment of their taking, meant to die.

I spoke to Tottenham today. It was my turn to supervise the cleaning of their sties. Tottenham prides himself on his cleanliness. We spoke of the middle passage and its terrible conditions. Tottenham has trouble imagining a time when creatures such as himself could ever have done such things to people like me. He told me that what the slavers had done was wrong and that their disgrace was his own. He understood why he lived as he did. Tottenham claimed that he was closer, because of his life, to those who endured the middle passage, than I. I struck him. He had no right to say such a thing.

I spoke with Father Kembo about what Tottenham had said.

I thought, though it angered me, that he had actually made some sense. I asked for time in the sties so that I might find out things I needed to know.

Father Kembo was displeased.

Tottenham was beaten.

I didn't like it. He was innocent.

Innocence. In-no-sense is s/he who is deserving of the term guilty. In-no-sense is s/he blameable for what has gone before.

What is an animal?

Can we judge an animal just by its form?

Can an animal rise above its birth?

314

For all their sins, they share our form. They are clearly not pigs, despite all we are taught. Can the pig speak our language? Can the pig express its pain as I have heard the whites do? Father Kembo takes a separate class and teaches them of their sins, but can the pig think or feel? Clearly they are different from other animals.

I cannot sleep. I am shamed. I shame my family. I shame my father with these thoughts. They belong in the classroom, not in the dark, not in secret.

Something keeps running around my mind. I shut it out, but it comes back all the time. Its power lies in its truth.

It is this. I am a human being. Therefore I should act as a human being. Surely humanness must be acted out. I can't believe that any good comes from punishing these poor creatures. My family constantly celebrate the achievements of these human beings who have been ignored in the great liestory. We celebrate the likes of George Polygreen Bridgetower, who Beethoven described as 'a very able virtuoso and an absolute master of his instrument'. We are right to do so, for these human beings knew what they were meant to achieve and defied the whites. Even though the whites have expunged them from their perverstories, we have found them. But can we ignore the fact that Beethoven's friendship transcended time and culture?

Likewise, if we praise the works of the composer Samuel Coleridge Taylor, we cannot ignore his friendship with the likes of John Thelwall. If our hearts break for the radical William Davidson, must we not mark the passing of the whites, Arthur Thistlewood, John Brunt, James Ings and Richard Tidd, who were hanged with him?

I dreamt of Tottenham last night. I often dream of him. In these dreams, we talk without restraint, we laugh freely. The other day I made a joke and he laughed for a moment. It was a wonderful sound. It stopped all too soon, lest someone else hear him. I like the sound of his joy. It is full of unsuppressed wonder.

I have shown Tottenham some of my reading. He is slow, but improves all the time. I delight in his education. Knowledge is the saviour of us all. Without wisdom how will he improve? I am older. I can see that with help he could be my equal by the time he reaches my age. It won't be easy, but it could be done. The words act, action, dunce, ace, neat, it, cat, cute, cut, tune, no, an, die, dune, den, note, nit, dote, one, dot, deacon, not, on, tied, tan, ton, nude, at, ion, iodate, eon, eat, tied and tone are all found within the word education. It is a big word.

My equal. Such weakness is unforgivable. The white has waged war on whatever differs from itself. It does not deserve equity. It does not deserve equality. It does not deserve kindness.

Martin found Tottenham with one of my books. Tottenham said he stole it. He was beaten. I was sick with fear that he would tell the truth, but he kept his silence. We had been taught to revel in truth, but I lie in bed at night petrified of a truth being exposed. I know that Tottenham's nights must be filled with the same fear. It links us together.

I watched Tottenham with Marcus today, and found him as charming as my brother. It was a horrifying moment. I was ashamed. But there it is.

I have come to know Tottenham. We both understand that we are friends. But Tottenham is not alone. The other whites are the same. It is not true to say that they do not count, just because I have not befriended them. I recognize them all as thinking, feeling beings.

This is madness. The whites are awful, and I should treat them as such. Innocence is no excuse. It never caused them to stop their activities or abuse. I have power. Why should it not be used as recklessly? Must I act with greater responsibility? Greater love?

We spoke today in the classroom of cruelty.

I raised the topic, because I was unable to maintain my silence and I believe that a family must be able to discuss anything.

The Chinese general Sun Tzu felt that in war a nation prepared for peace, and in peace prepared for war. I felt we should adopt this maxim. We are strong. Our home is secure. We could live out our lives in harmony with nature and see a cure to evil before we are done. We know the weakness of the white. Why do we not try to build its strengths? Instead of continuing the brutality and cruelty, we could build something inspiring. We could stop everything that has gone before and start fresh.

Father Kembo tried to discuss my proposals calmly, but I could see that he was angry. His anger touched off my brothers' temper. Martin reminded me that we were at war with the white – we were not in retreat or seclusion, but in preparation for the inevitable war that would come.

Everything I said, they countered. I could not win a debate against the three of them and Father. I could not reason with their anger. Words are powerful and my family are full of the power of their words. Still, their much-vaunted POW errs.

Father has taught me to argue. He has constantly asked 'Are you who you think you are?' I know who I am and I know what I know.

Father brought Tottenham before me and insisted that I beat him. I could not. He accused me of being weak, of betraying the family and my race. I was handed a stick, but could do nothing with it. One by one my brothers beat Tottenham. Marcus could hardly bring himself to raise the stick. Father beat him, until he attacked Tottenham. I know that Malcolm had difficulty. They are fine human beings. As for my brother Martin, he is a warrior and enjoys acting as one. Father rounded off the attack. I refused to join in. Tottenham was taken away and I was ordered to my bed.

Tottenham has gone. Father took him away. I cannot sleep. It is all my fault.

I am a human being. I know that this is wrong. It is wrong. Nothing beautiful is growing on this farm.

I will tell Father of my decision to leave. I want to go my own way. Ever since I can remember he has taught me to become the architect of my own life. I believe in his teachings. The time has come to walk in the white world and survive on my terms. Perhaps after I have been out there for a time, I will understand my failings and be able to correct them. Perhaps Father has spared me too much?

Gabriel put the paper down.

The children were asleep.

'Arthur, what happened next?'

'She asked to leave and, like any possessive father, I said no.' He paused for a moment. 'Roberta acted in accordance with her nature and tried to leave anyway. She was stopped.' He held out his hand for the folder.

'Are you familiar with Sun Tzu's methods of military analysis when determining the stronger of two opposing armies? He asks a number of specific unchanging questions.' Arthur looked at the sleeping children and ticked off on his fingers, 'On which side is discipline most rigorously enforced? On which side are the officers and men more highly trained? In which army is there greater constancy both in reward and punishment? I would remind you that the armies governed by Sun Tzu were invincible.'

Arthur paused. 'It's late. I must sleep.' He pushed himself up and placed Roberta's writings in the fire.

Gabriel removed the folder and smothered the flames.

'You're a sentimentalist, just like your father.' Arthur stoked up the coals. 'I like fire, it's been good to me. It never deviates from its role.'

'Matthew thought you had died in a fire.'

'Well, here I am. I did what I needed to do. That was all it took, the ability to fulfil my needs, to realize what was within my mind. Do you understand? From that moment on, you, these children, everyone, have lived my reality. Have you any idea of the responsibility that brings?'

'No.'

'Try to put yourself in my shoes for a moment. In the search for knowledge of my enemy, I stared into his evil and drew his venality into my consciousness. Every depravity, perversion and aberration was now in my mind, constantly screaming for release. Imagine spending every second of every day controlling each thought, knowing that if you relax for one moment, the tiniest, itsy-bitsy wrong might escape into the world and cause unimaginable damage. Can you begin to understand the control I have to exercise?'

'No,' said Gabriel softly.

Arthur knelt down beside Gabriel and took his hand. 'I have one more truth for you. Let us see what springs from its roots. Many years ago I had a friend. He had a wife. I felt she was not "right" for him. I suppose, in my heart of hearts, I wanted her gone. Do you understand what I am saying?'

It took some time for Gabriel to respond. 'Yes.'

'One night, perhaps it was a morning, it could have been over a coffee, it may well have been during an idle moment at work, I wished her gone. This thought sped from my mind and out into the world. It changed it for ever. She was my first real thought. Do you understand?'

They stared at each other.

Arthur stretched, got up and made his way to the stairs. He went up, floorboards creaking with his motion. A door closed.

Gabriel sat watching the glowing coals until he was ready to lie down. The children were deep in sleep. With Roberta's writings on his lap, he joined them.

*

Gabriel awoke with a stiff neck in the sharp morning light. The staleness in his mouth was unpleasant, and he headed automatically for his bathroom; but he was in Arthur's house.

The children were still asleep. Montreal and Wood Green huddled against each other. Trafalgar had cast off his blanket and rolled away from them. Gabriel picked up the blanket and went to cover him. In the light it seemed that the boy's skin had an odd blue tint to it. As Gabriel bent down, it occurred to him that Trafalgar wasn't breathing. A moment's hesitation. His hand reached out and lay on the boy's chest. There was no heartbeat.

Gabriel felt Wood Green's neck for a pulse. Nothing.

He opened Montreal's eyelids and found dilated pupils.

His hand began to shake. 'Not now, not now.' The tremors continued. He formed a fist and bit into a finger as hard as he could, drawing blood. He sucked the wound until he was calm. Blowing on the cut, he made his way to the stairs.

He found Marcus, Malcolm and Martin in their beds. Their clothes, washed and ironed, lay waiting on nearby chairs. Collages of their respective heroes hung on the walls alongside framed certificates of achievement from Arthur. A note rested beside each boy. The message was the same: 'A good soldier and a better son.' Their birth names, Andrew, Simon and Karl, followed.

Gabriel stayed with them for several hours.

Arthur lay in his bedroom, seemingly about to wake at any moment. The walls and shelves were bare. Everything had been packed into boxes. A few cans of petrol were lined up by his bed. A note in his hand contained a bad joke about the contents of his special chocolate and directions to burn the house. An envelope marked with a name Gabriel was unfamiliar with lay by his side. Gabriel opened the envelope.

Gabriel,

I hope you are strong enough to live in truth.

I leave your true name so that no one else will have power over you.

After Roberta's passing, I knew this had to come. It was just a matter of how. Thank you for your help.

Your Godfather.

Gabriel went through the boxes and removed some books and many writing pads filled with Arthur's handwriting, as well as essays and paintings that belonged to his former students. He carried them all to his car, passing the poisoned dogs who lay outside the house. The barns were silent.

Gabriel made several more trips back and forth from the lounge choosing material. One box contained the maths and English work of Trafalgar, Montreal and Wood Green. One was full of sketches by Roberta. Another contained photographs of all the children, at various graduation ceremonies and at play. Yet another was full of unsent mail. Marcus had written a love poem to Storm of the *X-Men*; Malcolm to Fidel Castro about amateur boxing, and to Stevie Wonder for advice; Martin to Nelson Mandela of the need for strength and to Prince Charles of the need for a republic. Roberta had written to Nina Simone, and Montreal to his parents.

When he was unable to pack anything more into his car, Gabriel poured petrol in and around the house. He watched it burn for a time before driving away.

He left the car to open the gate. As he leaned against the gate, drops of sweat fell from his face on to the ground. Head bowed, breathing heavily, he looked over the farm and the surrounding area. Nothing moved. He wiped his face with his shirt, but his eyes just filled again with tears. He waited to gather his strength, then turned and walked slowly back to the house.

Sparks jumped off the house and floated above Gabriel's head, before falling to the ground. He felt like shielding his face from the heat, but couldn't be bothered to make the effort. Instead, he walked over to the sties.

He studied Trafalgar's former home for a time before entering the sty. It was cool inside, almost damp. The darkness comforted him, as it had so many times before. He thought of Rachel, closed his eyes, and dreamed.

Gabriel walked through a field of rich green.

A group of travellers offered him a ride in the back of their van, but he declined and made his own way up a short hill. The sky was Noddy blue. A Devon-ice-cream sun, with light streaming out of it like perfect cones, smiled down at him.

He came across two men dressed in white, oiling their cricket bats. They greeted him and carried on with their conversation as if he were an old friend. The younger man, slightly sun-tanned, said, 'Harold's a might too serious for my liking. He comes out throwing bombs and leaves the field trying to knock our blocks off.'

His friend, slim of build and with an easy smile, answered, 'That's just his way. The public come to see him and he likes to give value.'

'True, but fun is fun. He should never forget that.'

'Cricket's never been fun to Harold. He comes from a hard school. You're as tough as he is, but you just make the game look too easy.'

'People say that, but I try, you know.'

'I know you do, it's just that we can't see it.'

'You should talk. I swear, last session, I thought you were falling asleep until I looked up at the score-board.'

'Yes, I played well today. Reminded me of my form before the war.'

A bell rang.

The two men got up and walked down the hill. At the bottom was an enormous cricket stadium. It must have housed over a million people, and each viewer, no matter how far back, seemed to have an equally good view. As the two men walked on to the pitch, an incredible roar went up. The men raised their bats in acknowledgement and a score-board flashed, HOBBS 149, TRUMPER 152.

Gabriel walked on.

He came to another field and carried on until he came to a small clearing filled with parked caravans and wagons. A number of people were comfortably seated in a circle. Within the ring stood a young girl, brown skinned and still covered in puppy fat. She was holding several puppets. A Master of Ceremonies appeared. 'We move on to our last piece, written by our resident poet and performed by her daughter. I present the story of the monkey and the old woman's foolish daughter.'

Some applause followed.

'Once upon a time,' began the girl, 'in a garden without life, a daughter who would never be as old as her mother watched a man walk by.' Her puppets began to enact the tale. 'She was young and impressionable and much taken with his fine figure and dancing eyes.' The man puppet's long eyelashes fluttered, drawing wry chuckles from the audience. The girl drew their attention back to herself. She was confident and assured, clearly the veteran of many performances. 'A long time ago, when the man had walked as a monkey, he had grown to despise his form, so he had convinced the second son of the First Man to murder his brother. The deed completed, he had taken the skin from the corpse and worn it as his own. All this was unknown to the lovesick girl, who gazed upon the features of her murdered ancestor and told her mother, "He is the most beautiful man in the world." ' The girl's voice had changed utterly, becoming adult and filled with longing, conjuring up the passion of a woman supposedly much older than herself.

'Her mother,' she continued in her detached narrator's voice, 'toiling as ever to remove foul roots and bitter sediment, looked up and recognized the look of her first son. Many years ago, when her husband still carried the scars of her birth, the monkey had visited her and offered her a secret from his foreskin. That secret had cost her dear. She returned to working the soil and told her daughter, "Look again." '

The girl puppet walked towards the marionette of the monkey, whose costume was bright and pretty, made from glistening silk. Excitable types in the crowd yelled at the puppet to stop, but it continued. The girl continued to play on their emotions. 'Her daughter obeyed her and found the face of her great-grandfather to be most favourable. The mother was not surprised for all her family found favour with each other.

'Sifting through the never-ending rocks, she recalled a time of endless light, when she had been able to shed her skin and the garden had shaped itself to her will. It was then that the monkey who walked disguised as a man had plucked fruit from the upside-down tree and shared it with her.

'Her daughter had never been outside the garden and was tired of planting seeds that refused to flower. "He would never hurt me," she insisted. "I would be happy with him." ' Groans from the audience. 'Her mother looked at the monkey that carried the flesh of her lost son and trusted that one day he would find release. Still, the dark would soon come and her husband would sneak back to visit her. He would talk of the lands he had seen and speak of their grandchildren who would never see her. They would make new plans and love each other. Then he would be off, searching again for the only seed in the entire world that would grow in their garden.

'The monkey who had stolen her son's face knew where the seed was buried, but he would never tell them, and she had tired of asking. "Mother," she heard her daughter say, "I will go with him." '

Cries of 'NO!' and 'Listen to your mother!' rang out, but the puppet ignored them.

'The woman turned and walked into her house. She had lost many daughters and countless sons to the monkey – one more would not be the end of her. She had promised to replenish the sterile earth. The garden would blossom and her word be of measure again. Her daughter never even said goodbye. She just pushed open the gate at the bottom of the garden and walked away as if it had always been her greatest wish.'

Boos and angry shouts came from the audience. The monkey puppet turned and gave them the finger. The girl played the audience for all it was worth, waiting for their anger to settle before ending with, 'She never saw her mother again. The monkey saw to that.'

The girl lowered the puppets. Applause rang out. The Master of Ceremonies came forward and thanked the audience. 'That will be all for today. We thank you for your attendance.'

The audience dispersed.

The Master of Ceremonies went with them.

The girl ran off to play with some of her friends.

A woman walked out of the nearby trees, rubbing her hands. She stopped when she saw Gabriel and smiled at him.

Gabriel walked towards her.

'Hello,' she said.

'Hello. I enjoyed your play.'

It was nothing, she told him. If truth be known, she was fed up with it. The audiences continued to like it, but she'd had enough. It was time for something new.

'I hope I can see more of your work.'

The woman told him he would be more than welcome.

He helped her pack away the puppets.

After sneaking glances at each other, they began to laugh.

She stroked his face. 'I'm glad you came,' she said.

'I'm glad too.'

She thought they were being too formal and gave him a hug. 'I love you,' she said, and it was the purest thing he'd ever heard.

He wanted to say something but kept quiet unless his voice made everything less ideal.

Then she was gone.

The puppets, the clearing, everything went with her.

He waited for a while, then walked back to where he'd come from. Once he got there, he carried on.

READ MORE IN PENGUIN

In every corner of the world, on every subject under the sun, Penguin represents quality and variety – the very best in publishing today.

For complete information about books available from Penguin – including Puffins, Penguin Classics and Arkana – and how to order them, write to us at the appropriate address below. Please note that for copyright reasons the selection of books varies from country to country.

In the United Kingdom: Please write to *Dept. EP, Penguin Books Ltd, Bath Road, Harmondsworth, West Drayton, Middlesex UB7 ODA*

In the United States: Please write to *Consumer Sales, Penguin USA, P.O. Box 999, Dept. 17109, Bergenfield, New Jersey 07621-0120*. VISA and MasterCard holders call 1-800-253-6476 to order Penguin titles

In Canada: Please write to *Penguin Books Canada Ltd, 10 Alcorn Avenue, Suite 300, Toronto, Ontario M4V 3B2*

In Australia: Please write to *Penguin Books Australia Ltd, P.O. Box 257, Ringwood, Victoria 3134*

In New Zealand: Please write to *Penguin Books (NZ) Ltd, Private Bag 102902, North Shore Mail Centre, Auckland 10*

In India: Please write to *Penguin Books India Pvt Ltd, 706 Eros Apartments, 56 Nehru Place, New Delhi 110 019*

In the Netherlands: Please write to *Penguin Books Netherlands bv, Postbus 3507, NL-1001 AH Amsterdam*

In Germany: Please write to *Penguin Books Deutschland GmbH, Metzlerstrasse 26, 60594 Frankfurt am Main*

In Spain: Please write to *Penguin Books S. A., Bravo Murillo 19, 1° B, 28015 Madrid*

In Italy: Please write to *Penguin Italia s.r.l., Via Felice Casati 20, I–20124 Milano*

In France: Please write to *Penguin France S. A., 17 rue Lejeune, F–31000 Toulouse*

In Japan: Please write to *Penguin Books Japan, Ishikiribashi Building, 2–5–4, Suido, Bunkyo-ku, Tokyo 112*

In South Africa: Please write to *Longman Penguin Southern Africa (Pty) Ltd, Private Bag X08, Bertsham 2013*

READ MORE IN PENGUIN

A CHOICE OF FICTION

What a Carve Up! Jonathan Coe

'"They're not monsters you know. Not really," says Mortimer Winshaw, heir to desolate Winshaw Towers, of his clan. Oh, but they are, really, real monsters. And Jonathan Coe's novel is, really, something to get excited about ... a big, hilarious, intricate, furious, moving treat of a novel' – *Guardian*

Partial Eclipse Lesley Glaister

Jennifer is in solitary confinement, imprisoned for an undisclosed crime. As she waits for time to pass she reflects on the events that brought her there: her strange home life with an eccentric grandmother and her wild love for Tom, a philandering musician. 'She has an uncomfortable knack of putting her finger on the things we most fear, of exposing the darkness within' – *Sunday Telegraph*

Ireland: Selected Stories William Trevor

'He is a master of understatement, a minimalist, using detail with the delicacy of a man stalking rare butterflies: his characters are not drawn, but pinned down – just one or two precise thrusts and there they are, revealed in all their subtlety of colour' – *Daily Telegraph*

Something to Remember Me By Saul Bellow

Dedicated to Bellow's children and grandchildren, *Something to Remember Me By* tells the wonderfully tender and funny story of a young man's sexual initiation and sexual guilt, one bleak Chicago winter's day in 1933. That story, narrated like a memoir, is collected here with Bellow's acclaimed novellas *The Bellarosa Connection* and *A Theft*.

No One Writes to the Colonel Gabriel García Márquez

In a decaying Colombian town, the Colonel and his ailing wife are living a hand-to-mouth existence, scraping together or borrowing the money for food and medicine. The Colonel's hopes for a better future lie in his rooster, which for him, and indeed the whole town, has become a symbol of defiance in the face of despair ...

READ MORE IN PENGUIN

A CHOICE OF FICTION

An Experiment in Love Hilary Mantel

It was the year after Chappaquiddick, and all spring Carmel had watery dreams about the disaster. Now she, Karina and Julianne were escaping the dreary north for a London University hall of residence. Awaiting them was a winter of new preoccupations – sex and politics, food and fertility – and a pointless grotesque tragedy of their own.

Jackson's Dilemma Iris Murdoch

At Penndean, preparations for the marriage of Edward Lannion and Marian Berran are under way. The wedding party is to arrive the day before, and Marian, who loves surprises, will come on the morning of the wedding. But as the guests anticipate the festivities, something shocking happens. 'A work of brilliance' – *Independent on Sunday*

The Vinegar Jar Berlie Doherty

From childhood on, Rose Doran's life has been one of lovelessness and loneliness. Smooth-talking William abandons her, along with his baby, Edmund. Rose seeks comfort in an unsatisfactory marriage to Gordon. But it is not until she meets Paedric, her mysterious neighbour, that her colourless life is transformed – with disturbing consequences.

Bright Lights, Big City Jay McInerney

Portraying a week in the life of a young journalist on a *New Yorker*-style magazine, Jay McInerney's debut novel explores hangover days and night life in the apartment blocks and clublands of eighties Manhattan. 'Deadly funny' – Raymond Carver

These Same Long Bones Gwendolyn M. Parker

Eleven-year-old Mattie died falling from her slide. No one in the prosperous community of Hay-Ti, the 'coloured' section of Durham, North Carolina, is unaffected. 'A thoughtful and generous-hearted novel that shows a life "both blessed and ... hard", sustained by human resilience and always aglow with insoluble mystery' – *The New York Times Book Review*